YITZHAK RABIN

Yitzhak Rabin

Soldier, Leader, Statesman

ITAMAR RABINOVICH

Yale

UNIVERSITY
PRESS
New Haven and London

Yitzhak Rabin was not a charismatic man, but rather a logical, skillful captain. He was not endowed with Ben Gurion's prophetic passion, nor with Levi Eshkol's warm gracefulness. He did not have Golda Meir's sweeping simplicity, nor Menachem Begin's populist energy. The crowd never responded to him by chanting "Rabin, Rabin." By being a careful engineer and a precise navigator, his personality embodied the spirit of new Israel, a country seeking not redemption but solutions.

—Amos Oz, 1996

CONTENTS

---◆◈◆---

Prologue
Yitzhak Rabin's Death, Yitzhak Rabin's Life

MOST DEATHS are simply the end of a life. A political assassination, however, is unlike any other form of death. It is a death that acquires its own significance; a death with consequences. An assassination is not only the terminal point of a person's life but also the starting point for a new reality the death itself has created. The slain leader will often become the subject of a new mythology as the violent act of his death is remembered and commemorated, casting a different light on the leader's life and tenure.

In the aftermath of Yitzhak Rabin's assassination in 1995, a shocked Israeli public searched for context and precedent. Abraham Lincoln's assassination was powerfully invoked, as Walt Whitman's "O Captain! My Captain!" was given a new Hebrew translation, and a popular melody was composed. But the analogy was erroneous. The body of Whitman's captain lay on a ship that had reached harbor. Lincoln had completed his mission; his assassination was an act of revenge against that achievement. A much closer analogy would be the attempts of the radical French Right and the Algerian settlers to assassinate Charles de Gaulle in order to stop peace negotiations with the Front de Libération Nationale.[1] Had they succeeded, the assassination could have aborted a solution to the Algerian problem. In fact, Rabin's assassin, Yigal Amir, a fanatical Orthodox Jew from a Yemenite family, was inspired by Jean-Marie Bastien-Thiry, the French officer executed in 1963 for the attempted assassination of de Gaulle. Amir saw a similarity between the French situation at the height of the Algerian crisis and Israel's predicament in the early and mid-1990s. To him, Rabin was an Israeli version of de Gaulle: a war hero who had deviated from the right path and had to be killed before a precious part of the nation's territory was given away.

There is another intriguing analogy made: to President John F. Kennedy's assassination. As in the case of Kennedy, there was incitement against Rabin before his assassination, with accusations of treason and worse. Prior to Kennedy's arrival in Dallas, the site of his assassination, handbills with photographs of the president were passed out around the city claiming he was "wanted for treasonous activities against the United States."[2] Similarly, Kennedy's assassination created a yearning for a kind of lost golden period, the image and myth of a Camelot that purportedly once existed. The writer Norman Mailer wrote, "For a time we felt the country was ours. Now it is theirs again."[3] In the aftermath of Rabin's assassination, his supporters, the Candles Generation, and many others also yearned for what came to be perceived as a golden age in Israel's history and politics. Thousands of young people holding burning candles kept vigil near Rabin's home and at the site of the assassination. For the past twenty years an annual rally is held on November 4, the day of the assassination, in which large numbers participate. At the end of 2015, in anticipation and in the aftermath of the

PROLOGUE

twentieth anniversary of the assassination, a wave of yearning for Rabin was evident in Israel, reflecting both the sense of loss and the broad dissatisfaction with the country's current leadership as well as its inability to cope with the endemic Palestinian problem.

Rabin's assassination also highlighted a stark contrast between "us" and "them." Amir killed a man whose life and career represented the essence of Israel's original establishment: East European origins, the Labor movement, Palmach (the elite military unit of prestate Israel) and Israel Defense Forces (IDF), a secular northern Tel Aviv. The years preceding the assassination were defined by a kind of culture war: a clash between the settlers, the radical Right, and a large part of the Orthodox community and the secular, moderate sector of the Israeli public, not just over the peace process but also over the country's larger orientation. Like Kennedy's assassination, Rabin's would have a dramatic impact on this culture war for years to come.

But as consequential as Rabin's assassination was, it is his life—his decisions and actions—not his death that defines his legacy. Kennedy's impact and legacy were shaped by the Cuban missile crisis, the Bay of Pigs, the Berlin speech, the drift into the Vietnam War, and the glamorous aura he created. Lincoln's legacy is that he ended slavery, preserved the Union, and gave the United States a model for presidential power. Rabin's legacy is shaped by his peace policy in his second tenure, the bold decisions he took on both the Palestinian and Syrian tracks, and the high quality of his leadership.

Rabin's life is a fascinating tale of a natural-born Israeli who grew up within Israel's prestate establishment, moving through the now-familiar stages of a Labor movement school, an agricultural school, Palmach, the 1948 war, and a military career. Rabin's talents and perseverance—and the occasional lucky turn —would eventually bring him to the top of the military pyramid and finally to the prime minister's chair. But it was neither

3

a smooth nor an easy ascent. Rabin did not possess the charisma of leaders such as Moshe Dayan and Yigal Alon, who were identified as such at a young age. He climbed slowly, becoming a true leader only in the 1980s. Rabin's first tenure, in the 1970s, was marred by his failure to appeal to the Israeli public. Not until his impressive performance as minister of defense in the 1980s did his unique blend of authority and credibility enable him to come back from the political wilderness and regain the prime minister's post.

In Rabin's second term his leadership evolved into statesmanship. He demonstrated the ability to make bold, historic decisions, to go against his own grain and carry his people with him. And Rabin's success continues today to illustrate a crucial aspect of Israel's current politics: that an effective peace policy can be waged—by a credible centrist leader with security credentials who can persuade an anxious Israeli public to make the concessions and take the risks that progress toward peace requires. In a country still grappling with the same fundamental problems as those in Rabin's era, the yearning for a leader of the stature and qualities of Yitzhak Rabin is painfully felt.

1

---◆I◆I◆---

The Making of a Soldier, 1922–1948

"EXCEPT FOR his intelligence and tenacity, he was an unlikely ambassador. Taciturn, shy, reflective, almost resentful of small talk, Rabin possessed few of the attributes commonly associated with diplomacy. Repetitious people bored him and the commonplace offended him; unfortunately for Rabin, both of these qualities are not exactly in short supply in Washington. He hated ambiguity which is the stuff of diplomacy. [But] his integrity and his analytical brilliance in cutting to the core of a problem were awesome."[1] This is how Henry Kissinger aptly and subtly portrayed Yitzhak Rabin, who worked with him closely in Washington between 1969 and 1973. The qualities that made him an unlikely yet very effective ambassador made him an even more unlikely politician. But some of these very qualities help explain his transition from an awkward politician to an impressive statesman.

Rabin was born in Jerusalem in 1922 to Rosa Cohen and

5

Nehemiah Rubichev (later Rabin). Of his childhood he wrote, "My path was determined decisively by the inspiration of my parents' personalities, by the inspiration of our home and also by the inspiration of the school I studied in. I practically saw myself throughout my childhood directed toward a life of agriculture, life in a kibbutz, and if I had ever been told I would become a military man, I would have reacted to it almost with ridicule."[2] Both of Rabin's parents were born in the Russian Empire, and both were radicalized by its dark autocracy; they arrived in Palestine in the aftermath of World War I. Rosa, nicknamed Red Rosa, was the dominant parent. Her powerful personality is illustrated in a photograph that captured her marching in a May Day parade in Tel Aviv, chin forward, her eyes and face exuding determination. Rosa was born in Gomel in 1890 to the wealthy Orthodox anti-Zionist Yitzhak Cohen, after whom she named her son. From a young age she stood out as a strong-minded individualist with leftist, populist, and anti-Zionist convictions. She was wary of organized, structured groups, so she did not join either the Russian Social Revolutionaries or the left-wing anti-Zionist Jewish Bund. Breaking the mold of a young girl from a traditional Orthodox Jewish family, Rosa put herself through a Russian polytechnic school, refusing to accept financial support from her wealthy father and sneaking away from home to attend school on the Sabbath. Her left-wing radicalism was channeled into a Russian-style populism of helping the poor and needy. She lived among Russian workers and was adored by them, chopping wood in forests belonging to the Russian grand prince that were leased by her family. This was a dangerous way of life, and it put her in the crosshairs of both the Tsarist and, subsequently, the Communist secret police. A genuine radical, she was disappointed with the Communist regime. Rosa ran a factory near St. Petersburg (later Leningrad) that became an ammunition factory. In 1919, when she was fired because of her refusal to join the party, the workers went on strike. She found herself stranded without work and marked as a dangerous person in politically tumultuous times.

A non-Zionist, Rosa decided to visit her family in Jerusalem to see whether she might find her place in Palestine. She wrote, in Yiddish, to Berl Katzenelson, a senior leader of the Labor movement whom she knew through family connections, and asked him to advise her as to whether "the land of Israel will solve my problem." Worried at the thought of leaving a life she knew, Rosa asked if he thought she could manage. "By traveling to the land of Israel I have to sever one way of life in order to start another; there is no way back," she wrote.[3] Rosa's uncle, Mordechai Ben Hillel Hacohen, had moved his family to Palestine in 1903 and lived in Jerusalem, and she planned to stay with him for a while. In December 1919 she boarded the *SS Ruslan* in Odessa, a ship that would become famous in Zionist mythology. On board was a group of pioneers bound for Kinneret, a kibbutz on the shores of Lake Tiberias.[4] The *SS Ruslan* docked in Jaffa on December 19, 1919.

Upon arriving in Jerusalem, Rosa was introduced by her cousin David Hacohen to Moshe Shertok (later Sharett), a future foreign minister and prime minister of Israel. Sharett gave Rosa a letter to take to his sister, a member of Kinneret, in which he asked her to look after the new arrival. In the letter Sharett described Rosa as "an 'important' young woman, an engineer, socialist but not Bolshevik, but worked for a few years in a Bolshevik factory near Petrograd. . . . She has not seen a Jewish face in years, and she is now anxious about it. She is also worried by collective life, which she is not used to. She is very lonely here. The Cohen home is suffocating to her—you know the type of an intelligent Russian girl of the high bourgeoisie who has severed all her ties with her family and social circle and can no longer tolerate them."[5]

Although she arrived in Palestine as a non-Zionist, Rosa

gradually became an ardent supporter of the movement. After a short stay in Kinneret, she moved to Jerusalem to live with her relatives. The Palestinian Arabs rioted in Jerusalem's Old City in 1920, and Rosa went to help the Jewish residents, both as a nurse and as a fighter, having gained experience in self-defense during the pogroms in Russia. She then moved to Haifa and became active in organizing Jewish labor in Haifa Port, supporting herself by working in a store belonging to her relatives.

Little is known about the early life of Rabin's father, Nehemiah Rubichev. Nehemia was born to a poor family in a small village near Kiev and joined revolutionary activity against the tsar's regime. He left for America to avoid being arrested, ending up in St. Louis, where he worked as a tailor and was active in Jewish trade unions. In 1917 Nehemiah tried to enlist in the Jewish Legion, organized by Ze'ev Jabotinsky, in order to fight alongside the British in Palestine, but he was rejected on medical grounds because he had a bad leg. Nehemiah changed his name to Rabin and tried again at another bureau, this time successfully. He arrived in Palestine and stayed. In 1920, as an early member of the first incarnation of the Haganah, the Jewish self-defense organization in Mandatory Palestine, Nehemiah took part in the defense of the Jewish Quarter in Jerusalem's Old City against Arab rioters. In Jerusalem's Old City he met Rosa, who volunteered her assistance in giving medical help. Nehemiah was arrested by the British authorities, who suppressed the riots but jailed the Jewish defenders for carrying weapons. Rosa and Nehemiah married in 1921, settling temporarily in Haifa. Rosa moved to Jerusalem to be near her family in anticipation of Yitzhak's birth, which occurred on March 1, 1922. The young family then moved to Tel Aviv in 1923, where Rosa worked in a bank and Nehemiah at the Palestine Electric Company. In 1924 their daughter, Rachel, was born.

The family lived modestly in a succession of two-room

apartments, described by some of Rabin's childhood friends as being spartan. His parents were fully engaged in public activities in addition to their work; both were involved in the Haganah, Nehemiah was active in trade union affairs, and Rosa in the Tel Aviv city council and numerous other benevolent organizations. It seems the family placed an accent on values rather than emotions; the children grew up mostly by themselves, Yitzhak often taking care of his sister. Friday night was family night. The small apartment, barely furnished, hosted numerous meetings of trade unionists and Haganah members as well as guests from out of town. Rosa was very active, well known, and well respected, but she refused to join a political party or to assume any public position of authority. She had a heart condition, and the children lived in constant fear of losing her. She would, in fact, die young, in 1937 at the age of forty-seven, when Yitzhak was fifteen. Her funeral was a large public event attended by thousands, including David Ben Gurion, the chair of the Jewish Agency, the principal organization of the Jewish community in prestate Israel. By then Ben Gurion was the Jewish community's unquestioned leader.

In many respects Rabin's childhood was typical of that of a boy growing up in the mainstream of the Labor movement in Mandatory Palestine. He went to a primary school affiliated with the Labor movement, joined a youth movement, continued his studies in agricultural school in a kibbutz east of Tel Aviv, and went on to the Kadoorie Agricultural High School, located at the foothills of Mount Tabor in the Galilee, one of the best schools in the country. The Kadoorie school—donated by a wealthy family in Hong Kong that built two schools in Mandatory Palestine, one for Jewish boys and one for Arab—was famous for its high academic standards and for its code of honor. Teachers left the classroom when pupils took a test, trusting them to refrain from copying. At Kadoorie Rabin blossomed. He was a late bloomer, having had difficulties with reading and writing during his first two years in elementary school. The arrival of Eliezer Smoli, a writer and an inspiring teacher, resolved that issue. This late blossoming was typical of Rabin, who would have late starts in other phases of his life as well. With Smoli's help Rabin did well in the difficult admission tests at the Kadoorie school, and he went on to distinguish himself as an exceptional student who received a special prize at graduation from the British high commissioner. Rabin was entitled to a stipend from the government that would enable him to go to the United States and study water engineering in California. But events in Palestine and the outbreak of World War II interfered with this plan. In the Arab Revolt of 1936–39 Rabin was introduced to the security problems confronting the Jewish community and was given his first instruction in the use of weapons. Upon graduating, he could not go to California and went instead with his friends to live and work in a number of kibbutzim, though without actually joining one. In his memoirs and in other accounts of his childhood and early life Rabin mentions this fact but does not explain it. It seems that the individualist streak in his character ultimately prevented him from joining a collective.

There was, however, another important dimension to Rabin's life at this time. During the summer, when he was not in school, he would be sent to spend time with his mother's uncle, Mordechai Ben Hillel Hacohen, in Jerusalem. Ben Hillel was an impressive figure, a writer and an intellectual and a wealthy businessman. His immediate and extended family included some of the most prominent figures of the Jewish community in prestate Israel, or Yishuv. Ben Hillel's son, David Hacohen, lived in Haifa and became the liaison with British Intelligence during World War II. One of his daughters married Arthur Rupin, the head of the Economic Department of the Jewish Agency. Ben Hillel and his family were connected to the families of Moshe Shertok, Eliyahu Golomb, and Dov Hoz, some of the most prominent leaders at the time. During his stays with his great uncle, Rabin was exposed to an environment and way of life that were entirely different from what he was used to. The Hacohen house was spacious and elegant. In stark contrast to the small, barely furnished Rabin apartments in Tel Aviv, it included a large library that the young Rabin and his cousin Raphael Rupin were asked to organize as one of their summer chores. Rabin even joined his cousin on the tennis court, a game totally unknown in his proletarian Tel Aviv universe.

During his last stay with his relatives in Jerusalem, Rabin sent a revealing letter to his friend Hanna Guri (Rivlin). They belonged to a small group of students they named Telem, all of whose members went to the same schools in Tel Aviv and Givat Hashlosha and were part of the same Labor-affiliated youth movement. It was a close-knit group; the members discussed general and personal issues with the seriousness and openness typical of the youth movements of the time. Rabin's letter to Guri sheds light on how he himself viewed the shyness and reticence that were two of the defining elements of his character. On August 6, 1937, he wrote, "Am I the only member of Telem who keeps quiet? Never mind. This does not relieve me [of the duty] to articulate, but there are reasons for hindering articulation . . . if those who keep quiet want to be part of society, they have to express their feelings and if they fail to express them, it is because society prevented them from speaking and if there were any attempts on their part they were always met by the society with contempt. . . . I may have a sense of inferiority because I do not have the confidence that the members are interested in me."[6]

In 1941 Rabin enlisted in the Palmach. The Palmach, an acronym for the Hebrew Strike Units, was formed by the Jewish leadership that year with two ends in mind. One was to create a standing military force. The Haganah had a small apparatus but no full-time military force. In 1941 the prospect of a German invasion loomed large. The German field marshal Erwin Rommel was advancing in North Africa, and before he was defeated by Field Marshal Bernard Montgomery at El-Alamein it seemed likely his troops would overrun Egypt and invade Palestine. The Palmach's six companies were intended not to stop Rommel's army but to slow down its progress while the Jewish community would try to defend itself in the Carmel Mountains. At that time the Haganah and the Palmach collaborated closely with the British. In June 1941, as the British prepared to invade Syria and Lebanon, which were held by troops loyal to Vichy France, Haganah teams were allocated to assist them with reconnaissance and sabotage. Rabin, who was in Kibbutz Ramat Yohanan at the time, was asked by the local security chief if he was willing to volunteer for a mission. Rabin said yes and was interviewed by one of the Haganah's young stars, Moshe Dayan. It was the first encounter between two men whose paths would cross often and meaningfully and with more downs than ups. Rabin wrote of the interview in his memoirs: "He asked about the type of weapon I could use; I told him that I was acquainted with the revolver, rifle and hand grenade but nothing heavier or more sophisticated. Another couple of questions and then he muttered drily, 'You are suitable.'"[7] Rabin joined Dayan's team when it entered Lebanon on June 7 in support of the Australian unit tasked with the actual invasion. This was the operation during which Dayan lost his eye: while looking through his binoculars he was hit by a French sharpshooter and from then on wore the eye patch that became part of his persona and image. As a junior member of the team, Rabin was given the assignment of climbing telephone poles and cutting the lines, his first combat experience. He subsequently joined the newly established Palmach.

Rabin rose through the ranks to become the operations officer—in fact, the right-hand man of Yigal Alon, the Palmach's commander. After the foundation of the Palmach in 1941, the Jewish leadership had to contend with how to maintain the military force. Budgetary constraints led to the Palmach's adoption by the Kibbutz movement, particularly Hakibbutz Hameuchad, a group identified with Faction B, one of the components of Mapai, the dominant party in the Labor movement in prestate Israel and in the early years of Israeli politics. Faction B's leader, Yitzhak Tabenkin, was considered a rival of Ben Gurion (in 1944 Faction B seceded from Mapai and formed a new party named Achdut Haavoda). By this time Ben Gurion had become the leader of the Yishuv, or the Jewish community in Mandatory Palestine. Ben Gurion was not fond of the Palmach. He believed that the best option of the young generation of the Jewish community in Palestine during World War II was to join the British army fighting in Europe. This would be a way to contribute to the war against the Nazis and to help thousands of young Jewish men acquire military experience in the ranks of a major modern army. Ben Gurion, a politician as well as a statesman, was also wary of the Palmach's political orientation. In any event, the Palmach's units stayed mostly in kibbutzim, splitting their time between work and training. This worked as a way for a financially strapped community to maintain a standing military force.

Rabin was sent to the first squad commanders' course of the Palmach, commanded by Alon, a handsome, charismatic man a few years older than Rabin. A native of Kfar Tavor, an agricultural settlement in the foothills of Mount Tabor, Alon was a member of Kibbutz Ginosar on the shores of Lake Tiberias and, like Rabin, was a graduate of the Kadoorie school. This was to be one of the most important relationships of Rabin's early career, as Alon was responsible for his swift rise through the ranks: he discovered Rabin's talents, cultivated him, and would make him his operations officer / deputy. In 1942 Rabin was appointed as an instructor and then promoted to platoon commander. One of the other platoon commanders at the time remembered him years later as being characterized by "original thinking, not bogged down by conventional patterns, asking questions, reflecting on things, raising subjects that not everybody was willing to accept, dismissing popular and well-known people and making light of them, and cultivating people who understood him and followed his way. All told, he was a serious young man and a serious commander who did his job but was not considered anything special."[8]

In 1944 the Palmach shifted from an organization built around companies to one built around battalions. Rabin was promoted to battalion instructor, which in practice meant acting as deputy commander of a battalion, and by 1945 he commanded a major course for squad commanders. In this position Rabin began to distinguish himself. His profound understanding of command and military matters and his talent for instruction turned the course into a memorable experience for many and helped build Rabin's reputation. One of the graduates called it the most significant military course he attended during his career, including a stint at the prestigious École de guerre in France.

In 1945 Rabin had his first experience as a commander of a large-scale military operation. In its early years the Palmach's activity was predicated on collaboration with the British against an anticipated German invasion. Once this danger was over, the collaboration came to an end. The British became a rival, if not an enemy, and the Palmach's operations began to be directed against them. Illegal Jewish immigration to Palestine was at that time a major point of contention between the Yishuv and the British authorities. To the Yishuv, the idea that the British would be denying access to survivors of the Holocaust in Europe was abhorrent. To the British, this policy was in line with their role as an arbiter of the conflict between Jews and Arabs in Palestine. Illegal immigrants captured aboard ships coming to Palestine were put in a camp in Atlit, south of Haifa. The Palmach was assigned by the Haganah headquarters with storming the camp, freeing the detainees, and distributing them in Jewish villages. Battalion Commander Nahum Sarig was in charge of the operation, with Rabin as one of his deputies. The operation was a success. On the next mission, Rabin and his men were directed to blow up British train lines, which they did successfully with no losses. His third operation was to be an attack on the British police station in the town of Jenin. By now, collaboration with the British was replaced by open hostility, as the former partners in the war against Nazi Germany were now seen as supporters of the Palestinian Arabs and an obstacle to Jewish statehood in Palestine. But Rabin was injured in a motorcycle accident and bedridden for several months. While recovering, Rabin wrote often to his sister Rachel, who at a young age joined Kibbutz Manarah on the Lebanese border, where she still lives today. Rabin's letters to her reflect their warm relationship and a light, humorous side he shared only with his intimate circle—a contrast to his more often serious, gruff persona. On January 17, 1946, he wrote, "Since my 'limited' time is now rationally divided between absolute and semi-idleness I finally found the time to write a work of literature that is now in front of you. First, I have to render some details on the main object, namely, my glorious leg, wrapped in a cast, one of the honorable Dr. Pizer's creations." Another letter is written as a parody of biblical style, and another is signed, "Your limping brother."

On June 29, 1946, a day known in Israeli history as Black Saturday, British authorities arrested hundreds of the Haganah commanders and Yishuv leaders, placing them in a detention camp in Rafah in the northern Sinai. Rabin, still in a cast, was among those arrested, and he would spend several months in British detention, during which his wounded leg continued to be treated. The Israeli writer Nathan Shacham, himself a Palmach member and also a detainee, was struck by Rabin's serious, commanding presence. He recorded his first meeting with Rabin in Rafah:

> The awe he inspired in me when I first met him did not lessen upon subsequent closer acquaintance. Although I did not appreciate his uncouth tongue, unintentionally insulting, and the dismissive hand motion, occasionally even more offensive, and although I strongly opposed several of his public statements—all these years my respect for him did not diminish. His honesty covered all his faults. . . . I saw him for the first time . . . at the Rafah detention camp. . . . I stood behind the fence to meet a senior security man held in the other camp. . . . Next to him limped a fair-haired young man, his leg in a cast. . . . I felt uncomfortable under the frozen gaze of the young stranger. . . . The fair-haired young man's stern gaze forced me to speak briefly and to the point. I was later told it was Yitzhak Rabin, a young commander whose reputation preceded him. I was not an innocent underground boy, particularly impressed by famous persons . . . and yet I was deeply impressed by the seriousness of the blue-eyed, blond boy. . . . He did not utter a word, just fixed me with his cold gaze—not quite into my face but staring at some point, somewhat to the right of my right ear. . . . Anyway, when he was staring at that point to the side of my right ear—where he always looked when he listened to others, unless he reached a conclusion that the man had spoken enough, and then fixed him with a gaze, saying clearly without words— he managed, so I thought, to read me like an open book and found in me that frivolousness due to which he and I cannot be friends. Men of action are not friends with people of imagination, who view their experiences from outside.[9]

At the end of 1946, after five months of detention, Rabin was released from Rafah when the British decided to end this phase of their conflict with the Yishuv's leadership. Rabin was appointed commander of the Palmach's second regiment. The

Palmach was expanding as part of the Yishuv's preparation for the anticipated inevitable collision with the Palestinian Arabs and the Arab states. Ben Gurion created the security portfolio in the Jewish Agency and became the Yishuv's de facto minister of defense. He had come to the conclusion years earlier that the establishment of a Jewish state in Palestine would mean war with the Palestinians and that the Arab states would join the war. He took the defense portfolio in order to prepare for such a war; preparations went into high gear. This effort underscored the existing tension between the Palmach leadership and officers who had come back from service in the British army. The Palmach tradition emphasized the individual fighter and spontaneity, while the tradition of the Jewish Brigade in the British army emphasized well-rehearsed procedure. Ben Gurion's sympathies lay with the British tradition. He was dismissive of the Palmach's military value and suspicious of its affiliation with his rivals in the Labor and Kibbutz movements. These tensions remained important throughout and in the immediate aftermath of the 1948 war. Into the early 1950s Ben Gurion missed no opportunity in trying to promote officers who came from the British and other regular armies and to delay the promotion of Palmach officers. Only later, in the 1960s, did the Palmach officers who remained in the IDF assume the chief role in leading it.

Rabin did not remain a battalion commander for long. Alon, who had a high regard for Rabin's skills as a military planner and staff officer, brought him to the Palmach's headquarters as an operations officer and his deputy. The Palmach's first commander was Yitzhak Sadeh, an older, heroic figure with Russian military experience. The political leadership preferred Alon as the commander of the Palmach and kept Sadeh as a field commander. At the Palmach headquarters Rabin's main responsibility as of late 1947 and early 1948 was to plan the convoys of civilian and military supplies that traveled along the winding road through the Judean hills, rising from the coastal plain to Jerusalem and to other beleaguered Jewish centers and villages. This remained Rabin's responsibility until he was appointed commander of the Palmach's Harel Brigade. Securing the convoys meant defending them as well as trying to capture the areas and villages along the road to Jerusalem. At certain points Rabin's brigade was sent into Jerusalem to participate in the battle over the city.

Israel's War of Independence was a landmark in Rabin's political career and one of the most formative periods of his life, catapulting him from a midlevel officer in the Palmach to one of the IDF's best-known senior officers. Rabin would take part in some of the war's most difficult and important campaigns, emerging from it rich in military and political experience. The fighting in Jerusalem and on the road to Jerusalem in particular, where his brigade would suffer heavy losses, would have a deep and lasting impact on the young officer.

The War of Independence lasted over a year and was a difficult, costly effort. The Yishuv lost 1 percent of its population: six thousand out of six hundred thousand. At certain points, particularly in the early spring of 1948, it seemed the Jewish side was about to lose the war. The civil war in Palestine officially erupted in the aftermath of the UN Partition Resolution on November 29, 1947, but violence had begun prior to that date. The civil war between the Jewish and Arab communities lasted from November 1947 to May 15, 1948. During this first phase Palestinian irregulars and Arab volunteers attacked isolated Jewish settlements and ambushed Jewish traffic. A special effort was invested in blocking the road to Jerusalem. In the Partition Plan, Jerusalem was designated as an international city, but both sides invested great effort in trying to secure control of the city, understanding correctly that it was the key to the country's future. Blocking the road to Jerusalem was relatively easy for the Palestinians, who controlled the hilltops commanding the empty riverbed through which the winding road to Jerusalem ran. Getting reinforcements and supplies to the besieged city was a major challenge for the Yishuv's political and military leadership, and Rabin's job in the Palmach headquarters was the planning of these convoys. On April 15, 1948, he was appointed commander of the new Harel Brigade (not really a full-fledged brigade in that it consisted of two rather than three battalions). During the next two months Rabin and his men fought in some of the war's fiercest battles.

These were awesome, dangerous tasks for Rabin and his men, owing certainly to the war but also to political maneuvering within the military. Dealing with difficult leaders and discord within and without the ranks was one of many challenges. On several occasions during these arduous weeks Rabin questioned the wisdom of the orders he was given.

One of Rabin's two battalion commanders, Yosef (Yosef'le) Tabenkin—the son of Yitzhak Tabenkin, the leader of Hakibbutz Hameuchad and Achdut Haavoda (one of the Labor movement's political factions), a prince of the Kibbutz movement—considered himself superior to Rabin and refused to accept his authority.[10] Rabin and Tabenkin had clashed in the past, and in fact the leadership had in part appointed Rabin because of their own inability to get along with Tabenkin. Tabenkin simply did not follow Rabin's orders and instructions, and his regiment acted on its own most of the time rather than as a unit of the Harel Brigade. This was one of the reasons the brigade was not used as a full-fledged entity but as a series of smaller units. In Jerusalem the Harel Brigade was asked to support the efforts of the Etzyoni Brigade, commanded by David Shealtiel, another hard-to-control commander whose military skills were questionable. There was also the troubling fact that until May 15 the British army was still in Jerusalem and on several occasions obstructed the IDF efforts. After May 15 the Jordanian army, the Arab Legion, joined the fray. It was the best existing Arab army,

and King Abdullah of Jordan was determined to take posses-
sion of as large a part of Jerusalem as he could.

Rabin and his men were successful with their mission in
the southern part of Jerusalem but less so in its northern part
and in the approaches to it. Shealtiel pressured Rabin to support his effort to save the Jewish Quarter of Jerusalem's Old
City. Rabin thought Shealtiel's plan was absolutely misguided
but as a fellow commander could not deny his request. Rabin's
men, under protest, participated in Shealtiel's attempt. The
mission failed badly. The Harel fighters withdrew from the
Jewish Quarter, and the Jewish Quarter eventually surrendered
to the Jordanian Arab Legion. The episode became a matter of
controversy between Rabin and Shealtiel and left a permanent
scar on Rabin.

The fighting on the road to Jerusalem exacted an atrocious
toll on the Harel Brigade. The casualty rate was 50 percent,
and Rabin's men were left dazed and in a state of shock. The
novelist Yoram Kanyuk, one of his soldiers, wrote in his novel
1948, "Before departing for battle, we used to tell the elders of
the Kibbutz: 'Dig the graves as soon as possible because we are
on the way.' "[11] So dazed were the Harel fighters that when, on
May 14, 1948, "an ancient radio in Kibbutz Ma'aleh Hachami-
sha, a few miles outside Jerusalem, conveyed Ben Gurion's voice
to us," Rabin wrote in his memoirs, "as he proclaimed the establishment of the State of Israel, our weary troops strained to
catch the portent of his words. One soldier was curled up in the
corner in a state of complete exhaustion, opened a bleary eye,
and pleaded: 'Hey guys, turn it off. I am dying for some sleep.
We can hear the fine words tomorrow.' . . . None of us had ever
dreamed this was how we would greet the birth of our state."[12]

Rabin emerged from the fighting for Jerusalem experienced
but embittered. As he wrote in his memoirs, he could not understand why the Yishuv's leadership had not prepared earlier
and better for the inevitable war: "This [May 20, 1948] was for

me a bitter day, a day of soul searching. During the period of the convoys, in the days of fierce fighting in Jerusalem, prior to and after the invasion of the regular Arab armies, I was bothered by the question, why has this war caught us so ill prepared? Was it necessary?"[13]

On the eve of the first truce, on June 11, 1948, Alon reassigned Rabin. Alon and the American volunteer Col. Mickey Marcus (Stone) were assigned a relatively large force and ordered by Ben Gurion to secure the road to Jerusalem. The goal was to control key positions further away from the city, such as the Palestinian town of Ramallah and the stronghold of Latrun.[14]

Ben Gurion had assigned prime importance to Jewish control of Jerusalem and the roads leading to it ever since the beginning of the war, and prior to the truce he wanted to establish that Israel had free access to the city. Latrun was a key point on the road from Tel Aviv to Jerusalem; earlier IDF attempts to conquer it had failed, and capturing the town became an obsession for Ben Gurion. By June 10 Alon and Marcus concluded that their forces were exhausted and in no position to attack Latrun. They also knew by that time that an alternative road to Jerusalem, nicknamed the Burma Road, had been discovered and was being prepared for use by the IDF. The two senior officers were afraid of confronting Ben Gurion personally with the news that they could not and did not want to launch another attack on Latrun, so they asked Rabin to do it in their stead. Rabin knew full well he would be exposed to the "Old Man's" wrath, and he was right. Ben Gurion was so angry he told the young Rabin that "Yigal Alon should be shot."

When Colonel Stone was killed in a tragic accident by an IDF guard who took him for an intruder, Rabin became Alon's deputy and chief of operations. The period of the first truce was used to plan the next phase of the campaign to secure the road to Jerusalem as well as the young state's control of the area between Jerusalem and Tel Aviv. The IDF's command were worried by the prospect of an effort by the Jordanian army to cut through this area and threaten Tel Aviv and the coastal area. But planning and preparation during this time were overshadowed by two awkward political issues, both of which involved Rabin.

One was the *Altalena* affair. The *Altalena* was a ship sent to Israel from France by the Irgun, or Etzel, the acronym for Irgun Tzevai Leumi, the right-wing underground affiliated with the revisionist movement and headed by Menachem Begin. It was loaded with weapons provided by the French government. The French were persuaded to support this right-wing organization in order to weaken the left-wing component of the Israeli leadership and to support the Irgun's military efforts in Jerusalem to undermine the position of Abdullah, seen by the French as a British agent. The Irgun had disbanded upon the establishment of the State of Israel but not in Jerusalem, which was designated as an international city by the Partition Plan. The *Altalena* arrived on the Israeli coast north of Tel Aviv on June 20, moved to Tel Aviv on June 22, and anchored near the Ritz Hotel, the home of the Palmach headquarters. Ben Gurion demanded the total surrender of the fighters aboard the ship. He was adamant that if Israel was to survive, the authority of the state could not be contested and private armies and militias could not be tolerated. Much about the *Altalena* affair is contested to this day, but there is no disputing the fact that Irgun men disembarked from the ship to the coast, and fighting erupted between them and the small force manning the Palmach headquarters. The prospect of a Jewish civil war was real and frightening. Rabin happened to be at Palmach headquarters at the time visiting his girlfriend, Leah. Being the senior officer on the spot, he took charge of the fighting against the Irgun men. On the whole, Rabin's role in the *Altalena* affair was quite minor, limited to the fighting on the beach, while the major roles were played by Ben Gurion and

Alon. Ben Gurion ordered the bombardment of the ship by the IDF artillery, and the ship was sunk. He referred proudly to this action by dubbing the cannon that sank the *Altalena* the Holy Cannon. Alon was put in charge of a larger operation against the Irgun in the Tel Aviv area in the aftermath of the fighting on the beach.

The *Altalena* episode would remain a controversial point of tension between the Right and the Left in Israeli politics in the coming decades. In a peculiar twist of fate, Ben Gurion's relationship with the Irgun leader Begin improved after 1967. In June 1967 Begin and his party joined a national unity government and remained part of it until the summer of 1970, bringing them into the mainstream of Israeli politics. Ben Gurion himself was retired by then and was above the fray of Israel's routine politics. Because of this, in right-wing mythology Ben Gurion's role in the affair was reduced, and his responsibility for sinking the *Altalena* was shifted to others, first to Israel Galili and then, in the mid-1990s—when Rabin was being demonized by the Israeli Right for signing the Oslo Accords—added to Rabin's own list of sins.

Rabin was less directly involved in a second major political conflict during this period. It began with a dispute over the appointment of a commander for the Central Front, considered the crucial front in the next phase of the fighting. The underlying issue was again Ben Gurion's hostile attitude to the Palmach. The IDF's senior leadership wanted Alon as commander. From its inception the Palmach had been affiliated with Hakibbutz Hameuchad and Achdut Haavoda, and its leader, Yitzhak Tabenkin, was Ben Gurion's rival. Achdut Haavoda joined Hashomer Hatzair in January 1948 to form Mapam, an acronym for the Hebrew name for the United Workers' Party. Hashomer Hatzair was a Marxist Zionist movement, while Achdut Haavoda combined socialism with Israeli nationalism. To Ben Gurion, this United Workers' Party, a pro-Soviet political movement, was suspicious, and he viewed the Palmach as to some extent its private army. Ben Gurion respected Alon's military and leadership skills but was less appreciative of his ambition and character. Ben Gurion's choice, Mordechai Maklef, on the other hand, had served in the British army. When Ben Gurion, clashing with the IDF leaders, insisted on appointing him to head the Central Command, several generals tendered their resignation. A commission of five cabinet members was appointed to mediate. The committee, which held its meetings between July 3 and 6 and called several witnesses, Rabin among them, clearly saw its mandate as much broader than the issue of Ben Gurion's relationship with Alon. Its questioning of Rabin focused on the failure to save the Old City, and Rabin complained about the decision made at the time to terminate the single command for military operations in Jerusalem: "I believe that at the start of the operation there was a single command, Yitzhak Sadeh was there, he was head of 'the Jebusite Staff.' In any event, this command, . . . I believe it was important at the time. I was not the one to demand that the command above me and Shealtiel be removed. I believe that it was wrong to empower David Shealtiel with the authority to issue orders since he was merely responsible for the city. Whether there were military failures is difficult to say, because if something is said, it needs to be proven and for this the whole issue of the defense of Jerusalem will have to be unraveled."[15] Rabin believed the importance of the episode lay in its exacerbation of the tension and lack of confidence between Ben Gurion and the Palmach and the shadow it cast on its senior commanders. As Alon's deputy and protégé, Rabin could not avoid being affected by Ben Gurion's negative attitude toward Alon, and his progression in the IDF was thus delayed in 1948 and in subsequent years.

By the time fighting renewed after the end of the first truce on July 11, 1948, two crucial decisions had been made: to invest the IDF's major efforts in the Central Command rather than in the south and to entrust the command of the operation to Alon. The operation was given the code name LRLR (Lydda— Ramleh—Latrun—Ramallah), subsequently renamed Operation Danny. It was to be conducted in two phases: the conquest of Lydda and Ramleh, to consolidate the young state's control of the center of the country; then of Latrun and Ramallah, to secure the road to Jerusalem. The first part of the operation was completed successfully, and two aspects of it registered in Israel's collective memory. One was Dayan's daring raid facilitating Lydda's capture, an event that helped build his reputation as an unconventional, brilliant field commander. The other was the large-scale expulsion of Arab civilians.

The issue of the expulsion has loomed large in the subsequent historiographic and political debate over right and wrong in the 1948 war and over Israel's moral rectitude. As a senior staff officer, Rabin was not directly involved in the fighting, but he did play a role in the expulsion. He wrote about it quite frankly in his memoirs in a section of the book that was censored in 1979 by the ministerial committee in charge of vetting memoirs and accounts written by public servants. The book's English translator, however, Peretz Kidron, was a radical left-wing activist who leaked the censored passages to the international press:

> While the fighting was in progress we had to grapple with a troublesome problem . . . : the fate of the civilian population of Lydda and Ramleh numbering some 50 thousand. Not even Ben Gurion offered any solution, and during the discussions at the operational headquarters he remained silent as was his habit in such situations. Clearly we could not leave Lod's hostile and armed population in our rear where it could endanger the supply route to Yiftah (Brigade) which was advancing eastward. We walked outside, Ben Gurion accom-

panying us. Alon repeated his question: "What is to be done with the population?" Ben Gurion waved his hand in a gesture and said, "Drive them out."

Alon and I had a consultation. I agreed it was essential to drive the inhabitants out. We took them on foot towards the Beit Horon road, assessing that the [Jordanian] Legion would be obliged to look after them.

"Driving out" is a term with a harsh ring. Psychologically, this was one of the most difficult actions we undertook.[16]

The Lydda affair became a milestone in the debate over the Palestinian refugee issue. Some thirty years later the Israeli writer Ari Shavit, in *My Promised Land*, endowed the fate of Lydda with almost mythical proportions: "Lydda is our 'black box.' In it lie the dark secrets of Zionism. The truth is that Zionism could not bear Lydda. . . . If Zionism was to be, Lydda could not be. If Lydda was to be, Zionism could not be. In retrospect, it is all too clear."[17]

Whatever perspective one adopts in the second decade of the twenty-first century, it is far removed from the considerations the political and military leadership had to take into account in July 1948 as the issue of the civilian population of Lydda and Ramleh was discussed.[18]

Operation Danny's second part ended in failure: Both Latrun and Ramallah remained under Jordanian control, part of the West Bank until 1967. But the operation cemented the relationship between Alon and Rabin as chief of operations and de facto second in command. As Alon's biographer describes it, "Here the combination between him [Alon] and Rabin was ideal. Alon provided the leadership, his endless optimism, the self-confidence he radiated as well as the boldness in planning. Rabin, on the other hand, was the one who translated the ideas into detailed, precise, operational plans that calculated risks versus prospects. Together they were a winning team. For the soldiers, Alon was the great military leader, for whom they were willing to invest extra effort. Rabin was an excellent number two but without the qualities that turned Yigal into an object of his soldiers' admiration."[19]

The second truce, after July 21, 1948, was used by the IDF to prepare for the next phase of the war. The balance had by then clearly shifted in Israel's favor. New and better weapons had arrived, more men were mobilized, and the lessons of the previous round of fighting were implemented. The IDF would soon shift to an offensive mode and exploit the advantage it now enjoyed in order to end the war by obtaining a clear victory. But the truce could be and was used for other purposes as well.

Rabin took advantage of the lull in the fighting to marry his girlfriend of several years, Leah Schlosberg. Rabin was a handsome young man, considered attractive to many young women in the Palmach and in the kibbutzim where he spent time, but he fell in love with the attractive, vivacious Schlosberg. They were a couple for several years, the so-called poster couple of the Palmach. Leah's background—she was born in Germany to an upper-middle-class, German Jewish family—was dramatically different from Yitzhak's. She was strong-minded and well-read, had a taste for art and literature, and rarely shied away from expressing her opinion. Their union was to be a successful one. Later, when Rabin became chief of staff, ambassador, and prime minister, Leah would become a public figure as well, flourishing in Washington circles, where she distinguished herself as an active and successful diplomatic hostess. Given Rabin's shyness and introverted character, Leah played an important role in conducting the couple's social life. Rabin wrote of their relationship in his memoirs:

> Ours was a wartime romance. It began with a chance encounter in a Tel Aviv street in 1944: a glance, a word, a stirring

within, and then a further meeting. But there were obstacles to the deepening relationship. I was in the Palmach and leaves were rare. We grew closer in 1945, when Leah joined the Palmach, and served in the battalion in which I was deputy commander—one of the rare occasions in our life together where she was under *my* command. I did my best to pay frequent visits to the kibbutz where she was stationed and we took frequent rides on my motorcycle. . . . As we began to weave our dreams, along came the British and arrested me; our only link was by letter. Then came the War of Independence with its bitter fighting and heavy toll in lives. Personal plans were set aside, and Leah managed to complete her studies at the teachers' seminary. During the second truce we decided to seize the opportunity and sealed our ties.[20]

Typically for those years, the young couple could not afford their own apartment and moved into a room in Leah's parents' home in central Tel Aviv. It was only in 1952 that they moved into their own house in a housing project for IDF senior officers.

The second event took place at Kibbutz Na'an starting on September 14, 1948. Several dozen Palmach senior officers were invited to a meeting with Ben Gurion. The Old Man sweetened a bitter pill by complimenting the Palmach on the contribution they had made to the war but then told his audience there was no justification for keeping the Palmach's separate staff: the state had an army, and the Palmach had to be an integral part of it. Its three brigades were to be kept in their entirety but placed under the full authority of the respective regional commands. Rabin refrained from taking part in the ensuing debate. He agreed with the essence of Ben Gurion's position, though he believed the Palmach's staff should be kept and given a special mission in order to preserve its legacy and spirit. But he realized that presenting this complex view would be perceived as lending support to Ben Gurion's decision. As was suspected, this was not the end of the process, and Ben

Gurion would later completely dismantle the Palmach. To him, this was in line with his conduct in the *Altalena* affair. If the new state was to survive, there had to be only one army: private armies could not be tolerated. By the end of September 1948 Israel was ready to renew the fighting and bring the war to an end. The choice of taking up the battle on the southern front was obvious, as the Egyptian army was in control of the Negev, the country's large, arid, sparsely populated southern area. This was Israel's land reserve, and the Red Sea at its southernmost tip offered future naval access to Africa and Asia. Folke Bernadotte, the UN mediator, who would be assassinated by the Stern Gang, a radical nationalist underground movement, on September 17, recommended in his report, published posthumously on September 20, that the southern Negev be taken away from Israel and exchanged for another part of the country. Egypt and possibly Great Britain saw the southern Negev as a land bridge connecting Egypt, still a British protectorate, to the eastern part of the Arab world. It was time to act.

The southern front was assigned four brigades. Alon was the commander, and Rabin was once again his deputy and chief operations officer. But the division of labor between the two now underwent a change, as Rabin would play a more important and salient role in these operations. Previously seen as Alon's right-hand man, he began to be seen on his own as a first-class military planner, the officer who meticulously mapped out the major operations in the south and then supervised their implementation.

Between October 1948 and March 1949 the IDF would complete three major operations in the south: Yoav, from October 15–22, 1948; Chorev, from December 22, 1948–January 7, 1949; and Uvda, from March 6–10, 1949. Operation Yoav accomplished its mission and opened the road to the Negev, driving a wedge into the Egyptian army's deployment. Operation Chorev, which sought to drive the Egyptian army out of the territory of Mandatory Palestine, was accomplished with the exception of the "Faloujah Pocket," where a significant Egyptian force was besieged. The victorious Israeli troops penetrated the Sinai Peninsula, Egyptian national territory. Under international pressure and always mindful of the political limits of any military action, Ben Gurion instructed the unhappy Alon and Rabin to withdraw their troops to the international border. During Operations Yoav and Chorev the IDF encountered stiff Egyptian opposition, but Israel's army now operated on a different scale, conducting complex and combined land, air, and naval operations. The success of Operation Chorev finally brought Egypt to the negotiating table. On January 12, 1949, the armistice negotiations were launched at the Roses Hotel on the Greek isle of Rhodes, under the chairmanship of Ralph Bunche, the new UN mediator. The IDF's second in command, Yigael Yadin, headed the military team that formed part of the Israeli delegation. Rabin was a member of the team as the representative of the southern front and the delegation's expert on the actual issues under discussion. Alon, still smarting under the impact of the order to withdraw from the Sinai, refused to attend. Rabin, too, was unhappy with the whole procedure, feeling the IDF was denied the opportunity to inflict a total defeat on the Egyptian army and thereby obtain greater leverage in the talks. During the negotiations he objected to the Egyptian demand that the area known as Awjah al-Hafir be demilitarized. The Foreign Office diplomats took a softer line. They attached great importance to arriving at an early conclusion of an armistice with the senior Arab state and were willing to make concessions on military issues. Rabin's outlook and mood during the meetings are reflected in a letter he wrote to Alon on February 10, 1949:

> I am convinced, based on everything that I saw and heard here, that the Egyptians are very much in need of the ar-

mistice agreement, that will extricate the brigade from the Pocket [the one besieged in the Falouja Pocket], and will reduce the forces in the coastal sector. In my view, any concession now is premature and unnecessary. In my view we have more breathing space than the Egyptians and can persist more than them in a war of nerves. I am almost certain that we will be successful in it. And if not, we will always be able to make a concession. . . . I am sick and tired of politics and diplomacy.[21]

The Egyptian–Israeli negotiations were concluded on February 24, 1949. Rabin and his colleagues were overruled. As a compromise of sorts, Rabin was allowed to leave on February 20, four days prior to the signing, so as to spare him the need to be a signatory to an agreement he objected to.

The Rhodes negotiations were Rabin's first diplomatic experience and first real interaction with non-Palestinian Arabs. He took from the meetings a lesson that would stay with him in the coming decades: it was not in Israel's interest to negotiate with an Arab collective. In such a negotiation the group dynamics tilted the Arab group toward following the lead of the most radical state. Israel does better when it deals separately with individual Arab states.

There was a second lesson to be taken from the Rhodes negotiations. Egypt was the one Arab state with a sense of raison d'état. Its leaders were the first to conclude that it was in their interest to end the war; their agreement with Israel was signed on February 24, 1949. Other Arab states, Syria in particular, took their time, and their negotiations were not concluded until July 1949. Even while the talks were still unfolding, Israel completed its southward drive and—through Operation Uvda—took control of the whole Negev, obtaining a foothold on the Red Sea in Umm Rashrash, present-day Eilat. It was an impressive logistical exploit, taking a large military force through uncharted territory.

When the war ended in 1948 Rabin was a lieutenant colonel, second to Alon in the Southern Command. He had emerged with a reputation as a first-rate military planner and staff officer. He had a wealth of experience won on the field, in senior staff posts, and at the negotiating table. But the war's most enduring legacy for Rabin was the one he took away from the difficult fighting on the road to Jerusalem. As he wrote time and again in his memoirs, Rabin felt that the IDF had not been sufficiently well prepared prior to the 1948 war and that his men and others paid dearly for it. He vowed that such unreadiness would not be repeated.

2

◆｜◆｜◆

From Independence to the Six-Day War,
1949–1967

As THE final weeks of the war drew to a close and a new, postwar routine began to emerge, the tension between Ben Gurion and the Palmach's leadership rose to a new level. Some of the Palmach's senior commanders were pushed out of the IDF, while others chose to leave in protest. Rabin chose to stay. In his memoirs he explained: "Standing now at a crossroad in my personal life, I felt a profound sense of moral responsibility, a kind of debt of honor toward the men whose courage and whose very bodies had blocked the Arab advance. . . . At the most tragic moments of the war . . . many of my fellow officers and I undertook a personal commitment. . . . We would dedicate our life to ensuring that the state of Israel would never again be unprepared to meet aggression. . . . We built a mighty army."[1]

But there was more to it than that. For one thing, options in the young, poor state were limited. Rabin identified with the

Palmach, but he was also the independent loner—Rosa's son—who did not join a kibbutz or Achdut Haavoda, who made his own decisions. It was this same Rabin who, at the meeting in Kibbutz Na'an held by Ben Gurion with the Palmach's leadership to air their differences, chose to keep quiet. Rabin in fact agreed with the substance of Ben Gurion's decision to dismantle the Palmach's general staff but did not want to side with the Old Man against his comrades. Rabin was close to Achdut Haavoda, but he refrained from actually joining the party. As he wrote to his sister in the mid-1940s, "I am not a party member and despite my identification in some issues with the movement of Achdut Haavoda, I fail to see in it any vision, any will to take the initiative, to lead and to show the way; it is rather a middle of the road entity that wishes to point to a path somewhat different from that of the existing leadership."[2]

All this did not affect his loyalty to Alon, who was removed by Ben Gurion from his post at the Southern Command and replaced by Dayan. Alon was actually in Europe visiting the French army, and, despite being undermined at home, he inexplicably extended this visit. Alon's career peaked during the 1948 war and began to decline in its immediate aftermath. This episode was an early indication that Alon's personality had undergone a profound change. Rabin kept Alon informed while he was abroad and fought on his behalf. He described to Alon his efforts on his behalf by quoting a letter he had written to Chief of Staff Yaacov Dori on October 12, 1949: "Demanding a written explanation with regard to you. I also added an oral demand for a meeting with him. Despite three requests in one day to his aide-de-camp, I got no answer." The letters he sent to Alon were written in a primitive code, and the code name chosen for Dayan was "the antiques dealer." They were critical of Dayan. In a letter to Alon on October 23, Rabin wrote, "Dayan showed up. I am breaking him in. The guy has no idea. In my view, he lacks minimal military understanding on a scale larger than a company or a battalion. Totally tactless in dealing with people."[3]

The dislike and lack of appreciation were mutual. Dayan wasted no time in removing Rabin from his post as second in command in the Southern Command. Rabin was appointed commander of the 12th Brigade, which in the standard of those days qualified as an armored brigade. This arrangement did not last for long. The 12th Brigade was seen as a Palmach Brigade, and it was disbanded under the pretext that all armored elements should be concentrated in the 7th Brigade. Rabin sent an angry letter to the chief of staff criticizing the decision. "I wonder why and to what end?" he wrote. "It occurs to me that there might be two reasons: Either personal arguments against me that I cannot understand or arguments against the Brigade because of its Palmach origins."[4]

Tensions surrounding the Palmach issue came to a head on October 24, the date set for a Palmach rally intended both as a farewell event and an act of protest. The IDF's general staff issued an order forbidding officers on active duty from participating in what they defined as a political event. It was very important to Ben Gurion that Rabin in particular not take part, as he was the ranking Palmach officer in the IDF. His participation—or absence—would be noted. Ben Gurion, who had something of a soft spot for Rabin, may also have wanted to protect him from the consequences of directly disobeying an order. He invited him for a discussion at his home late in the afternoon of that day. As Rabin describes it in his memoirs, when he was just preparing to leave, the Old Man invited him to stay for dinner. Rabin declined and went to the rally, knowing full well he would pay a price for this act of defiance. Staying in the IDF was one thing, loyalty to his friends and colleagues was another.

Ben Gurion was incensed. He held Rabin's conduct against him and delayed his promotion by a decade. Ben Gurion was not the only politician angered by the incident. At a cabinet meeting the leader of the Mizrachi (later the National Religious) Party, Moshe Haim Shapira, argued that "Rabin is not just a young man who was confused by the two commands— he sat with Mr. Ben Gurion, argued with him, poured [out] his heart and then when he faced the dilemma of what is more important—party discipline or military discipline—preferred the party discipline. It means that the deputy commander of a front who in a first test, when he confronted such a choice, decided in favor of the party. And what happens if the party orders him to hurt the government—he will once again face the choice, the party or the government, and I do not know how he will come out of this test. . . . I am saying openly: I am not willing to deposit the fate of a brigade in the hands of a commander who could violate discipline in such fashion." This was not the last clash between Shapira and Rabin.

The incident was brought to an end when Chief of Staff Dori took disciplinary action on October 21, 1949. Rabin's encounter with Dori, transcribed in the archives, was a rare moment: few senior officers on their way to supreme command are disciplined for failure to obey an order. Rabin's responses to Dori were short, dry, and matter of fact:

> DORI: You were summoned to a disciplinary trial for breach of discipline. Did you receive the order forbidding participation in the rally?
>
> RABIN: I received the order.
>
> DORI: Did you participate?
>
> RABIN: Yes.
>
> DORI: How does the failure to comply with the order square with the oath you took to obey all instructions issued to you by the supreme command?
>
> RABIN: It does not square. I admit breaching the order. I had a sense of a personal loyalty towards friends . . . it was

a matter of friendship. . . . I felt that I had to meet with my friends.

DORI: Was there another order?

RABIN: There was no other command, it was a personal decision. It is true that there was a failure to comply with a command but I did not receive a command from another source.

DORI: How does it square with the oath?

RABIN: It is true that there was a command, but there is no law forbidding a soldier as a citizen to participate while on leave in rallies.

Rabin was given a severe reprimand and extricated from the predicament of this period by Haim Laskov, who invited him to join and then replace himself as commandant of the School for Battalion Commanders, a new military course founded soon after the end of the war as part of the institutionalization of the IDF. Rabin invited several of his Palmach colleagues to join him as instructors. To some of them this became an incentive for staying in, or returning to, the IDF. Laskov, formerly a major in the Jewish Brigade of the British army, was a model of the former British officer that Ben Gurion preferred as an antithesis to the Palmach officers. But despite their different military backgrounds, Laskov and Rabin got along famously. Their collaboration and the role played by their colleagues were crucial in integrating the lessons of the 1948 war as well as the two different military traditions into the IDF's distinctive doctrine. The fifty students of the school went on over the following years to become the core of the IDF's command, commanders and trainees together developing a new professional language in Hebrew. Rabin's meticulous approach occasionally proved exasperating to the students, but they accepted and respected his authority.[5] Rabin had an excellent memory and combined analytical skills with attention to detail. He insisted on precision and perfection, qualities that were not always appreciated by the people working under him.

Rabin's next posting was as head of the General Headquarters' (GHQ) Department of Operations, a position he held from January 1951 to December 1952. This was a key position in the GHQ's most important division. The department was responsible for three areas: operations, current security, and the organization and mobilization of the reserves. The documents written by Rabin during this period reflect his mastery of military affairs, from matters of doctrine to command and control to tactics.[6] His comments on a research paper prepared by the IDF's Planning Department are a fine example of his performance in this capacity. He was keen and incisive, demonstrated a profound understanding of the role of the air force in modern warfare, and insisted that the air force's role and performance be determined not by the air force itself but by the General Staff. Rabin's main contribution to the IDF's work and methodology during this period was effecting a transition from the wartime military planning of 1948 to a more orderly, systematic type of planning required by the postwar IDF, illustrated by a paper he wrote on December 24, 1951, "War Planning in the IDF." Rabin drew a distinction between strategic and operational planning, thus resolving the dilemma facing every modern army. Planning for a hypothetical scenario could produce rigidity; the challenge of the planner is to keep an element of flexibility that enables the army's leadership to cope with the actual reality it may meet when a military plan prepared in advance has to be applied to unforeseen circumstances.

During this period Rabin built his standing and reputation as a military thinker, planner, and unusually efficient staff officer. General Yisrael Tal, the legendary architect of the IDF's armored corps, described Rabin as "the highest intellectual authority on military matters."[7] Another IDF general, Elad Peled, wrote, "Yitzhak was regarded by the representatives of the 1948 generation in the IDF as the most senior military professional. . . . In every exercise, in every maneuver, in any discussion that he attends people listen to him and know that he is the 'Admor' [Hasidic rabbi], the professional."[8]

Rabin's rise in the IDF's pecking order was demonstrated by Chief of Staff Mordechai Maklef's initiative in 1953 to appoint him as chief of operations—and thus his second in command, instead of Dayan, with whom Maklef did not get along. But Ben Gurion, who was fond and deeply appreciative of Dayan and perhaps still smarting from Rabin's disobedience over the Palmach rally, nipped Maklef's initiative in the bud.

Rabin and his family were actually in England at the British army's Staff College in Camberley at this time, during 1953. Rabin was one of the first officers to be sent to a Western military college as part of a policy designed to protect the IDF from the potential provincialism of a small army of an isolated country and to integrate Israel in practice, if not formally, into the Western defense establishment. For Rabin it was an opportunity to be exposed to the outside world, to learn from the rich experience of a great army, to improve his command of English, and to spend some leisurely time with his wife, Leah, and their daughter, Dalia (their son, Yuval, would be born in 1955). Upon Rabin's return, Dayan, now the chief of staff, showed he held no grudges by appointing him chief of the Instruction Division at GHQ as well as promoting him to major general. Indeed, Dayan went to great lengths to persuade the minister of defense, Pinchas Lavon, to agree to Rabin's promotion. Rabin was still considered by Mapai's leadership as not politically reliable owing to his breach of discipline at the Palmach rally. Dayan told Lavon that the Instruction Division had no troops under its command and that therefore Rabin could not, even if he wanted, fail to carry out an order he did not agree with. Lavon still resisted, remarking that the IDF at that point had too many major generals. Dayan wrote that he agreed with him but asked to make an exception in Rabin's case. Lavon finally assented. Dayan's biographer, Shabtai Teveth, who knew Dayan and Rabin well, rightly commends Dayan in this episode for promoting Rabin despite the awkward relationship between the two. Dayan, explains Teveth, was determined to transform the spirit of the IDF and saw Rabin as the right candidate for translating his ideas into an orderly, effective system of instruction. Despite Dayan's political support, however, there was constant tension between the two men. They managed to work together effectively, but their personal relationship remained uneasy. Teveth wrote,

> A partial explanation is their very different characters. Rabin was not fond of Dayan's modus operandi. But there were also differences characteristic of the gap between a distinctive field commander and a distinctive staff officer, between a natural or charismatic leader and an excellent professional or technocrat, between a man operating according to his senses and practical wisdom and a rational man of sound logic, between someone comfortable with other people and a shy person. To this should be added Rabin's tendency to make critical, biting comments about his superiors. . . . It was Rabin who coined the phrase that haunted Dayan for a long time— "He is a user of force, not a builder of one."[9]

In the IDF organizational culture it has been common for officers to serve three to four years in a senior position and then move on. Rabin's next posting, as general officer commanding, Northern Command, which he held from April 1956 to April 1959, was quite different. Instead of holding a senior staff position, he was now in command of a territorial entity, responsible for security in a part of the country bordering Syria and Lebanon. The main challenge was managing the difficult border relationship with Syria. The Armistice Agreements of 1949 were seen at the time as temporary arrangements, to be replaced by peace treaties. This failed to happen, and the conflict festered.

Syria's politics were becoming militarized and radicalized; it had gone through four military coups between 1949 and 1954. By the mid-1950s, beneath the surface of a parliamentary regime, political power and influence were held by radical ideological parties and military factions. The complex, awkward arrangements regarding both agricultural work in the demilitarized areas and water issues around Lake Tiberias and the Jordan River were sources of ongoing friction. Israel and Syria would collide many times over Syrian access to Lake Tiberias, Israel's most important water reservoir. The 1949 Armistice Agreement with Syria defined the small territory west of the international border between Syria and Palestine, held by the Syrian army at the war's end, as demilitarized zones. Israel's sovereignty in this territory was limited, and Syria objected to Israel's right to cultivate land in the demilitarized zones that had been Arab-owned before the 1948 war. Whenever Israeli tractors worked in these lots they were fired upon from the commanding heights of the Golan. Rabin was a staunch guardian of Israel's position vis-à-vis Syria and emerged from his three years in the Northern Command with a perception of Syria as a bitter enemy and a strong sense of the strategic and tactical significance of the Golan Heights. As general officer commanding of the Northern Command, Rabin had no involvement in the Sinai campaign of 1956, Dayan's springboard to fame and glory. The Sinai campaign was fought in the South and had no direct repercussions on Israel's relations with Syria.

The end of his tenure at the Northern Command in 1959 marked an important year for Rabin. For a while it seemed to be the end of his military career. Dayan, in his final year as chief of staff of the IDF, had tried to steer Rabin out of the army by suggesting that at the end of his term they both enroll at the Hebrew University. Rabin at the time insisted he was interested only in studying abroad: his old dream of studying water engineering in the United States. Dayan, in his capacity as chief of staff, ruled it out, and Rabin stayed in the army. Thanks to his friendlier relationship with Laskov, Dayan's successor, Laskov arranged for Rabin, who had completed his tour of duty in the North, to study at Harvard University in Cambridge, Massachusetts. Rabin and his family prepared to depart for Cambridge in the summer of 1959, but in April of that year a reserves call-up exercise was mismanaged by the IDF and caused a war scare. Ben Gurion removed the head of the IDF's Staff Division and the Director of Military Intelligence from their positions, and Rabin was appointed as head of the Staff Division at GHQ. He now held the third most senior position in the IDF after Chief of Staff Laskov and his deputy, Zvi ("Chera") Tsur, and became a serious candidate to replace Laskov at the end of his term.

In his new capacity as head of Staff Division, Rabin joined the small group that shaped Israel's national security policy, expanding his activity beyond the strict confines of military matters. Ben Gurion was busy building "the alliance of the periphery," a partnership with Israel's regional neighbors Turkey, Iran, and Ethiopia opposed to the Soviet Union and to the revolutionary Pan-Arabism of Egypt's president Gamal Abdel Nasser. Rabin made several trips to Ethiopia, offering advice and instruction to its military. As the foreign minister, Golda Meir cultivated relations with Africa, and Rabin was sent to the Congo. He took part in the debate on procurement policy and found himself in disagreement with the influential director general of the Ministry of Defense, Shimon Peres. The conflict between the civilian leadership of the defense establishment and the top echelons of the military is endemic in Israel—and in almost any other country. In this case, Rabin argued that decisions regarding procurement had to be made by the military leadership rather than by the civilian bureaucracy. There were many other such issues on which Peres and Rabin held opposing views. While Peres advocated a European orientation (France and Germany) in procurement, Rabin and others wanted Israel to turn a still-reluctant United States into a major source of military equipment. Peres, regarded as the father of Israel's defense industries, believed in local production whereas Rabin preferred buying off the shelf abroad. Peres was the main force behind the Dimona nuclear reactor project, about which Rabin, along with his friends in the Achdut Haavoda faction Galili and Alon, was dubious. He believed in conventional deterrence and preferred to allocate Israel's limited resources to building up the IDF rather than to the expensive nuclear project. Rabin changed his mind in 1963 when he became persuaded that Israel would be hard put to sustain an endless, conventional arms race with the Arab world. These would be the roots of the rivalry and bad blood between Rabin and Peres that became such an important issue in Israeli politics in the 1970s.

The major military event of this period came to be known as Rotem: the remilitarization of Sinai by Egypt in 1960. Egypt was, at that time (February 1958–September 1961), united with Syria in the framework of the United Arab Republic (UAR). Escalating tension on the Israeli–Syrian border generated by friction over the demilitarized areas and fear of a massive Israeli attack prompted Egypt to send a large number of tanks to the Sinai in violation of arrangements made in 1957. Israel was caught by surprise, but the tension was eventually defused since neither party had an interest in a military clash. It was a case of successful crisis management. One of Rabin's major efforts in the coming years would be to develop the intelligence capacity that would prevent another such surprise.

The early end of Laskov's term as chief of staff was another milestone in Rabin's slow progression to the top of the IDF's pyramid. Ben Gurion was fond of Laskov, but the chief of staff's conflicts with Peres and with several senior officers had exacted a price. Rabin believed he was entitled to succeed Laskov as chief of staff, but Ben Gurion decided in favor of Tsur. He invited

Rabin to a meeting to explain his choice. Rabin knew full well that Peres had pushed for his choice, Tsur, but this was not mentioned by Ben Gurion. In a personal letter to his friend Uzi Narkis, who served as the military attaché in Paris, Rabin wrote, "Ben Gurion offered a broad set of explanations, starting with Chera's seniority etc. . . . He also mentioned two 'sins'—first the fact that I disobeyed his order at the time and went to the Palmach rally . . . the second he thinks I am a bit cautious. . . . Later I asked him whether I should stay at the IDF and in my present position . . . should an undesirable personal relationship [with Tsur] develop. In short, he almost jumped up off his chair and asked me how I dare entertain such thoughts etc. etc. In any event it turned out that he agrees that in addition to my position as Chief of the Staff Division, I will receive the status of Deputy Chief of Staff, but the offer did not come from him."[10]

Rabin was indeed given the title of deputy chief of staff, another step in his arduous voyage to the chief of staff position. But the journey's final leg was not smooth. His question to Ben Gurion about possible tension between him and Tsur was prescient. In early December 1960 Tsur spoke positively about Rabin to Ben Gurion. Ben Gurion wrote in his diary on December 8 that "Yitzhak—in Tsur's opinion—rather than Haim [Laskov] manages the army, and he is a good manager. Knows the work. Works quietly." But once Tsur actually replaced Laskov, the relationship between Rabin and Tsur deteriorated. Tsur did not want him as his deputy, and, after a period of joint work punctuated by grievances, told him he wanted to replace him. Ironically, Rabin's main supporter in his conflict with Tsur was Ben Gurion, and when Tsur wanted to ease him out, Rabin insisted they go see Ben Gurion in order to resolve the conflict. Rabin was now focused on becoming chief of staff and stayed on target. On February 26, 1963, Ben Gurion wrote in his diary about the prospect of a "study leave" he suggested to Rabin. "I plan," he wrote, "to keep Tsur in his post for another two years and, if I stay in my position—the post of Chief of Staff is reserved to him, To Yitzhak." But Rabin brushed aside the idea of a study leave and decided to stay put. He knew full well it would be too risky to be abroad while waiting for a promotion.

It was the right move. In the spring of 1963 Ben Gurion decided to retire from politics. Before leaving he asked his successor, Levi Eshkol, to respect his promise to Rabin. Eshkol obliged and, to boot, decided to end Tsur's term after three years. Rabin became chief of staff on January 1, 1964.

The senior leadership of the IDF in those years was composed of a small group of able and ambitious men, some of whom were friends, others bitter rivals. The competition for senior posts was fierce but moderated by a sense of membership in the same club. Some of these relationships, good and bad, lingered over the coming decades, as several senior officers and defense officials went into politics and continued to compete for power and influence. Rabin's relations with Alon, Dayan, Peres, Ariel Sharon, Ezer Weizman, Haim Bar-Lev, and Aharon Yariv were all shaped in the 1940s and 1950s and continued to be an important part of his universe well into the 1990s.

After having formed his government on June 26, 1963, Eshkol had two important meetings with the IDF's general staff in which he was given thorough briefings on the army's current state and what it was planning. In the second meeting, held on July 8, Weizman, commander of the air force, argued that Israel's current borders posed a danger and threatened the safety of the air force and its airfields. The IDF, he said, should strive to expand its borders even if this was incongruent with "the political approach." Rabin, who, as chief of the Staff Division, presented a platform for discussion, had a different view: "We do not believe that in order to implement the state's mission, to guarantee its existence—the condition is to improve the borders. . . . As for the IDF's tasks— . . . we put under first priority defense of the state and its territorial integrity and the protection of its sovereign rights within its territory and outside it as first priority. If this is the purpose, it is better to achieve it without war."[11]

This statement was reflective of Rabin's conception of the national security of the country and his approach to the issue of resorting to military action: essentially defensive. He believed in deterrence rather than the preemptive use of force. Given Israel's small size, the Arab advantage in territory, and the size of the Arab armies, Rabin subscribed to the doctrine that in the event of war Israel should rely not on defense but on the rapid transfer of the war to the enemy's territory. As chief of staff, Rabin would build the force and oversee the planning for implementing his concept of Israel's national security.

Rabin's slow progression to the top of the IDF's pyramid had one positive result: He became chief of staff as the undisputed leader of the IDF's senior corps, authoritative and powerful. Rabin was the oldest chief of staff of the IDF at the time, being the first officer over the age of forty to hold the position. By serving in several positions at the IDF, Rabin had accumulated experience and depth that added to the authority he already had among his colleagues and subordinates.

Rabin assembled a team that is still considered the IDF's best General Staff ever. Ezer Weizman, Haim Bar-Lev, Aharon Yariv, Zvi Zamir, Yeshayahu Gavish, Amos Chorev, and David Elazar were some of its prominent members. Rabin also made a point of including three unorthodox officers: Ariel Sharon, Matti Peled, and Israel Tal. It was a formula that provided originality and freshness to a team composed of excellent, traditional generals. Promoting Sharon was the fulfillment of a promise Rabin made to Ben Gurion to look after Sharon. Ben Gurion was aware of the problematic side of Sharon's character—he was considered undisciplined and capable of lying—but admired him as a great soldier, and Rabin shared Ben Gurion's view. In 1964 Sharon was a colonel, the commander of an unimportant base, and seemed to be at the gloomy end of his military career. Rabin appointed him as second in command to the General Officer Commanding of the Northern Command. Rabin told Sharon that if he behaved properly for one year he would promote him. The year went well, and one year later he appointed Sharon as head of instruction in the IDF, promoting him to the rank of general.

As chief of staff, Rabin continued to combine comprehensive overview with an exceptional command of detail. On the eve of operations and in their aftermath he used to go out to the field and study the minutest detail of each exercise by speaking to junior officers and regular soldiers. Famous for his awkwardness and his impatience with long-winded discussions in staff meetings, Rabin displayed unusual patience and calm grace when talking to soldiers.

Between 1949 and 1964 Rabin held several positions that played an important role in building the IDF and crafting its doctrine. He naturally continued to do so as the IDF's chief of staff. Of particular importance would be his collaboration with Weizman in the development of Kurnass, the secret plan for destroying Arab air forces crafted as Israel's opening gambit should another war prove to be inevitable.

THE ROAD TO WAR

When Rabin began his term as the IDF's chief of staff in January 1964, the Israeli intelligence estimate was that the Arab world was not likely to initiate a war in the foreseeable future. In January 1964 a large part of the Egyptian army was bogged down in Yemen in a hopeless effort to help the Republican regime there defeat a tribal rebellion supported primarily by Saudi Arabia. On his first day in office Rabin presented his view of Israel's national security position to the members of his General Staff: "I believe that there is no danger of an immediate attack on Israel as long as we are able to maintain a reasonable balance of power, at least at its present level. It is important to tilt that balance in our favor. I believe it is possible to maintain a balance of power that in practice would mean unwillingness and reluctance to become embroiled with us in the future as well."[12]

However, three developments were unfolding at the time that would alter the Arab–Israeli equation, culminating three and a half years later in the crisis of May 1967 and the Six-Day War. These were the decline of Nasserism and Nasser's regime in Egypt; the revival of Palestinian nationalism; and the radicalization of Syrian politics.

The failed adventure in Yemen was just one aspect of the decline of Nasserism after its heyday in the late 1950s. Syria broke away from its union with Egypt in September 1961, in what the American scholar Malcolm Kerr called the "Arab Cold War" of the early 1960s against both the conservative Arab states and the Ba'ath Party regimes in Syria and Iraq; Egypt became more of a client than an ally of the Soviet Union; and Nasser was hard put to deal with political and economic challenges at home. One of these challenges, not fully understood in Israel at the time, was Nasser's loss of control over the military, which became the private preserve of his deputy, Field Marshal Abd al-Hakim Amer.

During the peak period of Nasserism most Palestinians were enthusiastic supporters of it. They felt their redemption would come once he united the Arab world and developed the formidable force required to defeat Israel. But as Nasserism began to decline, a variety of Palestinian groups, some of them Islamist in orientation, began to organize to act on their own—most notably Yasser Arafat's Fath. Fath (in Arabic, "conquest") is the reversed acronym for the Arabic Movement for the Liberation of Palestine. Founded in the late 1950s and remaining underground until 1965, Fath was a nationalist Palestinian group touched by an Islamist flavor whose vision was to resuscitate the Palestinian dimension of the Arab–Israeli conflict after the defeat and dispersion of 1948–49.

But the single most important development leading to the crisis of May 1967 was the radicalization of Syrian politics. Three and a half years of a failed union with Egypt that lasted from February 1958 until September 1961 revived the sense of Syrian distinctiveness. Syria seceded from the union, but secession was easier than rebuilding a stable polity. Egypt refused to recognize the newly independent Syria, and Nasser was still influential enough to deny the new Syria any legitimacy. He pounded Syria's new rulers as traitors to the cause of pan-Arab nationalism, castigating them for undermining its most meaningful achievement: the first union between two Arab states.

In March 1963 a group of officers affiliated with the Ba'ath Party staged a coup in Syria and established the Ba'ath regime there. Like Nasserism, the Ba'ath stood for Arab unity and a version of Arab socialism, but after a period of close cooperation in the late 1950s Nasser and the Ba'ath became bitter rivals. Having seized power in Syria, the Ba'ath regime rested on a very narrow political basis, supported by a military faction and the small radical left wing of the party and resented by the majority of Sunni Muslim Arabs. Toward the end of 1963 the group sought to turn a challenge into an opportunity. Israel announced it was about to complete the overland water carrier, pumping water out of Lake Tiberias and bringing it to the south of the country. This project was seen by the Arab world as a dramatic turning point because, with water soon to be available in the arid southern part of Israel, Israel would be able to increase its population and consolidate its existence. In the 1950s Syria's conservative rulers had been successful in stopping the first effort to build the project. How could their radical successors overcome the humiliation of failing to stop the project's new incarnation? The solution devised by the leadership of the Ba'ath regime was to announce that Syria would go to war to stop the project. This was not merely a face-saving formula but a threat directed at Egypt: should Syria's radical new leaders actually go to war against Israel and be defeated, would Egypt be able to stay out of that war? This was a risk Nasser could not take. In order to restrain the Syrians, he convened an Arab summit in January 1964.

The purpose of this conference was to deal with the new Israeli challenge. Nasser was hoping for an Arab consensus to restrain Syria. But the Cairo summit's scope broadened: the Arab response would not just deal with Israel's water carrier but also formulate a comprehensive strategy against the Zionist enemy. Three major resolutions were made: first, to divert the tributaries of the Jordan; second, to form a "unified Arab command" in order to protect the diversion works; and third, to form the Palestine Liberation Organization (PLO) in order to create, for the first time since 1949, a Palestinian entity that would transform the Palestinian problem from a problem of refugees to a clash of entities with Israel. Like his Ba'athist rivals, Nasser was attempting to turn adversity to advantage. More than simply restraining Syria, he was trying—by establishing the Unified Arab Command that was to rely on Egypt's military power—to exert pressure on Saudi Arabia that would allow him to exit honorably from Yemen. The onus would be on Saudi Arabia to agree to a political solution in Yemen that would enable Egypt to bring its troops home and put them under the new Unified Arab Command. The formation of the PLO was directed not just at Israel but also at Jordan, one of Egypt's conservative Arab enemies. Abdullah, the grandfather of King Hussein of Jordan, had annexed the West Bank and given the Palestinians Jordanian citizenship. The formation of a new Palestinian entity was a direct threat to Jordan by claiming the allegiance of its Palestinian population.

The Cairo summit was the first in a series of conferences that became the framework for inter-Arab relations. The summit's major decisions were implemented in short order. A Unified Arab Command was formed under the command of an Egyptian general; the PLO was formed under Ahmad Shuqeiri, an Egyptian protégé; and plans were made for diverting the tributaries of the Jordan in Syria and Lebanon. The implementation of these resolutions exacerbated the Arab–Israeli conflict and led to the crisis of May 1967. The establishment of the PLO prompted the authentic Palestinian groups which had begun to crystalize in the 1950s to come to the surface. Their attitude to the Arab states was complex: they needed and wanted their support, but they had learned in 1948 that they had to control their own destiny rather than be a tool of Arab politics. In January 1965 the first terrorist act was staged by Fath when it tried to sabotage Israel's National Water Carrier. This marked the beginning of the organization's path to reviving the Palestinian nationalist movement and turning it into an independent actor in Arab politics.

As Syria started the groundwork for the diversion of the sources of the Jordan, a new dimension was added to its conflict with Israel. The Syrian front had been the most active line of confrontation in the Arab–Israeli conflict since 1949. Most of the incidents had to do with disputes over the demilitarized zones and fishing rights in Lake Tiberias. Israel was determined to prevent Syria from completing the diversion works and to use force if necessary. In 1964 and 1965 the IDF, led and prodded by Rabin, demonstrated it could destroy the Syrian equipment with tank fire, thus limiting the engagement rather than getting drawn into a large-scale conflict. Syria retaliated by taking Fath under its wing and supporting its terrorist activities, launched primarily through Jordan's territory. This was not only a way of getting back at Israel but also a demonstration of the Syrian regime's claim that it had adopted a "Popular War of Liberation" against Israel. The regime's spokesmen argued that, as in Vietnam, the way to confront a militarily superior enemy was to abandon the methods of classical warfare and to adopt so-called popular ones. This was a thinly veiled criticism of Egypt and its traditional ways. By encouraging Fath to carry out its terrorist activities through Jordan, Syria was seeking to provoke conflict between this conservative Arab rival and Israel and thereby reduce the risk of Israeli retaliation against itself.

In short order a cycle of violence was created. Israeli destruction of Syrian diversion equipment would generate a Syrian retaliation, either along its own Armistice Lines or via a Fath terrorist squad. Israel would retaliate against that attack, and a new round of violence would begin. Syria easily escalated the conflict by shelling Israeli villages from its dominant positions in the Golan Heights. In November 1964 Rabin obtained Eshkol's permission to use the air force to silence Syria's artillery. Rabin argued that given the massive use of American air power in Vietnam, Washington would find it difficult to criticize Israel's resorting to aerial superiority in order to protect its civilian population.

The Syrian coup d'état, on February 23, 1966, brought to power the radical wing of the Ba'ath and its military allies and once again escalated the conflict. The new regime was more radical than the one it replaced and more clearly dominated by members of the country's minority communities, Alawites, Druze, and Ismailis. It rested on an extremely narrow basis and seemed several times to be on the verge of collapse. Its leaders were willing to resort to a more adventurist policy, initiating direct and indirect attacks on Israel, that worried their Soviet patrons as well as Egypt. Nasser was worried by two prospects: the regime's collapse and possible replacement by a conservative regime allied with his Arab rivals and a full-blown war with Israel that would force him to get off the fence. He was therefore willing to recognize the Syrian state's legitimacy by reestablishing diplomatic relations and then went further by signing a defense treaty with Damascus in November 1966. If Nasser was hoping these concessions would serve to calm the tension, he was quickly disappointed. In August 1966 a major clash developed above Lake Tiberias, and on April 7, 1967, six Syrian air force jets were shot down by the Israeli air force close to Damascus. A perfect vicious cycle was fueled by Syria's radical rulers, reckless adventurism, and Rabin's and his generals' conviction that increasingly powerful responses were the only effective way to restrain the Syrians. The dovish wing of the cabinet, led by National Religious Party (NRP) ministers, was consistently opposed to this line—particularly to employing the air force—but with a few exceptions Eshkol tended to accommodate Rabin's preferences. At different periods in Israel's history the formulation of national security policy would be divided between the prime minister, the minister of defense, and the chief of staff. Between 1964 and 1967, Eshkol, as both prime minister and minister of defense, tended to defer to Rabin, who became the chief architect of national security policy. Characteristically, Rabin dealt both with the large picture and with such details as the use of tank fire against the Syrian tractors engaged in the effort to divert the tributaries of the Jordan River.

There was a Jordanian dimension to this process. In November 1966 an explosive device laid by a Palestinian squad dispatched from Syria through Jordan claimed the lives of four Israeli soldiers. Israel knew full well where the squad originated but decided to retaliate not against Syria but against Jordan, arguing that it was responsible for sealing off its borders and territory against such activity. The retaliatory Israeli attack, against the police station in the village of Samu' near Hebron in the southern West Bank, was a massive operation and a gross error of judgment. Syria and Egypt, Jordan's radical Arab foes, criticized Jordan's conservative, pro-Western Hashemite regime for being unable to defend the national territory and its population and called on it to introduce mandatory military service. This would have meant a Palestinization of the Jordanian army and the loss of the regime's mainstay, namely, the loyalty of the Bedouin officers in its armed forces. Jordan responded by taunting the Nasserist regime for "hiding under the skirts of the UN soldiers" who in 1957 had been stationed along the border with Israel and in the Straits of Tiran. It was a classic case of Kerr's "Arab Cold War." The linkage between the inter-Arab bickering and the Arab–Israeli conflict contributed in a major way to the escalation that culminated in the May 1967 crisis.

Egypt's military leadership was unwilling to accept the humiliation caused by the Jordanian taunting. In the aftermath of the Egyptian defeat in June 1967 Field Marshall Abd al-Hakim Amer and several other senior officers were court-martialed in Egypt for their role prior to and during the war. The protocols of the court-martial shed light on the prewar decisions made by Egypt. It was revealed that while on a trip to Pakistan in November 1966 Amer sent a cable to Nasser demanding the removal of the UN peacekeepers and the remilitarization of the Sinai Peninsula. Amer's argument was that the Egyptian army could hold the IDF back in the Sinai should Israel decide to go to war over the collapse of the post-Sinai-war security regime. An oblique paragraph in Rabin's memoirs indicates that Israel's defense establishment was aware of Amer's position but failed to give it proper significance. As late as spring of 1967 it still believed Egypt would not be drawn into war "over a Syrian tractor," as Nasser stated.

Rabin shared this assessment. As he saw it, Israel had found a solution to the diversion challenge but had no adequate response to Syria's sponsorship of terrorist activities. He and his colleagues in the General Staff came to the conclusion in late

1966 (and held onto it until May 1967) that only a large-scale military operation against Syria would put an end to this challenge and that Egypt would not join the fray. In an interview he gave to the IDF's weekly magazine on the eve of the Jewish new year in September 1966, Rabin explained that unlike Egypt, Jordan, and Lebanon, who opposed terrorist activity, Syria sponsored it. This called for a different kind of response. "The response to Syria's activity," he said, "needs to be directed against the perpetrators and against the regime that supports them. . . . Here the purpose should be changing the regime's decisions and the removal of the motivation of these activities. The problem with Syria is thus in essence a collision with the regime."

Rabin did not quite threaten to topple the Ba'ath regime, but his statement was widely perceived as doing just that. It generated a storm of protest, and Eshkol reprimanded his chief of staff. But he did so privately and then issued a milder statement on September 18 which stated, "Israel does not intervene in the domestic affairs of other states and their regimes."

This was not Eshkol's first reprimand of Rabin. In September 1964 he wrote Rabin "an absolutely private letter" criticizing him for making comments of a political diplomatic nature to the media. Such comments, he wrote, should not be made unless absolutely essential, and if that was the case, it was necessary "to coordinate them with the relevant actors." Eshkol's military assistant noted in his diary that this reprimand served a subtler purpose as well. Their good relationship notwithstanding, Eshkol was envious of Rabin's popularity and exploited his slip of the tongue to rebuke him and instruct him to clear interview requests with himself. But the prime minister treaded softly when dealing with Rabin and let the director general of his ministry, Yaacov Herzog, negotiate the text of the cabinet's statement regarding Rabin's own statement. Rabin was not much impressed by Eshkol's displeasure and by media criticism. On September 26, 1966, speaking at a meeting of the IDF's General Staff, he said, "I issued an order to all of our people not to enter into discussion, debate, lecture or guidance, to be outside the issue. Let them write what they want; tomorrow there will be a new newspaper. The IDF's PR activity will continue even though in the first phase I asked those who are about to speak to exercise greater caution. In any event, in anticipation of the Sinai campaign day, there will be public appearance by officers, because at this phase I received no instruction to stop, and of my own initiative I certainly do not intend to do so."[13] Rabin was respectful of the military's subordination to the political level and not fully attuned to the political and diplomatic repercussions of statements to the media, but he was clearly determined to remain in charge of all aspects of the IDF's activities.

THE CRISIS OF MAY 1967

In the second week of May 1967 a crisis erupted that almost immediately led to the Six-Day War. Independence Day, May 14, is Israel's most important secular holiday. In May 1967 preparations for the holiday were overshadowed by tension and controversy. The government had decided to hold the traditional military parade in Jerusalem. The decision was contested by Jordan, who argued this was an infringement of the 1949 Armistice Agreement between the two countries. The government responded by scaling down the military parade and dividing the celebration into two parts: a festive ceremony at the Hebrew University's stadium on May 14 and a small military parade on May 15. This decision was criticized by Ben Gurion, who argued that his successor, Eshkol, was "soft on security." This controversy took place against the backdrop of mounting tensions on the Syrian and Jordanian borders. The planners of the festive ceremony to be held on May 14 decided to include in the program a reading of a poem written in 1956 by Israel's national poet, Nathan Alterman, that was in effect a harbinger of the

Sinai campaign launched a few months later. Alterman's verse, read over loudspeakers, was a dire warning to the Arab world and, in retrospect, prophetic: "Oh Araby, calculate your path in time. The string is getting thinner and thinner . . . shake off hallucinatory dreams, this may be the last hour." At this very moment Rabin received and transmitted to Eshkol the first news that Egyptian armored units were rolling from the Egyptian mainland into the Sinai Peninsula.

The remilitarization of Sinai, a clear violation of the 1957 arrangements, soon grew in scope and was conducted in a demonstrative fashion. The Egyptian units moved openly, some of them through the streets of Cairo, for all the world to see. Eshkol and Rabin shared the assessment that this was a repetition of the measures taken by Egypt in 1960 in the Rotem case. Rabin ordered the IDF to take limited precautionary measures. We now know that Egypt's move in May 1967 may in fact have been prompted by false information it had been fed by the Soviet Union, namely, that Israel had amassed at least eleven brigades in preparation for a major assault on Syria. Moscow's motivation in feeding this information to Egypt and Syria is still not clear: was it meant to induce Egypt to repeat the Rotem maneuver and thus deter Israel from taking further action against its tottering Syrian client? or was it more sinister? In any event, it produced an avalanche of events no one had anticipated. A wave of enthusiasm swept Egypt and the Arab world in the wake of the remilitarization of Sinai. Nasser and his associates felt that Nasserism, having been in decline for the past few years, was experiencing a revival. Drunk with ego and emboldened, Nasser threw caution to the wind. He demanded that the UN remove its peacekeepers from the Egyptian–Israeli border in the Sinai and concentrate them in Gaza. He did not demand that they be removed from Gaza and the Tiran Straits. U Thant, the UN secretary general, inexplicably chose to inform the Egyptian government that he did not believe in half measures, and when the Egyptians extended the demand to include the Tiran Straits, he accepted it. Not surprisingly, the next step was the declaration of an embargo on Israeli ships and certain goods shipped to the port of Eilat in non-Israeli ships. Israel defined the embargo as a casus belli, and war seemed imminent, if not inevitable.

Israel was now in the midst of a severe crisis. Early discussions with the administration of Lyndon Johnson in Washington indicated it had no appetite for taking any action to defuse the crisis. As time went by, it seemed even that the administration tended instead toward opening a dialogue with an empowered Egypt. Syria was Egypt's ally, and Jordan seemed to be crumbling under the pressure; a war on three fronts had to be taken into account. Rabin and his GHQ colleagues faced a major challenge alone. They mobilized reserves, reviewing several plans for what seemed an inevitable war. The IDF had been built by Rabin to deal with an Arab attack on several fronts and had several contingency plans for alternative scenarios. But Israel could not afford to maintain a large number of reservists mobilized over time; the cost to the country's economy was prohibitive. There were indications Egypt might not wait for an Israeli attack and instead choose to initiate. Other indications raised the fear of an aerial raid against the Israeli nuclear reactor in Dimona. A wide gap in opinion opened up between the cabinet and the GHQ. The dovish ministers who had been critical of the army's activism since 1964 were now vociferously critical of a GHQ that, as they saw it, drove the country to the brink of disaster. Rabin, until recently respected by the cabinet and seen by its members as almost one of them, a virtual minister of defense, lost much of his standing because of the inaccurate estimates of Arab conduct and the feeling that he had led the IDF and the country to the edge of an abyss. The generals, on the other hand, had an entirely different view of the situation. Particularly after the closure of the straits, they believed Israel should go to war. Time was not on Israel's side. Also at stake was the country's ability to deter its Arab enemies. It had already been corroded by the failure to respond to Egypt's initial challenge and would continue to decline as the government hesitated and searched for a diplomatic solution. The consensus among the generals was that Israel could win the war.

The primary advocate of a diplomatic solution was the country's chief diplomat, Foreign Minister Abba Eban. Early on, a controversy erupted between Eban and the military (military intelligence, in particular) over the interpretation of Washington's true position. As a rule, American leaders and spokesmen warned Israel not to resort to war, and Eban argued that their statements should be taken literally. Military intelligence contended that such admonitions should be taken with a grain of salt, that the president and other figures in the administration actually expected Israel to resolve the crisis by itself since they had no desire or intention to send or participate in a flotilla that would break the siege. But neither the U.S. president nor any senior official wanted to be on record as having encouraged another country to go to war. They therefore opted to offer Israeli interlocutors a mixed message, warning Israel against war but sending indirect signals that it had to act by itself in order to break the siege and remove the larger Egyptian threat.

Eban was opposed to the military option. He persuaded Eshkol that he should travel to Paris and Washington to seek a solution with the help of Charles de Gaulle and Johnson. His trip delayed a decision to launch war and became the source of fresh controversy, based on his report that Johnson promised to organize a multinational naval force in order to break the siege. Skeptics persuaded Eshkol to double-check by sending Johnson a personal message thanking him for taking this position.

Johnson sent his national security advisor, Walt Rostow, to tell the minister in the Israeli embassy the president had made no such promise.[14]

This course of events put Rabin in a predicament. He had built the IDF into a formidable military force led by the best General Staff and capable of defending Israel against an Arab coalition. Together with Weizman, he helped build the air force to the point of implementing Kurnass, the secret plan for eliminating the Arab air forces in a preemptive attack that would give the IDF a massive initial advantage should war prove to be inevitable. For three and a half years Rabin had been an authoritative, popular chief of staff successfully negotiating the relationship between the generals and the cabinet and viewed by each as one of them. But now he was uncomfortably sandwiched between the politicians and the generals, his stature diminished by the crisis and the absence of a clear solution. He himself believed Israel had to go to war, but he refrained from banging on Eshkol's or the cabinet's desk. His customary caution and his concept of his role and position prevented him from doing that. Since he had lost his quasi-ministerial position and since Eshkol was not quite a full-fledged minister of defense, he had no authoritative senior political figure to rely on and share the burden with.

On May 22, one day before the announcement of the Egyptian blockade, Rabin sought the advice of two people he respected. The first was Ben Gurion. Ben Gurion was cordial; Rabin briefed him on the military situation and was embarrassed to discover how detached the great man was from Israel's new realities and the IDF's capabilities. The Old Man was very critical, primarily of Eshkol, but he did not spare Rabin: "You brought the country to a very severe situation, you bear the responsibility. One must not launch war. We are isolated."[15]

Rabin next went to see Dayan. As noted, their relationship had long been tense; in 1965 Dayan joined Ben Gurion in leaving Mapai to form a new party, Rafi. As a Rafi member, Dayan was in the opposition, and from his perch in the Knesset's Foreign and Defense Affairs Committee had been critical of Eshkol's and Rabin's policies since the mid-1960s. But tensions aside, Rabin held Dayan in esteem. This meeting, however, would not offer him any comfort or guidance either. As he put it in his memoirs, he was not pleased by Dayan's criticism, even though Dayan, unlike Ben Gurion, did not couch it in personal terms. According to Dayan, the government was wrong to test Nasser's leadership in the Arab world and push him into a corner by acting against Syria and Jordan. By so doing, he maintained, Israel forced Nasser to defend his prestige in his own country and in the Arab world and created a severe escalation in the Middle East. In Dayan's view, Nasser was likely to escalate his conduct, among other things by blocking the straits, which would cause Israel to act.[16]

The next day, May 23, after the closure of the straits, Rabin had an even harsher confrontation, this one with the minister of interior, Moshe Haim Shapira, the leader of the NRP. At that time the NRP was moderate, and Shapira, a member of the Ministerial Defense Committee, was the most consistent opponent of military action. In the aftermath of the committee's meeting Rabin met with him in private and was subjected to a critical barrage. "Do you really think the team Eshkol–Rabin should be bolder, more courageous, than the team Ben Gurion–Dayan?" he asked. "Why? . . . Ben Gurion did not go to war even though Egypt encouraged terrorist activities against Israel and armed the terrorists and protected them. When did Ben Gurion go to war, in 1956? Only when two fundamental conditions were met: Israel did not go by itself. France and England . . . undertook to destroy the Egyptian air force and navy. . . . The British and French navies defended the coasts of Israel. The safety of the civilian population was guaranteed. How do you dare go to war and all the conditions are against us?"[17] This was the same Shapira who after the Palmach rally demanded tougher action against Rabin. Whether a grudge against Rabin or a manifestation of the minister's dovishness, there was no mistaking the harshness of his criticism.

The three difficult meetings took their toll on Rabin. He found it difficult to cope with the mounting cross-pressures: even after the closing of the straits the cabinet remained reluctant to vote for war, while his generals became more militant and agitated. Rabin was consumed by doubt and a sense of guilt regarding his role in the escalation of the years 1964–67, specifically the Samu' operation and some of his statements. As he said to his second in command, Weizman, "I cannot escape the feeling that together with the political level I have my share in getting Israel into a severe situation—the most severe since its war of independence."

On the evening of May 23 Rabin succumbed to the combined impact of physical exhaustion and acute anxiety. He wrote in his memoirs in 1979 that he could not explain to himself "why I reached mental and physical exhaustion." He attributed it to the toll taken by more than a week of unending work, sleeplessness, and chain smoking as well as to a sense of guilt over his mistakes. That evening he invited Weizman to his home. What followed is a matter of controversy. According to Rabin, he was primarily interested in sharing his thoughts and concerns "to seek to relieve this great distress by exposing myself to another person. I am a closed man, this time I had such a pressing need." He told Weizman he "had a sense of fatigue and distress," that he felt responsible for his share in leading Israel to the current crisis. In a cri de coeur he asked Weizman if he should quit his position. Weizman disabused him of the idea and left. Leah called the IDF's surgeon general, who gave Rabin a shot that put him to sleep. On the twenty-fifth, Rabin resumed his responsibilities. The episode was kept a secret, the version offered to his colleagues being that he succumbed to "nicotine poisoning."

Weizman's version of the event is quite different and less flattering to Rabin. Their relationship always had its ups and downs; Rabin's later decision to appoint Haim Bar-Lev over Weizman as deputy chief of staff did not improve it. In his memoirs Weizman wrote that ever since the outbreak of the crisis in mid-May he had felt that "the state and stability of the Chief of Staff, Yitzhak Rabin, [were] fraying. It was manifested through changes of decisions, in expressions of anxiety regarding the future and inability to make decisions. Rabin generated insecurity around him. It was visible in meetings with the prime minister and in sessions of the General Staff." According to Weizman, when he went to see Rabin at his home he saw "a broken and despondent man." Rabin took responsibility for his mistakes, said Weizman, and told him he wanted to quit, offering him the chief of staff position. Weizman gallantly rejected the offer and told Rabin to regroup, to become the victorious chief of staff of the imminent war, which would be successful. This is a problematic version of events. Weizman, as second in command, would certainly have acted for Rabin until he regrouped, but the appointing of a chief of staff of the IDF was the cabinet's prerogative.

On the twenty-fourth, while Rabin was recuperating, Weizman was a very active substitute and convened the General Staff to deal with its war plans. Rabin was back at the helm on May 25, but it took some time for him to fully regain control of matters. His colleagues and the prime minister were supportive, and the incident was kept secret until 1974, when Weizman publicized it in order to help Peres in his contest with Rabin.

When Rabin returned to his post the cabinet was still not ready to go to war. Public and political pressure built up, and Eshkol's standing in the country plummeted when he stuttered during a speech to the nation. Eshkol was pressured to give up the defense portfolio as well as to bring Dayan in in some capacity. Dayan said initially he wanted to become general officer commanding of the Southern Command. Eshkol agreed, hoping this would relieve the pressure to appoint Dayan as minister of defense. Rabin was obviously unhappy with the idea, knowing full well Dayan would not accept his authority as his nominal superior, but he did not object. Eventually, Rafi and the right-wing Gahal, a merger of the nationalist Herut with the liberal conservative General Zionists, headed by Begin, joined the coalition to form a national unity government, and Dayan was appointed minister of defense. Bar Lev was appointed deputy chief of staff. These larger groundswell changes paved the way for a decision to go to war, facilitated by dispatching Meir Amit, the head of the Mossad, the national intelligence agency, to Washington to establish through his own channels that the Johnson administration was not opposed to Israel's action.

Once launched, the Six-Day War turned out to be a brilliant military success. Its impact was dramatically enhanced by the sharp contrast between the prewar anxiety and the magnitude and swiftness of the victory. In six days the IDF destroyed three Arab air forces and conquered the Sinai and the Gaza Strip, the Golan Heights, and the West Bank from Egypt, Syria, and Jordan.

Despite the success of the war, the collaboration and coordination between Dayan and Rabin was far from perfect. Dayan complained that the IDF reached the Suez Canal against his wishes, while Rabin discovered after the fact that Dayan had gone over his head and, in the nick of time, ordered (in a phone call!) the commander of the Northern Command to capture the Golan Heights. But the magnitude of the victory obscured these problems. And there was enough glory to go around for both Dayan and Rabin. Rabin's high moment in the war's aftermath was the speech he delivered on June 28, 1967, at the

Hebrew University's amphitheater on Mount Scopus. Mount Scopus was the university's original campus and remained an enclave in Jordanian-held Jerusalem after 1948. It was one of the manifestations of Israel's and Jerusalem's new realities that the university held its commencement ceremony on Mount Scopus and bestowed an honorary doctorate on the victorious chief of staff of the IDF. Rabin won many accolades for his acceptance speech. Among other things, he said, "The whole nation was swept by joy and yet we encounter again and again a strange phenomenon among the fighters. They cannot be fully happy and more than an element of sadness and bewilderment is added to their celebration and some of them do not celebrate at all. The fighters in the front lines saw with their own eyes not just the glory of victory but also its price—their comrades fell next to them, covered by blood. And I know that the terrible price paid by the enemy has also deeply affected many of them. It is possible that the Jewish people have never been educated or accustomed to feel the joy of conquest and victory. Therefore, it is received with mixed feelings."

Only in the years that followed did the magnitude of the problems created by the victory become clear. The huge triumph of the military is retroactively seen as a mixed blessing. Israel won a great victory, and a huge crisis was converted into a new reality—with Israel looming as a military power and a major regional actor, having captured territory three times larger than its own. The territories captured in the war finally provided the bargaining chips for a peace settlement that had been absent since 1949. But in the subsequent absence of progress toward a settlement, the captured territories also became an albatross around the state's neck. The conquest of the West Bank brought back to the surface ideas and sentiments that had been dormant since 1948 and generated a messianic wave that transformed religious Zionism from a moderate wing of the Israeli political system into a radical nationalist party and movement.

The debate over the disposition of these territories, particularly the West Bank and the Gaza Strip, parts of the historic Land of Israel, has since divided Israeli society and the body politic. It was a peculiar twist of history that Rabin, the architect of the great military victory of 1967, was the prime minister who was called upon to grapple with this mixed blessing and paid for the effort with his life.

3

———◆◗◆◗◆———

Ambassador to Washington, 1968–1973

THE POST of Israel's ambassador in Washington, D.C., as I well know, is an unusual diplomatic position. Since World War II the Washington embassy has been the most senior and most important posting in foreign ministries. Given the crucial nature of Israel's relationship with the United States, the ambassador to Washington is in most cases a personal emissary of the prime minister: a trusted confidant or public figure, not necessarily a professional diplomat. Effective Israeli ambassadors have tended not to act as traditional diplomats but to become active figures in Washington politics, familiar faces on Capitol Hill and in the national media, interacting with the highest echelons of the White House, the State Department, and the Pentagon. This uniqueness of the position is due to the importance of Middle Eastern issues and Israel on the American political and national security agenda, and the Israeli ambassador's influence (perceived or real) on the American Jewish community. Much depends on the stature and ability of the individual ambassador; the powers that be in Washington waste no time in finding out whether the Israeli ambassador is an effective channel to the prime minister.

Yitzhak Rabin was undoubtedly one of Israel's most effective ambassadors. In the aftermath of the Six-Day War, Rabin had to calculate the next phase of his career. He wanted to enter politics and become a cabinet member but felt that his transition from the military to the political phase of his career would be facilitated by acquiring the experience a stint as ambassador in Washington could offer. He asked a surprised Eshkol to appoint him to the position, which Eshkol did, in the face of Foreign Minister Eban's initial opposition.

Rabin was unusually well qualified for the task despite the fact that his command of English was only adequate. He was a well-known, major figure, the victorious chief of staff of the Six-Day War, tightly connected to the prime minister and the rest of Israel's political establishment, and well versed in the main issues on the U.S.–Israeli agenda, which included the future of territories captured by Israel in June 1967 and Israel's quest for sophisticated U.S.-made weapon systems. To the Jewish community Rabin was a military hero, an architect of the war that had raised Israel's stature to new heights. To his interlocutors in the Johnson administration, on Capitol Hill, and in the media, he appeared to be a wise, authoritative figure, an effective channel to the prime minister and his (later, her) cabinet, and a ranking member of Israel's political elite in his own right.

It took Rabin some time to master his new position. Initially he wanted to focus on the senior levels of the executive branch and let his staff deal with what he viewed as "peripheral constituencies," such as Congress and the think tank and academic communities. As time went on, however, he would develop strong, fruitful relationships with these groups.

Rabin's relationship with the organized Jewish community

in America had its ups and downs. Johnson had a circle of Jewish friends and confidants—Abe Fortas, Abe Feinberg, Arthur Goldberg, Arthur and Mathilde Krim, to name a few—and he was used to discussing Israeli issues with them as well as garnering their assistance in fund-raising and building support for his controversial Vietnam policy. When Rabin first assumed his post, the deputy chief of mission (DCM) in the outgoing ambassador Avraham Harman's embassy, Ephraim ("Eppy") Evron, who managed to build a personal rapport with Johnson, played a key role in working with the president's Jewish circle. Johnson also got along famously with Eshkol; their personalities and political styles were, mutatis mutandis, alike.

Rabin attached great importance to the American Jewish community. He and Leah traveled extensively in the United States visiting Jewish communities, and they acquired a circle of close Jewish friends in Washington. But Rabin was not fond of the particular fashion in which the Israeli issue was dealt with by Johnson and his Jewish friends. He preferred to deal directly with the White House, and in short order he replaced Evron as DCM and appointed Shlomo Argov to that post. Johnson never warmed to Rabin and dealt with him formally, as most presidents do with most foreign ambassadors. Rabin would have to wait until Richard Nixon's election to have free access to the White House and a strong personal relationship with the president.

Nor did Rabin have a smooth relationship with the American Israel Public Affairs Committee (AIPAC), the organization known nowadays as the pro-Israel lobby. The AIPAC of the 1960s, headed by Isaiah ("Si") Kenen, a Canadian-born Zionist activist, was a far cry from the large, powerful AIPAC that, since the 1980s, has developed from a small, discreet group to a powerful grass-roots political organization. He and his successors wanted to be the key influencers of the U.S.–Israeli relationship on Capitol Hill and resented a powerful ambassador who wanted to manage his own relationship in Congress. In time,

Rabin, who initially believed he could accomplish much more by dealing directly with Congress and the executive branch, would find that influential American Jews like Max Fisher, the wealthy Republican businessman from Detroit, Arthur Burns, the head of the Federal Reserve, and Leonard Garment, Nixon's lawyer, could be very helpful to his mission.

During Rabin's tenure in Washington the agenda of the American–Israeli relationship was shaped by the aftermath of the Six-Day War and the diplomatic and military conflicts over the future of the territories captured by Israel in June 1967. In the immediate aftermath of the war, the Johnson administration supported the Israeli position that Israel should not withdraw from these territories for less than full peace. One clear lesson of the crisis of 1967 was that postwar arrangements such as those imposed by President Dwight Eisenhower in 1957 were inadequate, that the territories captured in 1967 were assets to be used to end the Arab–Israeli conflict or at least to put Arab–Israel relations on a sound footing. But the Johnson administration and its successors were adamant that an Arab–Israeli settlement "must not reflect the burden of conquest," that is, minor border rectifications could be contemplated but in return for peace Israel would have to withdraw from the territories captured in the June 1967 war.

This position was only partially congruent with Israel's own position, as, on June 19, the Israeli cabinet resolved that in return for full peace and adequate security arrangements it was willing to withdraw from the Sinai and the Golan Heights, but the resolution did not apply to the West Bank and the Gaza Strip. Israel held that the issue of sovereignty over Palestine west of the Jordan was open. This was a secret resolution, but the gist of it was conveyed by Foreign Minister Eban to U.S. Secretary of State Dean Rusk soon after it was made. Rabin himself was unaware of these developments when he was sent to Washington. Four months later, under the impact of the negative resolutions adopted at the Arab summit conference in Khartoum in September, the Israeli cabinet revoked the June 19 resolution, this time without informing the United States. The differences between the American and Israeli positions would surface time and again in the coming years, but in the second half of 1967 there was sufficient common ground to enable the United States to thwart efforts by the Soviet, Muslim, and Arab blocs in the UN to pass a resolution calling for a full Israeli withdrawal without the benefit of peace accords with the defeated Arab states. Finally, in November 1967 a compromise formula in the best tradition of "constructive ambiguity," drafted by the British diplomat Lord Caradon, proved acceptable to both sides and became Security Council Resolution 242.

One by-product of these developments was the appointment of the Swedish diplomat Gunnar Jarring as the mediator between Israel and its Arab antagonists. Jarring began shuttling between Israel and its neighbors, except for Syria, which at that point refused to accept SC 242. Jarring's efforts proved ineffective and were eventually supplemented by two diplomatic fora: the two-party talks of the United States and the Soviet Union and the four-party talks of the United States, the Soviet Union, Great Britain, and France. As Israel's ambassador to Washington, Rabin had to deal with both the U.S. view and the handling of Jarring's mission. Rabin's management of the U.S. angle produced frequent tensions with Israel's UN ambassador, Joseph Tekoa, who insisted that the Jarring mission was part of his portfolio.

When Jarring began his shuttle diplomacy, hostilities had resumed along the Suez Canal. What began as a series of isolated attacks and counterattacks in October 1967 developed by March 1969 into a full-fledged "War of Attrition" that lasted until August 1970. It was fought primarily between Egypt and Israel, but there was also significant fighting along the Israeli–Jordanian border with both Palestinian and Jordanian forces and occasionally in the Golan Heights and on the Lebanese–Israeli border. As the term "attrition" implies, the purpose of the Arab parties was not to achieve victory but to wear Israel down and create additional political and diplomatic pressure on the country and its main supporter, the United States.

As Israel's ambassador in Washington during these years, Rabin's principal mission was to help maintain Washington's support for the territorial status quo so long as a diplomatic settlement acceptable to Israel was not available; he also helped persuade reluctant American politicians and bureaucrats to provide Israel with sophisticated weapon systems. Rabin's tenure can be seen in three distinct periods, defined by his effectiveness and stature: an introductory phase from his arrival in March 1968 to January 1969, when Johnson departed from the White House; from January 1969 to September 1970, when his closeness to Kissinger and the Nixon White House culminated in the joint U.S.–Israeli action in Jordan; and from September 1970 to his return to Israel in March 1973, when he was at the height of his influence and effectiveness.

During his first few months in Washington, Rabin had to deal with a president who had announced he would not seek reelection and whose main interest was the bane of his administration, that is, the war in Vietnam and the country's mounting opposition to it. His interest in the Middle East and in Arab–Israeli relations was limited. By September 1968, in the absence of presidential focus, Washington's support for the territorial status quo in Israel had begun to fray. Rabin was asked by Secretary of State Rusk for Israel's response to Soviet offers to the United States to promote a diplomatic solution. The Soviet offers reflected Moscow's support for Egypt and were patently not acceptable to Israel. It was clear that the administration was entering into a dialogue with the Soviet Union that would weaken its original post–June 1967 position. In early November 1968 Rabin found out that in an earlier meeting in New

York Rusk had given Foreign Minister Mahmud Riyad of Egypt a seven-point plan for settling the Egyptian–Israeli and Arab–Israeli conflict. Under this plan Egypt, in return for a full Israeli withdrawal, would agree to a formal ending of the state of war and sign a joint (and ill-defined) document with Israel. The Palestinian refugee problem would be solved on the basis of a free choice by every refugee. Rabin was shocked and alarmed at receiving news of this proposed agreement. In the end the U.S. paper was rejected by Egypt, but the United States was not to be deterred. On September 19 Rusk invited Rabin for "a vigorous talk." He said it was "up to Israel to make its position clear, to move beyond generalities and get into specifics." Rabin argued back, urging Rusk "to reject the Russian plan. After all, it lacks the elements both Israel and America had agreed must be part of any political settlement in the Middle East. It did not mention peace and it did not include any concrete expression of recognition for Israel or acceptance of her existence." When Rusk asked whether it would be enough "for Israel and the Arabs to sign a joint multilateral document," Rabin explained that Israel "wanted a bilateral, contractual peace agreement with each and every neighboring Arab state."[1] Rabin left with the secretary a written aide-mémoire, but the gap between the State Department's and Israel's position was all too evident. The pressure continued when Rusk's deputy, Nicholas Katzenbach, invited Rabin on November 13 for a lengthy discussion. The talk revealed the growing distance between the U.S. and Israeli views of the border rectifications demanded by Israel in a peace settlement and the best diplomatic strategy to achieve it. Johnson's national security advisor, Walt Rostow, summed up the situation in a memorandum he submitted to the president on November 15, 1968: "Rabin feels we've changed our position and undermined Israel's bargaining position. The fact is that this has been our consistent position for over a year, but the Israelis have turned off their hearing aids on us. As for undermining their position, we can't afford to go along with their bazaar haggling if we're going to have any chance of peace."[2]

A great deal of Rabin's energy and time during this period was spent trying to stem this drift of Washington's toward a position closer to that of the Soviet Union, the European powers, and, of course, the Arab states. He was quite effective in his conversations with Kissinger but less so with the State Department.

Rabin's other main effort during this period was to secure the sale of fifty F4 Phantom jets Johnson had promised to Eshkol. It was a crucial issue. The sale would effect a substantial upgrade of Israel's air force and overall military capability and would be the first sale of a major advanced offensive weapon system by the United States to Israel, an important milestone in turning the country into Israel's chief source of military equipment. Johnson's promise to Eshkol was resisted by powerful elements in his administration, foremost among them Secretary of State Rusk and Secretary of Defense Clark Clifford. Some felt it would enhance Israel's military advantage over the Arabs to a dangerous level. Others saw it as a golden opportunity to revisit the issue of Israel's nuclear option and sought to create a linkage between the two issues by way of forcing Israel to offer greater transparency in return for receiving the Phantom jets. In Israel, Washington's ambassador, Walworth Barbour, dealt with Eshkol and his ministers while Eban negotiated with his counterpart, Rusk. But the main Israeli effort was invested in Rabin, who started his campaign in the State Department and ended up in a tug-of-war with the assistant secretary of defense, the formidable Paul Warnke.

The question of Israel's nuclear capability was not a novel issue to Rabin. Israel's national security establishment in the 1950s and 1960s was split over the nuclear question—between advocates of the nuclear option as the ultimate deterrent, led by Shimon Peres, and those who believed in conventional deterrence, identified with the Achdut Haavoda faction of the Labor Party and its security experts, Alon and Galili. Rabin began by supporting conventional deterrence, but by 1963 he had changed his mind and came to the conclusion that Israel would not be able, in the long run, to afford the cost of a conventional arms race.

Rabin's change of view happened to coincide with a period of massive U.S. pressure on Israel to come clean about its nuclear plan and capabilities that had begun under Kennedy and continued under Johnson. Eshkol is reported to have allayed Johnson's concerns with the formula "Israel will not be the first to introduce nuclear weapons to the Middle East," but the pressure was soon renewed. Rabin himself was exposed to it as chief of staff in 1965 in meetings with the imposing Averell Harriman, who at that time served as ambassador-at-large for the Johnson administration, and Robert Komer, a staff member of the National Security Council, who were dispatched to Israel by the Johnson administration. Harriman, subtly, and Komer, more bluntly, expressed their dissatisfaction with Eshkol's formula. Komer told Rabin, "If Israel goes in this direction, she might bring about the greatest crisis ever in its relationship with the United States."

Rabin and Warnke met several times in November 1968 to discuss—or rather argue about—the draconian Memorandum of Understanding the Pentagon was seeking to attach to the sale of the fifty Phantoms to Israel. The minutes of these meetings read like a description of an elaborate minuet: Rabin rejecting Warnke's efforts to impose a ban or at least limitations on Israel's nuclear and missile capabilities; Rabin fending off Warnke without actually admitting that Israel had such capabilities or intentions to develop them. When Warnke asks, "What was specifically meant by the word 'introduce'?," Rabin asks him for *his* definition of nuclear weapons, "since you are more familiar with these things than we are," and then asking

Warnke if he "consider[ed] a nuclear weapon one that has not been tested and has been done by a country without previous experience?" Rabin argued that all nuclear powers had tested their nuclear weapons and asked, "Do you really believe introduction comes before testing?"

Rabin nonetheless recognized that, sophistry aside, the give-and-take with Johnson's cabinet secretaries and their assistants was stale. He resorted to a different tactic. Through mutual Democratic friends, Rabin sent President Johnson a message that the Republican candidate, Nixon, if elected, would be committed to delivering the planes to Israel. This tactic may not have been elegant, but it was effective. In mid-January 1969, just before he left the White House, Johnson overruled his subordinates and ordered them to implement the sale. But negotiations were far from over. Rabin would have to go through a second round of sterile dialogue in 1969, initiated by Nixon's deputy secretary of state, and would again need to shift the discussion to a higher level. Not until December 1969 was the deal finally concluded, in a meeting Rabin arranged between Nixon and Golda Meir.

A new chapter in Washington's policy toward the Arab–Israeli conflict and in Rabin's tenure in Washington would begin with Nixon's inauguration on January 20, 1969. Nixon's secretary of state was William Rogers, a distinguished Republican lawyer. It did not take long for tensions to develop between Secretary of State Rogers and Nixon's brilliant national security advisor, Henry Kissinger. Bureaucratic rivalries are built into the American political system, and tension between the secretary of state and the national security advisor over the conduct of U.S. foreign policy is one of them. During Nixon's first years in office he kept Kissinger away from Middle Eastern issues, giving Rogers and the State Department primacy in this area. Nixon tended to view the Middle East and the Arab–Israeli conflict primarily through a global lens: as an area of intense conflict with the Soviet Union and a potential "powder keg," as Nixon used to put it. It was important to avoid a Soviet–American collision in the Middle East, but it was also important to prevent the Soviet Union from gaining ground in the region. This was the very point argued by Rogers and the State Department—that America's support for Israel was undermining the position of its moderate Arab allies, and it was therefore imperative to push for a swift resolution of the Arab–Israeli conflict even if this required a distancing from Israel and Washington's own original post–June 1967 policy.

Kissinger was critical of this policy. His rivalry with Rogers was exacerbated by his conviction that Rogers's and the State Department's policy made no sense. What was the point in forcing Israel to withdraw from the Sinai and return it to Nasser, Moscow's client? When the Egyptians and other Arabs discovered that Moscow could not return the lost territory to them and turned to Washington to obtain it, Washington's policy could change. Nixon kept listening to Kissinger's advice, but throughout 1969 he tended to support Rogers and the State Department. He gave them space to negotiate with the Soviet Union, Britain, and France in the framework of the two powers and the four powers groups and refused to sign new major agreements on arms supply with Israel.

Rabin had a preexisting personal relationship with Nixon. In 1966, when Nixon, at that time considered a spent force after losing both a presidential and a gubernatorial race, visited Israel and was given little attention by the government. Rabin, as chief of staff, hosted him in style and gave him a thorough tour. In 1968, on the eve of the presidential election, Rabin met with Nixon. Although he did not advertise it, Rabin privately expressed to his confidants his preference for Nixon over Hubert Humphrey. Rabin thus now had a friendly president in the White House, although his meetings with him were rare. His regular contact at the White House was Kissinger and, in the

State Department, the assistant secretary of state for Near Eastern affairs, Joseph Sisco.

Although he did not at that time deal directly with Middle East diplomacy, Kissinger was a very influential member of the administration and a first-rate guide to Washington politics, U.S. policy, and world affairs. In time Rabin and Kissinger became close friends, deeply appreciative of one another. Sisco was also a key player in this grouping. He was the principal U.S. foreign policy officer in charge of the Middle East, dealing with the influential Soviet ambassador to Washington, Anatoly Dobrynin, the Europeans, the Arabs, and, of course, the Israelis. Unlike most of his colleagues in the bureau, he was not an Arabist by training or inclination. He was also very skillful at sustaining a good personal relationship with both Rogers and Kissinger. Kissinger described him fondly but with a touch of irony: "Intense, gregarious, occasionally frenetic, Joseph Sisco was not a conventional foreign service officer. . . . He turned out to be a living proof of what imaginative leadership could achieve in the State Department. . . . Enormously inventive with the talent in the stratagems that are the lifeblood of Middle East diplomacy, sometimes offering more solutions than there were problems, Joseph Sisco seized the bureaucratic initiative and never surrendered it."[3]

As 1969 wore on, the State Department increased the pressure to implement policy geared toward a swift resolution and away from Washington's own original post–June 1967 policy. In October and December Nixon finally authorized the Rogers Plan. The plan represented everything Israel was opposed to: full Israeli withdrawal for less than contractual peace. Israel reacted sharply, denounced the plan, and launched a massive campaign against it in the Jewish community and on Capitol Hill. Nixon used Kissinger and Rabin to send a back-channel message that he was not entirely supportive of the plan. Kissinger also told Rabin repeatedly that the president was one of Israel's few friends in the executive branch, and it would be calamitous to antagonize him. And so the campaign orchestrated by Rabin targeted Rogers rather than Nixon. Rogers was understandably offended and took Rabin to task for it, complaining about being made into a scapegoat and being depicted as anti-Israel, when he was merely implementing American policy.[4] Rabin actually liked Rogers and had a high regard for him personally but profoundly disagreed with his policy and understood it would be a capital mistake to criticize Nixon personally.

While he was attempting to repudiate the political trends represented by the Rogers Plan, Rabin launched a more discreet effort directed at his own government. He argued repeatedly in his cables to the prime minister that Israel's failure to find an effective solution to the full-blown war of attrition launched by Egypt in March 1969 was undermining Israel's position in the United States. As he wrote in his memoirs: "Israel disappointed the US. It had no proper response to the war of attrition. . . . The Americans never admitted it and it's doubtful whether they would admit it now. But they assumed that Israel was powerful enough to inflict on Egypt a blow that would put an end to its will to continue the war of attrition. As the war continued, the US position in the Middle East kept eroding, and as the erosion kept growing so did US willingness to come to an agreement with the Soviet Union."[5]

Rabin argued over and over that this was neither his personal opinion nor his impression but that it was indicated to him by senior members of the administration. He tended to refer to his conversations with Sisco, trying to disguise the fact that his principal interlocutor was Kissinger (in the Israeli system, sensitive cables tended to leak or be leaked). Kissinger was critical of Rogers's and the State Department's line, tended to look at the Middle East in geopolitical terms, namely, as primarily an arena of Soviet–American rivalry, and was probably not averse to seeing Rogers and his policy defeated.

Rabin believed instead in the need to escalate the attacks on Egypt and to launch "deep-raid bombings" against strategic targets in order to bring Nasser to his knees. In Rabin's view, Nasser's capitulation or collapse would be construed as an American achievement and a blow to the Soviet Union and would reduce the pressure on both Washington and Jerusalem to accommodate Egyptian and Soviet pressures. This approach had its opponents and critics in the Israeli cabinet, first and foremost Eban. Eban and his loyalists were opposed to escalation as such and doubted that Rabin was on solid ground in interpreting and reporting the U.S. position. They found it difficult to believe the United States was encouraging Israel to escalate its military attacks rather than tone them down.

The acrimonious debate between the foreign minister and the Washington ambassador was yet another turn in a relationship going from bad to worse. As we have seen, Rabin and Eban had had a sharp disagreement in May 1967 when Eban argued in the Israeli cabinet that the United States did not want to see Israel go to war over the closure of the Tiran Straits. Later, when Rabin asked Eshkol to send him to Washington, Eban objected. Early in Rabin's tenure, Eban came to visit President Johnson at the White House. Eban snubbed Rabin by excluding him from the meeting and then dismissing him from his own office at the embassy in order to make a call on the secure line to Jerusalem. Rabin retaliated by aborting Eban's attempt to use a visit to New York to return to Washington. It was quite easy for an ambassador of Rabin's stature to persuade the prospective American host that the prime minister was not interested in having her foreign minister come to Washington at that particular time. In February 1969 Eshkol died and was replaced by Golda Meir, who had no time for Eban. The new prime minister wanted Rabin to report directly to her and bypass the foreign minister, further exacerbating their fraught relationship. She told Rabin it was her responsibility to update the foreign minister when necessary. This probably did not break Rabin's heart. Bypassing the foreign minister and his ministry had another advantage beyond fewer dealings with Eban: it was (and still is) a well-known fact that interesting, and all the more so provocative, telegrams tend to leak from the Foreign Ministry. Leaking was and is used by politicians and diplomats for various reasons, often to cultivate relations with journalists, to promote or obstruct a policy line, sometimes to embarrass the sender. Over the years different ambassadors had devised a whole set of measures in order to overcome this problem. Rabin did send regular cables and reports to the foreign minister and to the Foreign Ministry, but his most important and sensitive telegrams were sent to the prime minister through the Mossad communications channel. So in September 1969, during Meir's visit with Nixon, the two leaders, after preparation by Kissinger and Rabin, formally decided to bypass the State Department and Foreign Ministry and communicate directly through the national security advisor and the ambassador.

Rabin's disagreement with Eban and the Foreign Ministry's leadership over the recommendation to launch the policy of deep-raid bombing was particularly sharp. Eban and his associates disagreed with the substance of Rabin's recommendation as well as with what they saw as his tendency to generalize about U.S. policy on the basis of his conversations with Sisco. When Eban criticized him for this, Rabin responded pointedly, suggesting that Eban, who had failed to understand the subtlety of Washington's position in May 1967, continued to misunderstand U.S. policy.

Rabin was by no means deterred by the criticism. He continued to push for aggressive tactics and went so far as to suggest that Israel threaten to occupy Cairo. Needless to say, Eban was horrified. Rabin's outlook was most fully articulated in a cable he sent to Eban on April 17, 1970, with copies to Dayan, Aharon Yariv, the director of military intelligence and a friend of

Rabin's, and Simcha Dinitz (Director General of the PM's office), prompted by the knowledge that Dayan had asked Sisco a direct question during Sisco's visit to Israel:

> The guiding line in the US's approach to Israel's military operations is to avoid being drawn into a situation that can be defined as a collusion. . . . The US will absolutely refuse to say in advance in a clear and formal fashion "go for deep-raid bombing" in the same way it refused on the eve of the Six-Day War to tell us "start the war." Furthermore, any attempt by us to present such questions to a representative of the US government in order to receive a clear answer points to a wrong assessment in this cardinal matter. . . . [T]he US understands that Israel has the right to take independently military measures that it views as necessary for its security. If the US takes exception to these measures, it finds the way to clarify it to Israel. . . . Posing a direct question to Sisco with regard to deep-raid bombings is a small-scale repetition of our attempt on the eve of the Six-Day War to receive from the Americans a formal approval to go to war. . . . In my humble view posing this question will prompt the Americans to rethink the ability to discuss this delicate issue with us in the future. We will try to correct it in our contacts here.

Kissinger, who knew Rabin and Eban well and worked with both, saw their rivalry as more than a clash over policy and a place in the hierarchy. To him, it was a clash between "two very different persons: The urbane, complex, polished, Cambridge don and the tough, direct, prickly Sabra [native Israeli] military man."

Rabin did not have many friends and admirers in the Foreign Ministry, but those he did have, such as Moshe Bitan, the deputy director general for North America, thought Rabin conducted himself as a cabinet minister rather than as a diplomat. He mentioned in his diaries correspondence he had with Rabin's deputy in the embassy, Shlomo Argov, who wrote, "Your criticism of some of Yitzhak's telegrams are quite to the point. . . . I assume you have no argument with many of the things he says. The problem is that he says them in a style and a form that must also bother his friends. I try here and there to moderate his statements but as you can see, not very successfully."[6]

With Rabin's encouragement, but primarily owing to the mounting toll exacted by the War of Attrition, Israel would adopt the policy of deep-raid bombings Rabin so aggressively pushed for, using its aerial superiority to hit strategic targets deep inside Egypt. The new policy produced a swift escalation. A helpless Nasser traveled secretly to Moscow in January 1970 and told his Soviet patrons that unless they came to his aid he would resign. The Soviets responded, undertaking direct responsibility for defending Egypt's airspace, first, by sending several batteries of surface-to-air missiles (SAMs) operated by Soviet crews to Egypt, then by sending Soviet warplanes and pilots for combat missions along the Egyptian–Israeli front.

It was a new and dangerous phase of the Cold War in the Middle East: no longer war by proxy but with direct Soviet participation. Nixon's admonition that the Arab–Israeli conflict was a powder keg was now vindicated. The Israeli pilots did well in the one dogfight they had with Soviet pilots, but the SAM-6 missiles proved deadly. Whatever electronic defenses Israeli fighter jets had proved insufficient against them. The United States did not seem to possess (or did not wish to share) more advanced equipment. Israel lost several planes, and its political and military leadership were shaken by the direct clash with the Soviet Union. Rabin and his colleagues felt they could cope with Arab adversaries, but once the Soviet Union decided to intervene directly it could and should be checked only by the United States.

It was against this unfolding backdrop that the U.S. secretary of state released the Rogers Initiative. It was different from the Rogers Plan in that its focal point was an Egyptian–Israeli ceasefire in place but similar in that the ceasefire was linked to the quest for a comprehensive diplomatic solution in the spirit of the Rogers Plan. The Rogers Initiative intentionally had something for everybody: it would supposedly defuse a dangerous international crisis; it would extricate Israel from the predicament of a direct military conflict with the Soviet Union; and it would offer Egypt the prospect of a diplomatic process predicated on the original Rogers Plan.

It was precisely this final point that pitted Meir against the Rogers Initiative. She immediately sent Rabin a message for the president rejecting it. Rabin thought this was a grave error and was reluctant to pass it on to the president. He asked Meir to suspend the message and to allow him to fly to Israel in order to persuade her and the cabinet to adopt a different approach. It was unusual for an ambassador to take such a drastic step— and for a strong-minded prime minister like Meir to agree to it—but Rabin was not a conventional ambassador, and it was clearly a crucial moment worthy of further reflection. These were very tense weeks in Washington's relationship with Jerusalem. Meir was willing to accept the principle of the Rogers Initiative, namely, the cease-fire in place, even if this meant the resignation of the right-wing members of the national unity government; she could not, however, agree to language linking it to the original Rogers Plan. Telegrams and phone calls between the two capitals were frequent and heated. Meir called Sisco angrily on the phone, and Rabin was summoned to Kissinger for a dressing down. As Rabin puts it, "Thousands of words, many of them enraged. Golda scolded me furiously, but the entanglement remained unresolved."[7]

Despite the absence of a clear formal Israeli acceptance of the initiative, a cease-fire of ninety days went into effect on August 7, 1970, but the end of the fighting was soon overshadowed. Israel found out through aerial reconnaissance that the Russians and the Egyptians had violated the terms of the cease-fire in place (namely, based on a freezing of the status quo) and had moved several SAM-6 batteries toward the Suez Canal. The United States was skeptical, and it took a while for Israel to persuade the United States that the violation had occurred. There were genuine disagreements between Israeli and American imagery analysts, but the Americans' reluctance to accept the fact that the Soviets had cheated was evident and had serious implications for the relationship between the two superpowers.

However, once the United States did endorse the Israeli complaint, Washington and Jerusalem decided to stay with the Rogers Initiative. The United States undertook to limit the potential damage to Israel by providing the country with new sophisticated equipment. Yet the damage caused by the advancement of the antiaircraft missile batteries closer to the Suez Canal could not be undone, and the Israeli air force would pay dearly for it during the first days of the October War in 1973. The tug-of-war over the cease-fire along the Suez Canal finally ended on August 8, when the cease-fire between Israel and Egypt went into effect. However, the calm of August was soon to be overshadowed in September by two momentous developments.

The first of these developments was subsequently named Black September: King Hussein's military campaign launched on September 7 against the PLO in order to reassert his sovereignty and restore his control of Jordan's national territory. Hussein was prompted by egregious provocations: the attempt on his life on September 1 and the hijacking of three Western airliners by the Popular Front for the Liberation of Palestine. The planes landed, were parked, and were subsequently blown up in Zarqa in central Jordan. With determination and brutality Hussein's army defeated the PLO. This prompted Syria, the PLO's ally and protector, to intervene on the PLO's behalf by sending its tanks into Jordan's territory on September 18.

The move by a Soviet client to invade the territory of an American protégé was a move on the international chessboard and confronted the Nixon administration with an acute dilemma. At the height of the Vietnam War the last thing needed was a new military entanglement in the Middle East, but watching Jordan be invaded and defeated by Syria was equally unacceptable. The option chosen by Nixon and Kissinger was to ask Israel to save the Hashemite regime. It so happened that Meir was in New York, about to depart for Israel. Rabin was with her and was reached by an anxious Kissinger on the phone. The president and his national security advisor wanted to know whether Israel would be willing to use its army to save the king.

This was far from a simple decision. Israel needed clarifications and assurances from the United States. Most important, it wanted an umbrella against Soviet military intervention. The minutes of Rabin's telephone conversation with Kissinger on September 21 still convey the air of drama of those days:

> KISSINGER: We have asked Sisco to talk to you in a few minutes.... He will give you a reply which in principle is yes, but I would like to make the following suggestion. The less you say and reply is better. Just communicate with your government and then come in and see me. It is terribly important that we know who says what to whom and I will give you guidelines on that.
>
> RABIN: In the meantime I have instructions too. More detailed.[8]

Rabin was flown by the administration from New York to Washington in order to be closer to Kissinger. After much consideration, Israel's response was positive. In the end, actual military action was not required, as Israel's military moves on the ground and in the air sufficed. The commander of Syria's air force, Hafez al-Asad, refused to commit his jets, and without aerial support, Syria's tanks became sitting ducks. Jordan's own tanks and planes pushed back Syria's armored columns.

This was to be one of the high points of Rabin's tenure as ambassador, a demonstration of deft political and diplomatic give-and-take. Not only was the Nixon administration spared the need to intervene, but the president could argue that the Nixon Doctrine, that is, relying on regional allies rather than on American troops, was working. On September 25 Kissinger conveyed to Rabin a message to Meir from the grateful Nixon: "The President will never forget the role played by Israel in preventing a deterioration in Jordan and in checking the attempt to topple the regime. . . . The US is fortunate to have in Israel a Middle Eastern ally; what happened will be taken into account in any future development."[9]

The risk taken by Israel would pay great dividends over the next three years. It would set the stage for a period of unprecedented closeness and intimacy in Israel's relationship with Washington. But in retrospect it was a mixed blessing in that it reinforced Meir's policy of trying to freeze the status quo and contributed to the stalemate that would lead to the October War.

The second momentous event that occurred in September 1970 was Nasser's death from a heart attack on the twenty-eighth. It may well have been expedited by the tension and aggravation caused by Black September. Nasser's death marked the end of an era in Arab politics. It also brought to power Anwar Sadat and with him the October War and Israel's first peace treaty with an Arab country.

Intimacy and closeness with the White House did not mean Israel could rest on its laurels and perpetuate the status quo. The Rogers Initiative was tied to renewal of the quest for a settlement and, more specifically, to the revival of the Jarring mission. By December 1970 pressure from the State Department and the White House on Israel to move toward a settlement became more palpable. Prompted by this pressure, in October 1970 Meir and Dayan more forcefully raised with Kissinger the notion of an interim settlement predicated on an Israeli withdrawal from the eastern bank of the Suez Canal.

The Israeli idea of the interim settlement was given further impetus when Egypt conveyed a message to the United States expressing interest in the idea in January 1971, relaying that it preferred to do this through the United States, not through Jarring's efforts. Sadat was not taken seriously as Nasser's successor when he was chosen in September 1970. He was Nasser's deputy but was seen by Egypt's power brokers as a harmless transitional figure to be replaced once they sorted out their own differences. Sadat, however, proved to be ambitious and cunning and in short order consolidated his own power over the machinery of the Egyptian state. He had a complete program for transforming Egypt's domestic and external policies. Sadat was determined to shift from a Soviet to an American orientation and to disengage from the conflict with Israel. This was demonstrated in February 1971 by Egypt's response to the questions addressed by Jarring to Israel and Egypt: a dramatic statement of willingness "to enter into a peace agreement with Israel" in return for a full withdrawal.

Israel's diplomatic agenda and Rabin's in Washington were now shaped by the need to respond to Sadat's bold new diplomacy, to Washington's obvious eagerness to exploit the new opportunities offered by the change in Egypt, and to Jarring's and the State Department's understandable drive to start negotiations for a comprehensive Israeli–Egyptian settlement.

The United States was disappointed by Israel's evasive response to Jarring, nor was it enthused by Meir's concept of an interim settlement. The give-and-take over the interim agreement revolved around three issues:

1. The question of whether the United States was interested in a reopening of the Suez Canal. It was assumed the Pentagon preferred it remain closed so as to slow down Soviet shipments to the Vietcong. The U.S. position in 1971 was that it was better to keep the Canal closed, but in the interest of peace in the Middle East it was ready to help it reopen.

2. Egypt's insistence that the interim agreement be explicitly linked to progress toward a final deal. Sadat was clearly worried that by agreeing to an interim agreement he would be collaborating in postponing a comprehensive settlement to an indefinite future date.

3. The terms of the deal: the depth of Israel's withdrawal from the canal and the size and nature of Egypt's presence on its eastern bank.

As a condition for actually going along with the idea of the interim settlement Meir wanted Washington to formally abandon the Rogers Plan, and her own concept of the interim agreement offered was rather limited. In the coming months Rabin became a consistent and persistent advocate of Israeli flexibility in an effort to maintain Israel's credibility and the Nixon administration's goodwill. He was branded in the Israeli government as being dovish. In his conversations with his American interlocutors, Rabin kept referring to his dovish image and asked them not to embarrass him and complicate his relationship with the prime minister by referring to the flexible ideas he raised occasionally on his own. This was to no avail, and his relationship with Meir became strained. In reporting on one of his conversations with Kissinger, Rabin was trying "to forestall her anger." He admitted in his cable that "I may have gone beyond my powers on airing proposals for a partial settlement, but in view of my relationship with Kissinger and my confidence in him—and considering present political circumstances—I thought that Israel ought to make salient contribution to furthering the political process. We have a vital interest in inducing the president to disown the Rogers Plan and there is no sense in doing so unless we inject momentum into the political process in the context of the partial settlement."

The prime minister's response was in line with Rabin's

fears. After thanking him briefly for his report she called him a week later, "notifying me," Rabin wrote, "that the proposals I discussed with Kissinger were unacceptable to her. She regretted that I aired them, even privately, without first requesting permission. She also expressed her concern that Kissinger might have conveyed the main points of my proposal to the President, thereby weakening Israel's stand in our debate with the State Department over the terms for a partial settlement. Finally, the Prime Minister told me to notify Kissinger of her sharp reaction, ask him to overlook our private conversation and tell him to regard my proposals as null and void."[10]

The American–Israeli conversation over the interim settlement idea continued into 1973, but by then it was essentially sterile. Nixon and Kissinger did want to see progress between Egypt and Israel, but there was no sense of urgency. Nor did they want to seek out a confrontation with Meir when the November 1972 presidential elections were looming. Sadat, meanwhile, was moving in the right direction: in July 1972 he expelled the Soviet advisors from Egypt and opened a discreet channel with Kissinger through his national security advisor, Hafez Ismail. Kissinger's insistence in 1969 that Egypt should eventually see the light and turn to Washington and away from Moscow in order to regain the Sinai was finally paying off. Although Sadat did not fully sever his relationship with the Soviet Union, the process was unfolding, and Kissinger was willing to wait.

Meir, in turn, was marking time. She had no interest in a comprehensive or partial settlement, but she knew that in order to keep Nixon and Kissinger on her side she had to come up with positive ideas. In December 1971 she arrived for another meeting with the president with some new ideas for an interim settlement. She was now willing to agree that Israel's right to use the reopened Suez Canal be first recognized in principle, then implemented at a later phase. She proposed that the

IDF would withdraw to the western side of the Mitla and Gidi passes, and Egyptian technicians and policemen could be deployed in the area evacuated by Israel once the canal was reopened. This position was not acceptable to either Egypt or the United States, and in any event, the prime minister was not deeply invested in it. Rabin had been initially skeptical of the settlement idea but gradually warmed up to it; Meir told her American counterparts she accepted the idea under certain conditions, but it is doubtful she ever took the idea seriously. Dayan, an early advocate of the idea, abandoned it rather than fight over it with the prime minister.

Not much changed between December 1971 and the end of Rabin's mission to Washington, in March 1973. Nixon and Kissinger were fully aware of the prime minister's reluctance to move on either a full or a partial settlement, despite her stated position. Her argument was that there was not much she could do before the Israeli parliamentary elections, planned for October 1973, and Nixon and Kissinger were willing to wait before pushing more vigorously for movement. Meir's last meeting with Nixon and Kissinger during Rabin's tenure as ambassador took place between February 28 and March 1, 1973. The minutes of Rabin's conversations with Kissinger on the eve of that visit reflect the unusual intimacy and candor that came to characterize their relations. Kissinger prepared Rabin in great detail for the prime minister's conversations with the president, offering him tactical advice on how to maximize the effect of the meeting. Rabin, in turn, when asked by Kissinger for the rationale of an Israeli military action in Lebanon, told him that Dayan might have acted in order to obstruct the success of the prime minister's visit. In Rabin's words, "I do not know why the Prime Minister allowed the raid into Lebanon. When I was Chief of Staff whenever we were trying to achieve something from the United States in the political arena, I piped everything down. . . ." And when Kissinger asked him, "What do you think is the reason for these moves?" Rabin responded by saying, "Frankly, I think the only motive is Dayan's desire to prevent a successful visit by the Prime Minister, because his chances are better if she retires before the election. It is a political year." Kissinger reciprocated Rabin's unusual candor with a detailed description of the conversation he was about to have with Ismail.[11]

Meir was not the only person marking time in 1972. Rabin felt that his mission in Washington had run its course, that he had achieved the highpoint of his ambassadorship, that in order to move on in his political career he had to be in Israel, not out of it. His relationship with Meir had deteriorated. For some time Meir had not been pleased with Rabin's growing independence, and his tendency to lecture the cabinet, including herself, in his cables on the proper way to understand the ways of Washington. Rabin, acutely aware of the change in Washington's position due to the changes in Egypt represented by Sadat's regime and its determination to see some forward movement, kept pressing for an interim agreement. Meir was displeased with Rabin's line. She felt he "went native," as ambassadors tend to do, and was overly influenced by Sisco. During one of her visits she even asked Amos Eran, Rabin's aide and confidant in the embassy, "Tell me, did Sisco brainwash Rabin? What is it, does he accept all his positions? Does he have that kind of influence over him?"[12]

Rabin was aware of the shift in his relationship with the prime minister. He was also distressed by two other issues. One was the ceaseless campaign conducted against him by Eban, his subordinates in the Ministry of Foreign Affairs, and the cohort of journalists who took their cue from Eban and his men. And more important, Rabin felt that his quest for a cabinet position was going nowhere. At that point he had been let down three times by Meir and the Labor Party leadership during his tenure in Washington. The first episode had occurred in September 1969; earlier that year the party leadership had wanted him to fully join the political fray, to run for the Knesset, Israel's parliament, and become a cabinet member. This was early in Rabin's stay in Washington, so he declined. But in September Meir offered him a shortcut. During one of Rabin's visits to Israel to prepare her for a meeting with Nixon, Meir told him that after the next parliamentary elections (scheduled for October that year and on the assumption she would form the new government), she wanted him to join her cabinet as minister of education. Rabin gladly accepted and gallantly told the prime minister she should not feel bound by her promise, that he would fully understand if it turned out after the elections that it could not be implemented. And indeed, it was not. Rabin had been sorely used, not for the first or last time, as a counterweight to Dayan. The Labor Party leadership had been worried that Dayan might secede and run on his own.

Rabin wrote angrily about the episode in a letter to his father and sister:

> I do not know what exactly happened after the elections. When I was in Israel two weeks ago she [Meir] summoned me and explained that due to Washington's importance and the lack of a suitable person [to replace me] she decided that at this time I would stay in the US. I responded by saying that even though she asked me in September, I demanded nothing from her. Quite to the contrary, I left her a way out. I added that in September I had doubts whether she really wanted me to come. Furthermore, the whole media game that revolved around me and the cabinet was not dignified. Still, she owed me nothing and does not owe me an explanation. Unrelated to the positive qualities which make her the most suitable Prime Minister at this time, it is difficult for me to say that her behavior in this matter was something to be proud about. . . . Anyway I am not sorry that I stayed here.[13]

This episode played out in early 1970. In 1971 the issue of Rabin's joining the cabinet was raised again, several times. During a visit to Washington, the finance minister, Pinchas Sapir, a close associate of Meir, consulted with Rabin about inviting Haim Bar-Lev, his successor as chief of staff, to join the cabinet. Rabin felt awkward but spoke positively about Bar-Lev. Labor's leadership saw greater political value in recruiting "the fresher" Bar-Lev over Rabin. In June 1971, however, during Rabin's visit to Israel, Sapir tried to set the record straight and told Rabin he wanted him to join the cabinet prior to Bar-Lev, who was to end his military service in 1972. But there were opponents, first and foremost Eban. There was also the issue of finding a replacement for the ambassador post in Washington. General Yariv, the director of military intelligence, who was offered the position, declined. Meir told Rabin he had to stay on another year in Washington and would join the cabinet upon returning in 1972. And then, in March 1972, Bar-Lev indeed joined the cabinet.

Disheartened and disappointed, Rabin wrote a bitter letter to Meir. The letter is not dated and may or may not have been sent, but the text shows how despondent Rabin became and how frustrated he was:

> Dear Golda,
> I had some hesitations whether I should write you this letter. I finally decided to write it, hoping that it will be received in friendship and understanding. When I was in Israel and you decided, against my will, that I will stay here for another year, I accepted that decision with a heavy heart. All my concerns have been vindicated. A general and personal situation developed that became difficult and almost intolerable. Everything that you told me, twice, and was not implemented by you (namely, my joining the cabinet) turned my position into practically a subject of ridicule. It seems that it is almost common not to respect what is being said to me. . . . Of course, I am instructed by you to keep my mouth shut, and I cannot defend myself. . . . You never stood up to defend me.

I would not have needed it, had I been at home. I would have known how to do it myself.[14]

Rabin's and Meir's relationship was not helped when Rabin got into some trouble in the 1972 U.S. presidential election when he took a public position in support of Nixon against his Democratic opponent, George McGovern. Rabin saw Nixon as a genuine friend of Israel, felt beholden to him, and was concerned with McGovern's liberalism. In an interview on Israeli radio in June 1972 Rabin stated, "While we appreciate the support in the form of words, we are getting from one camp, we must prefer support in the form of deeds we are getting from the other camp." Rabin's remark produced angry reaction in both the United States and Israel. The *Washington Post* published an editorial critical of him titled "Israel's Undiplomatic Diplomat." Rabin, however, did not regret the incident and defended his conduct in his memoirs, published several years later: "In that interview I noted that never in America's history had a president gone so far in his pro-Israeli declarations or in expressing America's commitment to Israel's security as President Nixon had in his address to Congress following his return from Moscow. That was a fact and at most I was bringing it to the attention of the Israeli, not the American, public. I truly cannot understand how my words could have been interpreted as a 'campaign speech' when the campaign had yet to begin and I was at any rate addressing myself to a public that was not going to the polls."[15]

The incident did not develop into a serious issue. Neither McGovern nor the chairman of the Democratic Party, Lawrence O'Brien, saw any point in inflating it, and Rabin's and Israel's important friends in the Senate, Henry Jackson and Stuart Symington, wrote to Meir in support of Rabin. The incident died down shortly thereafter.

Rabin completed his mission in Washington and returned

to Israel in March 1973. He hosted Meir for the last time just before his departure, in February. Nixon, who was fond of Rabin, expressed his hope that he would be promoted upon returning to Israel. Meir responded, "It depends on his behavior." It was an obvious reflection of the tension that came to characterize Rabin's relationship with the prime minister and a difficult beginning to the next political chapter, in the spring of 1973.

Rabin's tenure in Washington was an important phase in both his career and his personal life. It helped him transition from a ranking army officer to a politician with rich, extensive diplomatic experience, a profound knowledge of the American political system and global politics, and a valuable network in the United States. Despite his rocky relationship with Meir toward the end, Rabin's mission in Washington was considered to be a success and a stepping-stone. But equally important was the impact America had on Rabin's persona. As he himself wrote, he was predisposed to fall in love with America by his father's stories and recollections. He returned to Israel as an admirer of the American political system and way of life. Rabin adopted American notions of a market economy, and his personal lifestyle was transformed. He developed a taste for whiskey and became an enthusiastic tennis player. The Rabins' intensive social life in Washington turned Leah into a very successful hostess and her husband into a more enthusiastic participant rather than the proverbial loner. Rosa Cohen's son had traveled a long way from her radical socialist values.

(Top left) Rosa Cohen, Rabin's mother, marching in a May Day procession in Tel Aviv. The Pinchas Lavon Institute for the Study of the Labor Movement.

(Top right) Rabin as a boy. Chana Rivlin, Yitzhak Rabin Center Archives.

(Bottom) With his mother. Courtesy IDF and Defense Establishment Archives.

(Top) With his father, Nehemiah, and sister Rachel. Courtesy IDF and Defense Establishment Archives.

(Bottom) The poster couple of the Palmach: Yitzhak and Leah Rabin. The National Photo Collection of Israel, Government Press Office.

(Top) Rabin and Yigal Alon. Courtesy IDF and Defense Establishment Archives.

(Bottom) With David Ben Gurion. Fritz Cohen, The National Photo Collection of Israel, Government Press Office.

(Top) With his children, Dalia and Youval, in his IDF office. Courtesy IDF and Defense Establishment Archives. Photograph by Avraham Vered.

(Bottom) Kissed by civilians after the June 1967 victory. Courtesy IDF and Defense Establishment Archives.

(Top) The Mount Scopus speech, 1967. Ilan Bruner, The National Photo Collection of Israel, Government Press Office.

(Bottom) Ambassador to Washington with Golda Meir. Moshe Milner, The National Photo Collection of Israel, Government Press Office.

(Top) Ambassador to Washington with President Richard Nixon. The National Photo Collection of Israel, Government Press Office.

(Bottom) As prime minister with Henry Kissinger. Ya'acov Sa'ar, The National Photo Collection of Israel, Government Press Office.

Prime minister. Ya'acov Sa'ar, The National Photo Collection of Israel,
Government Press Office.

(Top) With Ariel Sharon. Ya'acov Sa'ar, The National
Photo Collection of Israel, Government Press Office.

(Bottom) Prime minister with President Gerald Ford.
Ya'acov Sa'ar, The National Photo Collection of Israel,
Government Press Office.

(Top) The handshake with Yasser Arafat on the White House lawn. Avi Oha-yon, The National Photo Collection of Israel, Government Press Office.

(Bottom) President Bill Clinton fixing Rabin's bow tie at their last meeting. Avi Ohayon, The National Photo Collection of Israel, Government Press Office.

Signing the peace treaty with Jordan. Avi Ohayon, The National Photo Collection of Israel, Government Press Office.

(Top) Rabin and King Hussein, two friendly heavy smokers. Ya'acov Sa'ar, The National Photo Collection of Israel, Government Press Office.

(Bottom) Rabin and Peres in the Knesset. Nathan Alpert, The National Photo Collection of Israel, Government Press Office.

Rabin in midlife. The National Photo Collection of Israel, Government
Press Office.

(Top) With Leah. Fritz Cohen, The National Photo Collection of Israel, Government Press Office.

(Bottom) Rabin and King Hassan of Morocco. Avi Ohayon, The National Photo Collection of Israel, Government Press Office.

(Top) Signing the Oslo II agreement at the White House. Avi Ohayon, The National Photo Collection of Israel, Government Press Office.

(Bottom) With his Palmach comrades. Rachel Rabin-Ya'acov, Yitzhak Rabin Center Archives.

4

First Tenure, 1974–1977

On June 3, 1974, Yitzhak Rabin was confirmed by the Knesset as Israel's fifth prime minister. He was fifty-two years old, quite young in Israeli terms, and the first native-born Israeli to become his country's leader. When he returned from Washington in March 1973 Rabin did not expect to become the next head of government and was, in fact, not ready for it. He entered politics in the spring of 1973 expecting to be elected to the Knesset on the Labor Party's list and finally join the cabinet in the aftermath of the elections planned for October 1973. Dov Tzamir, a member of Kibbutz Bror Hail in the south of the country and representing the TAKAM (a Hebrew acronym of the United Kibbutz Movement) in the Labor Party's headquarters, took it upon himself to help Rabin, who was completely unfamiliar with the realities of party life, cross the line from policy to politics. Yoram Peri, the party's spokesman, also joined the small team. Both Tzamir and Peri had been at the party's headquarters when Rabin arrived, and they decided to introduce the fresh recruit to the Labor Party's and Israel's politics. Rabin was given a small office in party headquarters, and he and his two assistants began to tour the country in order to familiarize Rabin with the ways and the structure of the party. Rabin's transition from soldier and diplomat to politician and political leader was neither smooth nor easy. His fledgling political career had been transformed by the October War. During the months preceding the war Rabin participated in the Labor Party's campaign for the parliamentary elections. He crisscrossed the country with Tzamir or Peri, driven in a modest party car and speaking to party branches. Both Tzamir and Peri recall a disciplined, dedicated Rabin speaking seriously to party members and sympathizers, lecturing about Israel's geopolitical and international situation. He recoiled from "pressing the flesh" and engaging in chitchat but impressed the audience with his willingness to share his experiences with the party rank and file. When the war broke out he held no position. When it became obvious that the general officer commanding of the Southern Command could not cope with the challenge, the decision was made to dispatch a senior general to restore calm and order at the southern front. Dayan swiftly rejected the idea that Rabin should be that person. The choice fell instead on Haim Bar-Lev, and Rabin was asked by the minister of finance, Pinchas Sapir, to help with emergency fund-raising. This was not his preference, but he obliged.

After the war the time came for a political reckoning. The war ended with impressive Israeli achievements against both Egypt and Syria, but Israel's casualties were staggering. The intelligence failure on the eve of the war and the operational setbacks during its first days had to be investigated and accounted for. A judicial panel of inquiry headed by the president of the Supreme Court, the Agranat Commission, was formed to investigate the setbacks. Its report was scheduled to be released in April 1974. While the report was being prepared, the ebb and flow of political life continued with a semblance of normalcy. The October 1973 elections were postponed by Meir, scheduled instead to take place on December 31. In a clever political maneuver, Meir's government participated in an Arab–Israeli peace conference organized by Kissinger in Geneva on the eve of the elections. The Geneva conference was essentially a ceremonial affair designed to give the Soviet Union some role in the postwar peace process and to help Egypt move forward in that process under the cover of a quest for a comprehensive settlement. As Kissinger was well aware, the conference was a way for Meir to portray her government as moving toward the peace so many Israelis were yearning for after an atrocious war. Ultimately the tactic worked.

Under Meir's new government, new faces were added to the new cabinet: Rabin as minister of labor and Aharon Yariv as minister of transport. Yariv, the former head of military intelligence who negotiated successfully at war's end with the Egyptian general Abd al-Ghani Gamasi, became a popular, highly respected figure. He and Rabin had been friends and political allies since the early 1950s. During the process of government formation, history repeated itself. Rabin was again raised as an alternative to Dayan, but he was only to be disappointed. Dayan and his ally, Peres, initially declined to join Meir's postwar cabinet. Rabin was offered the Defense Ministry by Meir and was about to assume the office with Yariv as his deputy when Dayan and Peres changed their minds. An intelligence report warning that Syria was about to renew the war emerged, and Dayan and Peres seized the opportunity, deciding to join after all. Rabin was instead assigned to the junior Ministry of Labor. Rabin and Yariv were not happy partners in Meir's government, feeling that the pretense of normalcy in the aftermath of the October War was not a proper response to the depth of the crisis. They participated in the meetings of the Etgar Circle, a group composed mostly of retired senior officers who were unhappy with the state of affairs in the country and in the Labor Party at large. Their sessions were not secret and were nicknamed the Night of the Generals. Meir saw the circle's meetings as an act of disloyalty, another element of tension added to her prickly relationship with Rabin.

Meir was not happy either with Rabin's statement to a group of young Orthodox Zionists that was leaked to the Israeli press on April 23: "I am guided by an important principle— the people of Israel must know that in order to achieve peace among nations contact must be established that would lead to a political settlement. On Jerusalem I will not compromise; that is my focal point." He was then asked by National Religious Party (NRP) Minister Michael Hazani, "And Ramallah?" He answered, "That is not a question of life and death for me." A settler from the Etzion Bloc asked, "And what about me?," to which Rabin responded, "It won't be terrible if we go to Kfar Etzion with a visa." A girl in the audience then asked, "And what about all of the historical Land of Israel?" to which Rabin answered, "For me the Bible is not a land registry of the Middle East. It is a book that provides education in values and its purposes are different."[1] This was Rabin at his bluntest. In an Israel still reeling under the effects of the October War this far-reaching statement failed to cause the uproar it would have caused under different circumstances. But too much should not be read into it. It was not a harbinger of the Oslo Accords nearly two decades later but a reflection of Rabin's basic approach, namely, that the bulk of the West Bank must not be kept by Israel and certainly not settled by it.

In any event, Rabin's tenure as minister of labor was to be brief. On April 1, 1974, the Agranat Commission released its interim report. The commission decided to exclude the political level from its mandate and limited its conclusions and recommendations to the military. The chief of staff of the IDF and several senior intelligence officers were sacked by the commission. Meir and Dayan were exonerated by the commission, but not by the public. Massive demonstrations by reserve soldiers who had been released from service forced Meir to resign on April 11, 1974.

In the wake of Meir's resignation, the Labor Party leadership chose to rely on its parliamentary majority in order to form a new government. But who should be selected by the party as the new prime minister? The key person in Labor's old guard was Sapir, but he did not want to be prime minister. Another potential candidate, representing the Mapai faction's old guard, was Haim Tzadok, a prominent member of the Labor Party, a member of the Knesset, and a former cabinet minister—but Tzadok would run only if unopposed. Peres announced he was running as a candidate, and Tzadok declined to run. Peres himself was not a natural choice, as he was disliked by the elders of the Mapai faction and by the Achdut Haavoda faction. Alon, as one of the members of Achdut Haavoda, was not desirable as such and, to boot, had been closely identified with Meir's policies. Sapir's candidate of choice was Rabin, the victorious chief of staff of the IDF in 1967, a major asset in a country still shocked by the debacle of 1973, an effective ambassador in Washington, and untarnished by the October setback. Rabin was also close to Achdut Haavoda, the Rafi faction's traditional foe, but not quite a member. For Mapai's elders, this was an advantage. Sapir recruited Rabin after persuading him that under no circumstances would he himself be the candidate. Rabin was surprised by this turn of events but in short order warmed to the idea of seeking the prime ministership.

The die was cast, and a frantic race began. The candidate would need to be elected by a party center numbering about six hundred members. Peres had the support of the Rafi and part of the Mapai factions; Rabin was supported by the Achdut Haavoda faction and Sapir's followers in Mapai. Peres was a natural politician and a much better campaigner than Rabin. Rabin was not fond of the reality of party life or of political campaigning; he was unusually shy and introverted, awkward with unfamiliar people, uncomfortable with small talk and casual cordiality. His handshake was surprisingly limp, not what one expected of an authoritative, military figure. He was reluctant to open himself up to a complete stranger and did not enjoy or excel at cultivating individual party activists and members. Picking up the phone and asking a complete stranger for his vote was a herculean task for Rabin.

Rabin's account of the events leading up to his election in his memoirs was written during a particularly difficult period in both his career and his relationship with Peres. It was published in 1979, after his resignation and the party's defeat in the 1977 elections. He was at that time a backbencher in the ranks of an opposition party, watching Begin celebrating his great breakthrough: the peace with Egypt. Rabin held Peres responsible for his and his party's ouster from power and unleashed his anger and bitterness in the text. According to Rabin's account in his memoirs, Peres invited him to lunch at a Jerusalem restaurant and "treated me to some smooth talk: 'Let us learn from the experience of our older colleagues. Alon and Dayan fought each other, sapped each other's strength and neither of them became prime minister. Let's conclude a gentleman's agreement to hold a fair contest. Whoever loses will accept the decision in good spirit and be loyal to the winner.' I was wary and my inclination was not to believe a word he said. Moreover, I was determined that if he became prime minister, I would not set foot in the cabinet. But I certainly had no objection to the terms he suggested. So I replied tersely, 'Agreed.' "[2]

This tense truce was not to be maintained—or, in Rabin's

mind, respected. On the eve of the vote at the party's center in May 1974, Weizman dropped a bombshell with his story about Rabin's personal crisis in May 1967. The message intended was clear: a chief of staff who could not face the pressure of a national security crisis in 1967 was certainly not fit to be prime minister in 1974. Weizman was settling a score with the man who had preferred Bar-Lev over him for chief of staff in 1968, but he was also a friend and supporter of Peres. In Rabin's mind, this move was proof enough that Peres was not living up to their agreement. In any event, with the support of the formidable Sapir and his party machine Rabin won the vote, albeit narrowly: 298 votes for Rabin against 254 for Peres.

Bitter over the tension with Peres, Rabin would have happily excluded him from his cabinet but soon realized this was not feasible. The slim majority he had indicated that Peres had massive support that could not be ignored. Even Golda Meir, who as foreign minister had resented the "alternative foreign ministry" run by Peres in the Ministry of Defense, was not entirely unsupportive of him. Her relationship with Rabin had become strained, and, like so many other retired leaders, she was lukewarm at best toward her successor. The Rafi faction would also not vote for a government that did not include Peres in a senior position; lacking that vote, Rabin would not have a majority in the Knesset.

Rabin ended up offering Peres the powerful Ministry of Defense position. This was the first round of a joint journey by two political Siamese twins that would last for twenty-one years—twins who both disliked and appreciated each other, competed and partnered, eventually realizing they were joined at the hip and bound to collaborate with each other. They were dramatically different people, with diverse qualities and gifts. Peres was imaginative, creative, restlessly tinkering with new ideas, a natural and seasoned politician. Rabin was cerebral, an excellent analyst of the strategic environment with his feet firmly planted on the ground. Peres was a voracious reader, a friend of writers, poets, and artists, while Rabin preferred to apply his mind to practical issues and never pretended to have intellectual or artistic pursuits. Rabin was the quintessential Sabra, while Peres never managed to lose the scent of the diaspora-born Israeli. When they managed to collaborate, they formed an awesome, powerful team.

Meanwhile, in 1974 the formation of a new coalition under Rabin proved to be arduous. The NRP, Labor's traditional coalition partner, was undergoing a transformation from a dovish party to a hawkish one; in fact, the new political arm of the settlers' movement and its younger bidders for the leadership had reservations and conditions that initially kept it out of the coalition. The NRP's young guard were opposed to any territorial concessions and took a radical position on the issue known in Israeli public and political life as "Who is a Jew?" They insisted on a strictly Orthodox religious definition of the word "Jewish." Rabin started his term with a fragile coalition of only 61 out of 120 Members of the Knesset. Several months later, in late October 1974, the NRP joined the coalition. This in turn led to the departure of a small left-wing party, Ratz. The coalition now rested on a majority of 68. In order to add the NRP to his coalition, Rabin agreed that any territorial concession in the West Bank would require a referendum or a general election. Nor did the distribution of the party's ministerial portfolios proceed smoothly either. Rabin did not want Eban as his foreign minister and offered him the junior information ministry. Eban declined and stayed out. Rabin gave the Foreign Ministry to his old friend and former mentor Alon. His original candidates for minister of finance also declined, possibly because they suspected his government would not last long. Sapir exerted pressure on Yehoshua Rabinovich, Tel Aviv's former mayor, who reluctantly accepted. He would turn out to be a very effective, very loyal, and very helpful ally to Rabin.

The tasks and challenges facing the new prime minister were daunting. Rabin needed to rebuild the public's morale and confidence in the government in the aftermath of the October debacle; rehabilitate and reform the IDF and the economy; and deal with Washington's and the Arab world's expectation that the diplomatic process launched after the war would be continued. The October War, the oil embargo, and the quadrupling of oil prices launched the so-called Arab decade, marked by greater Arab wealth and influence in the global arena. In Israel the war deepened the fault lines. The advocates of peace (and the concessions it entailed) felt the war had demonstrated that the status quo was untenable, while the right wing argued it had in fact underscored the crucial importance of territorial assets. One of the consequences of the war was the emergence of Gush Emunim (the Bloc of the Faithful), the Orthodox Zionist settler movement that sought to settle the West Bank. Gush Emunim opposed any territorial concessions and claimed to represent a fresh new phase in the Zionist revolution against the backdrop of the gloomy aftermath of the October War. A messianic movement led by cunning manipulators of the Israeli political system, it would have an enormous impact on Israeli life and politics.

These difficult challenges had to be met by what was an inherently weak government. Rabin was not an elected prime minister, and he lacked the authority derived from a popular mandate. His coalition was narrow and fragile; despite its expansion from 61 to 71, it then shrank to 68 when the Ratz faction left the coalition. The NRP, rattled by internecine conflicts and becoming increasingly hawkish, was not a comfortable ally. Nor did Rabin have a firm grip on his own party. He had barely defeated Peres for the party's nomination. He did not have his own "camp" and had to rely instead on Mapai's old guard and on Achdut Haavoda. Rabin had won the party's nomination largely owing to the support of Sapir. Sapir declined to be either prime minister or minister of finance, stayed out of the government, and gradually lost his influence; and in any event he distanced himself from Rabin and his former protégé and successor in the Finance Ministry, Rabinovich. An atrocious workload left Rabin little time for building and cultivating support in the party's apparatus, rank and file, a task he disliked and performed poorly.

In theory Rabin could have chosen to deal with these difficulties by grabbing the bull by the horns, taking bold initiatives, and sweeping the country with the vision of a young prime minister representing a new era in Israeli politics. But this did not suit the Rabin of 1974. He was cautious by nature, an incrementalist. As a political leader he lacked confidence and experience. He was ever mindful of the presence and shadow of the previous generation of leaders, Meir in particular, and of the antagonism of Dayan and Eban. He was not ready to storm ahead, preferring to move cautiously and deliberately. Rabin chose to present his government as "a government of continuity and change." This was a mistake. The public, it turned out, was sick and tired of the old Labor Party, its leadership, and its legacy and wanted freshness and change, not sameness. The Israeli political sociologist Jonathan Shapiro argued that the powerful generation of the founding fathers in the Labor movement managed to suppress and dwarf their successors—and for Rabin at this time that seemed very much to be the case.[3]

Rabin's two principal allies in the cabinet were Minister of Finance Yehoshua Rabinovich, a deceptively gray Labor Party activist who excelled in his ministerial role, and Minister Without Portfolio Israel Galili, who was wise and experienced, a cunning politician, and a master wordsmith. Galili, the former chief of staff of the Haganah who had been deposed by Ben Gurion, was very hawkish, in the tradition of Yitzhak Tabenkin's wing of Achdut Haavoda. Rabin also tended to rely on the advice of Minister of Justice Haim Tzadok, another wise, experienced man. The prime minister's relationship with his foreign minister, Alon, was awkward. As we have seen, Alon had been his friend and mentor and was largely responsible for his swift rise in the Palmach and the IDF. The reversal of roles was uncomfortable for both. More profoundly, Rabin had lost respect for his former leader. Something snapped in Alon in 1949, when he was sacked by Ben Gurion. He did not stand up to Ben Gurion in 1949 and never recovered from that setback, losing the charisma and halo of the great war commander. The Alon of the mid-1970s also tended to be long-winded, and Rabin, never patient with people he did not appreciate, used to cut him short in cabinet meetings. This treatment did not go down well with Alon's admirers from his glorious days in the Palmach.

But Rabin's main political problem was his relationship with Peres. Their rivalry had deep roots, going back to the 1950s. There had been an almost inevitable clash between a powerful, ambitious director general (and subsequently deputy minister) of the Ministry of Defense, and an authoritative deputy and then chief of staff of the IDF, which was a classic case of the tension between the civilian political leadership of the defense establishment and the senior military. Rabin also knew that Peres, who had Ben Gurion's ear, was, to some extent, responsible for the appointment of his friend, Tsur, ahead of him as chief of staff in January 1961 and suspected that he continued to act against his candidacy in 1964. The contest for the party's nomination further soured an already bad relationship.

It was one thing for Rabin to have Peres as a competitor inside his cabinet and another altogether to have him as minister of defense. It is an especially powerful position in a country preoccupied with its security. The minister of defense oversees the IDF, the defense industries, and the administration of the territories captured in 1967. In the Israeli system there is no commander in chief; the chief of staff of the IDF reports to the cabinet through the minister of defense. Ben Gurion understood all of this and kept the defense portfolio in his hands. So did his successor Eshkol, and so did several other Israeli prime ministers, including Rabin in his second term. During his first term, however, Rabin was often frustrated by his inability to apply his profound knowledge and understanding of military affairs and Israel's national security issues through direct contact with Mota Gur, the chief of staff of the IDF. Peres saw any attempt in this direction as a serious undermining of his own authority, and Rabin saw Gur as an ally of Peres. In June he appointed Ariel Sharon as his advisor. Sharon was not appointed as an advisor on military or security affairs, but security was his métier, and both Peres and Gur resented his appointment.

Rabin and Peres could perhaps have overcome these huge obstacles and worked together more often than they did. When they were able to do so, these two very dissimilar men complemented one another and formed a very effective team. But most of the time this connection failed to happen; the relationship was poisonous from the outset. As Rabin saw it, Peres never accepted his failure to win in 1974 and was determined to defeat and unseat him. To Rabin (and others) it was considered unacceptable for a senior minister to sit in a prime minister's cabinet and hope and work to replace him. Rabin knew Peres kept in touch with Dayan and saw him as his Trojan horse. Where Rabin saw subversion and intrigue, Peres saw paranoia and persecution. Rabin's temper (he was known to have a short fuse) led to several outbursts against Peres for all to see; Peres was much better at controlling his emotions. This unhealthy state of affairs between the two leaders was worsened by the actions of their eager, often overzealous assistants and spokesmen, who kept stoking the fires with gossip and leaks to the media. The fact of the matter is Peres did well in this competition with Rabin: he had greater support in the Israeli press and was popular with the party's rank and file. When he competed against Rabin for the party's nomination a second time in February 1977, he came close to defeating the incumbent. Although the two men did, of course, work together much of the time and the cabinet and government did function, the Rabin–Peres rivalry cast a permanent shadow over Rabin's first tenure.

THE ROAD TO SINAI II

The negotiating and signing of the interim agreement with Egypt and of the memorandum of understanding with the United States that was attached to it constituted the major achievement of Rabin's first term. The agreement, known also as Sinai II, consolidated the immediate postwar arrangements of 1974, removed the danger of renewed hostilities with Egypt, laid the groundwork for the quest for a full-fledged peace agreement later in the decade, and raised Israel's relationship with the United States to a new level. It was not easily accomplished and took an intense diplomatic effort of more than a year. Getting there would produce a severe, albeit temporary, crisis in Israel's relationship with Washington and in Rabin's personal relationship with U.S. President Gerald Ford and Kissinger.

In June 1974 Nixon visited Israel as part of a Middle Eastern tour that was essentially a farewell tour by a beleaguered president soon to depart the White House. Rabin's discussions with him during the visit did not deal with the next phase of the peace process. It was agreed that the issue should be dealt with at the end of the summer, in August or September. But one important aspect of the issue was discussed between Kissinger and Foreign Minister Alon during Alon's visit to Washington in July, and that was the prospect of an interim agreement between Israel and Jordan. At the same time, King Hussein of Jordan visited Sadat in Cairo to discuss the prospect of their collaboration in the next phase of the peace process. Kissinger supported the idea of a modest agreement, one that would give Jordan a foothold in the area of Jericho, for two reasons. The first was the need to find a second Arab party to the next round of Arab–Israeli diplomacy. Egypt was to be the principal Arab partner, but Sadat did not want to be exposed to the charge that he was going it alone or making a separate deal with Israel. In the aftermath of the October War, Syria, his wartime ally, was his partner and signed its own disengagement agreement with Israel. There was no great enthusiasm anywhere for another joint effort with Syria. Asad was considered a difficult, problematic negotiating partner, still closely allied with the Soviet Union. It was also difficult to craft another partial agreement in the relatively small area of the Golan Heights. The second consideration had to do with the rising salience and influence of the PLO. By giving Jordan a foothold in the West Bank, its claim to that territory and the leading role as custodian of the Palestinian cause could be reinforced.

Rabin weighed the Jericho Plan but ultimately rejected it. He did support the notion of a territorial compromise with Jordan in the West Bank, but at that point of time he felt he did not have the political power to negotiate even a limited agreement over part of the West Bank. The Israeli right wing objected to any territorial concession, but its attachment to the West Bank, or Judea and Samaria in its parlance, was even stronger than to Sinai and the Golan. This was the Land of Israel, and any concession was anathema. Rabin was in his early weeks in power, and his government rested on a slim majority; there were members of his own party and coalition who would object to the idea. Meir and Galili were two hawkish leaders of Labor whose views were given special weight by Rabin. And if Rabin wanted to add the NRP to his coalition (as he eventually did), the NRP would never agree to such a concession. The idea was discussed in Rabin's cabinet; a majority of the ministers did not support it. And so Rabin rejected the notion of the Jericho Plan. Given the subsequent course of events, it was an understandable but regrettable decision. It was also indicative of Rabin's insecurity while in that early phase of his tenure. A different leader, even Rabin himself later in his career, might well have seized the opportunity and taken a bold step. But this was not the Rabin of the summer of 1974.

Kissinger, for his part, kept the ball in the air. On August 18, at the end of a visit by King Hussein in Washington, a joint statement was issued, which stated, "The discussions between His Majesty and the President and Secretary of State were a constructive contribution to the consultations now underway looking toward the next stage in negotiations for a just and durable peace in the Middle East. It was agreed that these consultations will continue with a view to addressing at an appropriately early date the issues of particular concern to Jordan, including a Jordanian–Israeli disengagement agreement."[4]

In response, the Israeli Foreign Ministry's spokesperson issued a statement saying, "The government of Israel is prepared, as it has repeatedly declared, to strive for a peace settlement with Jordan. Israel, however, has rejected and will reject the Jordanian demand for an Israeli withdrawal along the Jordan River as part of what Jordan terms 'disengagement of forces.'"[5]

On August 29, 1974, Rabin had his first secret meeting with King Hussein. They met eight times during Rabin's first term. Their relationship was sustained by common enmity to the PLO and Syria and by Israel's interest in the Hashemite regime's survival, but they could not come to an agreement on either a final or an interim settlement. Hussein would not budge from his position on a final status agreement; he was willing to offer Israel full peace but only in return for a full withdrawal, including from East Jerusalem. If Israel wanted to keep part of the West Bank, it should talk to the PLO. With regard to an interim settlement, he insisted on receiving a strip of land eight to ten kilometers along the Jordan valley. This would have protected the kingdom from a prospective Palestinian presence on the Jordan but was a nonstarter from Rabin's perspective owing to opposition inside the Labor Party and by the NRP to any territorial concessions in the West Bank.

The first real steps in the negotiations toward the next Israeli–Egyptian agreement were taken in September 1974. Rabin paid his first visit to the United States in his incarnation as Israel's prime minister. His host was President Gerald Ford, who had replaced Nixon. The two main items on Rabin's agenda with Ford and Kissinger were Israel's request for new arms supplies and Middle Eastern diplomacy. By that time Rabin had reached the conclusion that the next agreement would have to be negotiated with Egypt alone. Egypt was, in principle, ready to go it alone. Sadat did not wish to be bogged down by Asad, and in September he distanced himself from the partnership with Jordan he had envisaged in July. But there was to be a high price for a self-standing Israeli–Egyptian deal. Sadat explained to his American interlocutors that in order to cover his flank when making a separate deal, he would need better terms from Israel that would justify this breach of Arab solidarity.

The Ford administration sought to restart the peace process by negotiating fresh agreements between Israel and Egypt, preferably reinforced by an Israeli–Jordanian one. Rabin began his talks with Ford and Kissinger by insisting there had to be a political dimension to the next agreement with Egypt to make it qualitatively different from the largely military agreements negotiated in 1973 and 1974. Rabin preferred the step-by-step approach to the quest for a comprehensive settlement. But he knew—and was chided for it by his domestic critics—that it also had a significant downside: it could end up being a case of "salami tactics," with Israel stripped of its territorial assets in return for limited agreements and ending the process empty-handed. To counter this possibility, Rabin demanded that the next agreement with Egypt offer Israel an end to the state of war with Egypt in return for a limited Israeli withdrawal.

Rabin's American interlocutors told him that Sadat would

agree to end the state of war in return for a full Israeli withdrawal from the Sinai. This was not acceptable to Rabin. He then proposed a withdrawal of thirty to forty kilometers in return for nonbelligerency. That figure, he wrote in his memoirs, had already been mentioned during Meir's tenure. The territory to be included in a withdrawal of that distance included three sites over which the negotiations, the disagreements, and the agreements of the next year would focus: (1) the oil field at Abu Rodes; (2) the Mitla and Gidi passes, considered crucial to any offensive or defensive deployment and maneuver; and (3) the Israeli electronic monitoring station in Umm Khashiba, a highly valuable intelligence outpost. Sadat refused to offer nonbelligerency in return for a partial withdrawal and insisted on regaining all three sites in the next agreement with Israel.

This initial back and forth ended in September–October 1974 following the Arab summit conference in Rabat, initiating a hiatus of several months. For one thing, the Arab summit conference represented a setback for Jordan and an achievement for Syria and the PLO. Its resolutions reinforced the Arab recognition of the PLO as "the sole legitimate representative of the Palestinian people" and the sole legitimate claimant of the West Bank. Sadat completed the about-face he began in September and joined Syria, the PLO, and the Arab consensus. Could he really be relied on as a partner? A worried Rabin asked himself. Israel and the United States were also concerned by a planned visit to Cairo by the Soviet leader Leonid Brezhnev, unmistakably seeking to bring Egypt back into the fold. Washington and Jerusalem decided to await the outcome of Brezhnev's visit. But in the end Brezhnev's visit was canceled. Kissinger came to what he called "an exploratory shuttle" in the region on February 10, 1975, visiting Israel, Egypt, Jordan, Syria, and Saudi Arabia.

Rabin got himself into some trouble prior to Kissinger's arrival when he spoke rather freely to Yoel Marcus, an influential columnist for the Israeli daily *Haaretz*—not the first or last time Rabin got into trouble by speaking freely to the media. In this case his understanding with Marcus was that Marcus would be allowed to report the substance of Rabin's statements but not quote them directly. The result was an unusually candid exposition of Rabin's view of Israel's position and strategy attributed to Rabin himself. Israel, Rabin told Marcus, had to get through "seven lean years" (an allusion to Pharaoh's biblical dream deciphered by Joseph) and should therefore play for time. In the aftermath of the Arabs' resort to "the oil weapon" and the quadrupling of oil prices after the October War, Arab influence was at a peak. Israel could not expect to achieve great diplomatic successes and should therefore seek limited agreements that would enable it to make it through this difficult period. In the meantime its purpose should be "to drive a wedge" between Egypt and Syria and Egypt and the Soviet Union.[6]

This candid presentation raised a storm of protest in the media and by the opposition. Begin, the head of the opposition, insisting the Knesset should discuss the issue, vilified Rabin on both substance and style; the parliamentary opposition and several journalists took Rabin to task for bluntly exposing his strategy. A few weeks later John Lindsay, the former mayor of New York, came to Israel on behalf of ABC News and interviewed Rabin. Lindsay asked him what Israel was willing to offer to Egypt in return for nonbelligerency. Rabin's response was, with some qualifications, that Egypt could have the passes and the oil field. Another storm of protest followed. These were birth pangs of an unpolished politician too free with his opinions and remarks and as yet unlearned in how to deal with and manipulate the media.

Kissinger came briefly in February and returned in March 1975 to shuttle between Cairo and Jerusalem. Some progress was made, but gaps on three issues simply could not be bridged: the lines of Israeli withdrawal and Egypt's new deployment; the

Israeli monitoring station in Umm Khashiba; and the duration of the agreement, Sadat insisting on two years, while Israel wanted a longer period. On March 22 it became obvious that Kissinger's mediation efforts had failed. Rabin refused to accept Egypt's demands, particularly its insistence on including the strategic Mitla and Gidi passes in the area of Israeli withdrawal and refusal to add a political dimension to the agreement. Kissinger was supportive of the Egyptian position. An angry and emotional Kissinger left Israel. He blamed Israel and Rabin specifically for his failure. When Kissinger and Rabin worked intimately and effectively together during Rabin's years as ambassador, Kissinger was clearly the senior member of the duo. In 1974 and 1975 he was the secretary of state of a superpower, and Rabin was a prime minister—prime minister of a small country but still prime minister. When Rabin came to Washington for his first visit as prime minister, he noted wryly in his memoirs, he no longer called on Kissinger in the secretary of state's office; rather, Kissinger, as protocol required, came to see him at Blair House, the presidential guesthouse. The two needed time—and a crisis—in order to adjust their relations to the new circumstances. As Kissinger saw it, when Rabin invited him to perform his shuttle mediation in March, he implicitly committed himself to make it work. One does not invite the secretary of state of the United States to undertake an abortive mission.

The famous "senior source traveling with the Secretary of State" on Air Force 3 (a thinly veiled reference to Kissinger himself) lost no time in briefing the American press corps, blaming Rabin and Israel for the failure. This was followed by a message from President Ford to Rabin, informing him that, in view of the failure, the United States would have to reassess its policy in the region, or, in other words, its relationship with Israel. Thus a difficult six-month period known as "the reassessment" began. During this time no new agreements were made for arms deliveries to Israel but older agreements were kept. An open feud and a persistent negative campaign by the administration greatly undermined Israel's regional and international position and the government's standing at home. Rabin fought back by mobilizing the Jewish community and Israel's friends in Congress. In June a new effort to resolve the crisis was launched. Rabin came to Washington, met with Ford and Kissinger, and together they reexamined creative solutions to the deadlock. Ford and Kissinger resorted to a threat: that a continuation of the impasse would lead to a convening of the Geneva conference, where the search for a comprehensive solution would be renewed. They knew very well that Israel was adamantly opposed to the idea of convening a forum that would include the Soviet Union and Syria and would create new pressure to add the Palestinian issue to the agenda.

By July 1 Rabin had reached a decision to seek a swift end to the crisis. He dispatched Ambassador Dinitz to meet Kissinger in the Virgin Islands with a clear message that he was determined to find a compromise. In the coming weeks the compromise would be facilitated by two developments: first, Rabin agreed to a line east to the Mitla and Gidi passes that would enable Egypt to gain control of the passes but would still keep Israel deployed in a satisfactory defensive position; second, the idea of an American military presence, later transformed to U.S. personnel manning the monitoring station, surfaced.

It took some time for tempers to cool and for confidence to be restored between the Ford administration and the Rabin government. The U.S. president warned the Israeli prime minister that conduct such as that which Rabin had engaged in jeopardized future cooperation between the two countries. But these difficulties were resolved when Rabin agreed to make the concessions he had refused to make in March. Rabin invited Kissinger to renew his shuttling between Cairo and Jerusalem on August 21. This time it was absolutely understood that Kissinger was invited in order to complete his mission.

A dark, ominous shadow was cast over Kissinger's visits to Israel in this period by the violent and ugly demonstrations of Gush Emunim. Its leaders saw the Sinai as part of the Land of Israel and were opposed to any territorial concessions. They cast aspersions on Kissinger, denouncing him as a "Jewboy" and "the husband of the gentile woman," and rioted in Jerusalem and other locations. It was one of Rabin's character traits that opposition to his policies, particularly ugly opposition, served only to reinforce his resolve. In harsh terms he ordered the police to disperse the demonstrators of Gush Emunim and its leaders, by force if necessary. In a press interview Rabin said, "A settlement movement . . . is like a cancer in the social and democratic tissue of the state of Israel, a group that takes the law into its own hands. . . . With a historical perspective, people will question what Israel was doing in 1976 (*sic*), and in what a lousy and unimportant place. A mystical debate focused on the existential problem of the existence of Israel. It's unbelievable . . . what is settlement anyway? What sort of struggle is it? What does it mean?"[7]

Twenty years later the demonstrations and incitement from the same quarters would be directed at Rabin himself.

By August 31 the Egyptian–Israeli part of the agreement had been completed. It took another night to complete the U.S.–Israeli memorandum of understanding and therefore end the odyssey to reach the agreement on September 1, 1975.

The interim agreement drew on the 1974 Egyptian–Israeli disengagement agreement. Rabin was unable to get the non-belligerency clause he originally wanted, but the two parties committed themselves to resolve the conflict between them by peaceful means and not to resort to the threat or the use of force against each other. The UN force would continue its role.

Egypt agreed to allow nonmilitary cargos destined for or coming from Israel to pass through the Suez Canal. The agreement would remain in force until superseded by a new one. The arrangements for U.S. manning and supervision of the early warning stations in the buffer zones were spelled out in detail. From Rabin's point of view the memorandum of understanding signed between the United States and Israel was just as important as the Egyptian–Israeli agreement. It dealt with military assistance, oil supply, financial aid, and diplomatic issues. The two countries agreed that the next step with Egypt should be a final peace agreement. The same should apply to Jordan. Washington agreed to consult promptly with Israel in the event of any threat to it from a "world power." The freeze of new arms agreements, which began in April, was ended. A special memorandum dealing with the Geneva conference was signed. Washington committed not to recognize or negotiate with the PLO until it recognized Israel's right to exist and accepted Security Council resolutions 242 and 338. It also committed to carefully coordinate its strategy with Israel should a Geneva conference be convened and agreed to keep the negotiations on a bilateral basis. Ford also wrote a letter to Rabin stating that "the US did not develop a final position on the borders [between Israel and Syria]. Should it do so, it will give great weight to Israel's position that any peace agreement with Syria must be predicated on Israel remaining on the Golan Heights."[8] At the same time, in its side letters to Egypt the United States committed itself to bringing about further negotiations between Syria and Israel.

Having signed the interim agreement with Egypt on September 1, 1975, Rabin expected to be able to rest on his laurels for some time. He knew full well he would have to move forward in the peace process, and he anticipated that the next phase would be another Israeli–Egyptian agreement—a long-term one predicated on Israeli withdrawal from about half of the Sinai to the El-Arish–Ras Muhammad line, in return for ending the state of war between Egypt and Israel. But it soon became apparent that the status quo could not be paused. There was growing criticism in Washington of Kissinger's step-by-step diplomacy. Its critics argued it was time to shift to a quest for a comprehensive settlement and to add the Palestinian issue to its agenda. Kissinger had to manage Syria's unhappiness with being left out as well as Arab pressure for dealing with the Palestinian issue. On September 29, 1975, Kissinger told the Arab representatives to the UN that "the United States would consider ways of working for an overall settlement" and that he would begin to refine his thinking on how the legitimate interests of the Palestinian people could be met.[9] Another step in the same direction was taken when the deputy assistant secretary of state for Near Eastern affairs, Harold ("Hal") Saunders, testified before the House Committee on International Affairs on November 12, 1975. The committee, chaired by Congressman Lee Hamilton, was holding hearings on the Palestinian question, in itself an indication that the issue was gaining recognition in Washington. Saunders's testimony, presented also as a written text, defined the Palestinian dimension of the Arab–Israeli hostilities as "the heart of the conflict." This was a very significant choice of words. If the Palestinian issue was the heart of the conflict, any attempt at a resolution that did not address it would be limited and temporary. Saunders further stated that "the legitimate interest of the Palestinians must be taken into account in the negotiations of an Arab–Israeli peace."[10]

ISRAEL, SYRIA, AND LEBANON

Rabin was worried by these developments as well as by Kissinger's efforts to placate Asad. The Syrian–Israeli disengagement agreement of 1974 stipulated that the mandate of the UN peacekeeping force in the Golan (UNDOF) had to be renewed every six months. This gave Syria an excellent means of pressuring Israel. As the time for renewal approached, Asad skillfully created the impression that Syria was about to object to the renewal and thereby produce a crisis. Syria's response to the Egyptian–Israeli interim agreement of 1975 was fierce. It denounced Egypt, accusing it of selling out and making a separate deal with Israel. While Syria was left out of Kissinger's Arab–Israeli diplomacy, it was building up its regional position. After years of instability, Asad, who took full power in November 1970, managed to build a stable and increasingly powerful state in Syria and began to pursue the ambitious policy of extending his hegemony over his weaker Arab neighbors Lebanon, Jordan, and the Palestinians. Whatever Kissinger could offer Asad by way of a second modest agreement on the Golan was unsatisfactory, and Kissinger tried to mollify him in other ways. One of them was his willingness to go along with a joint Syrian–Russian move to have the PLO invited to a Security Council discussion in January 1976. Rabin responded angrily. In his view the United States, Israel, and Egypt had just concluded a major step in their negotiation, and Washington, by going along with a Russian–Syrian countermeasure, was undermining its own policy and Israel's position. This caused another (brief) period of tension in Jerusalem's relationship with Washington and certainly in Rabin's personal relationship with Kissinger.

But in early 1976 the triangular relationship between the United States, Israel, and Syria would be transformed by the Lebanese civil war. The war erupted in April 1975 and was waged between a Christian-dominated coalition seeking to preserve the political status quo in the Arab world's only parliamentary democracy and a revisionist coalition composed of Muslim, Palestinian, and left-wing Lebanese who were seeking to reverse it. Syria and Israel were, not surprisingly, on different sides of this conflict. Syria had irredentist claims on the whole—or at least on parts of Lebanon—and supported the revisionist camp. Israel was worried by the potential transformation of its friendliest Arab neighbor; by the prospect of the country's takeover by radical elements; by further empowerment of the PLO's position on its northern border; and by the extension of Syria's influence. Rabin was wary of being drawn into the civil war and limited Israel's direct involvement to South Lebanon. He endorsed Peres's policy of extending humanitarian help (known as "the good fence" policy) and authorized the cultivation of a small local militia in the south in order to help the local population defend itself from the penetration of hostile elements in the vicinity of the border area. But he rejected the requests of the senior Christian Maronite leadership for direct intervention. Rabin met with the two senior Maronite leaders, Camille Chamoun and Pierre Jumayyil, on board an Israeli navy boat. His message to them was that Israel would not go beyond "helping you to help yourselves." That help consisted of the provision of military equipment and military training.

However, in the spring of 1976 an important change could be detected in Syria's policy. Asad changed his calculus and came to believe that a radical victory could jeopardize his own country by dragging it into an unwanted war with Israel. He shifted his policy to support the status quo camp, and when he encountered opposition by his former allies was ready to send his army across the border. He then turned to the United States in order to ascertain that his military intervention in Lebanon would not provoke an Israeli reaction; Kissinger was happy to mediate. Rabin could see the upside of Syria's stabilizing role in Lebanon, but he did not want the Syrians too close to the Lebanese–Israeli border or too free to flex their military muscle. He insisted on four conditions:

> 1. that the Syrian army refrain from crossing a virtual red line running some forty kilometers north of the Israeli border;

2. that they not deploy ground-to-air missiles in Lebanon;

3. that they not use their air force to attack ground targets in Lebanon; and

4. that the Israeli air force retain its freedom of action in Lebanon.

Asad agreed. The episode, since known as the Red Line Agreement, would lead to Syria's military intervention in Lebanon and to the establishment of Syrian hegemony in that country.

For Israel, this was a mixed blessing. For several years the Syrian army was split between the two countries, and the threat it posed to Israel was thereby reduced. Syria inflicted heavy casualties on the PLO, and its preoccupation with Lebanon blunted the edge of its campaign against the Sinai II Agreement. More broadly, the Lebanese issue captured Arab attention and diverted it for some time from the Palestinian one. But eventually there was no escaping the Palestinian issue. The PLO took over South Lebanon and turned it into a new operational base, a substitute for the one it lost in Jordan. These developments would unfold in their entirety after the establishment of Begin's government in Israel and would prompt him to adopt an entirely different policy from Rabin's. For the time being, though, Syria kept the Red Line agreement. In late 1976, after Jimmy Carter's victory in the American presidential election, the Syrians made an effort to test Jerusalem's and Washington's resolve and sent troops south of the Red Line. Rabin's response was swift: he reinforced Israel's deployment on the Lebanese border, thus persuading the Syrians to withdraw.

RABIN, THE PALESTINIAN ISSUE, AND THE SETTLER MOVEMENT

As Israel's new prime minister, Rabin had a very clear view on the Palestinian issue. He believed that Jordan was Israel's partner in resolving, or at least dealing with, the Palestinian issue and that a solution should be based on a territorial compromise with Jordan in the West Bank. He was adamantly opposed to having any dealings with the PLO but was open-minded when other, nonofficial Israelis, such as the retired general Matti Peled or the journalist Uri Avneri, would meet with PLO representatives, even though that was nominally forbidden by law. During Rabin's first months in power, however, it became obvious that neither a final nor an interim deal with Jordan was feasible since Rabin felt he did not have the political power to offer territorial concessions in the West Bank, and it was up to Israel to continue to administer the West Bank and Gaza.

One of the main challenges deriving from the persistence of the status quo in the West Bank and Gaza was the issue of Israeli settlements. Rabin himself supported the establishment of settlements in the Golan Heights, in sparsely populated parts of the West Bank, and in areas around Jerusalem that were designated to become part of Israel once a final status agreement could be reached. But his policy encountered challenges inside his party and coalition as well as from the relatively newly established Gush Emunim. Some of his closest allies, such as Galili, a leader of the Achdut Haavoda faction, were quite hawkish. Peres, at that time, supported Dayan's concept of a "functional compromise" in the West Bank. This concept advocated a division of labor between Israel, who would control the entire territory and be responsible for security, and an Arab partner who would be responsible for the civilian administration.

Gush Emunim persisted in its efforts to establish settlements in Samaria, the hilly, populated part of the West Bank. Their first success was in a former Jordanian military camp, Ein Yabrud, that eventually and subtly became a settlement known as Ofra. The leaders of the settlers' movement became very adept at manipulating the Israeli political system. In this case they persuaded Minister of Defense Peres, who was responsible for the administration of the West Bank, to adopt a policy of passive acceptance of their low-key installation in Ein Yabrud in the guise of a work camp. This was the first settlement built in the hilly part of the West Bank, an area supposedly reserved for a future agreement with either Jordan or a Palestinian entity. Even more prominent were Gush Emunim's repeated efforts to settle in Sebastia, near Nablus, an attempt which came to a head in December 1975. Their timing was well chosen. In Jerusalem a large Jewish gathering was held in response to the resolution passed in the UN General Assembly denouncing Zionism as a form of racism, the result of Soviet–Arab cooperation in the UN designed to undermine Israel's legitimacy. When Rabin was informed of Gush Emunim's attempt to settle Sebastia he confronted a complex political situation. His defense minister, Peres, was sympathetic to, if not even supportive of, the settlers. Other allies in Rabin's party also had a soft spot for the settlers, who skillfully depicted themselves as a movement following in the footsteps of Labor Zionism's pioneers in earlier years. The chief of staff of the IDF, Motta Gur, said he would need five thousand soldiers and three days to evacuate the settlers. The NRP members in Rabin's government and coalition were openly supportive of the settlers. The prospect of a massive, violent, perhaps bloody confrontation between the IDF and the settlers while a large show of Jewish solidarity was taking place in Jerusalem was problematic to say the least. Rabin enlisted his advisor Sharon, himself a patron of the settlers, to seek a solution. Rabin's childhood friend, the poet Haim Guri, who was there as a journalist, was also drafted as a mediator. The upshot was a compromise that allowed thirty settlers to remain in an IDF camp in Qadum. Only later did Rabin find out that thirty settlers became thirty *families* of settlers. The thirty families did eventually establish a new settlement, known as Qdumim. In December 1975 the government decided it would revisit the issue six months later, and it did indeed discuss the issue in May 1976. Once again, Rabin could not build a consensus, and a way out was found by a decision not to decide.

The Sebastia affair was a turning point in several respects. It was a defining event in the history of Gush Emunim and the settlers' movement, leading to additional settlements in Samaria. It also exposed the weakness of Rabin and his government. It was a moment that called for a show of political courage and a determination that the Rabin of 1975 was still lacking. It was also yet another important moment that worsened the relationship between Rabin and Peres. Rabin was critical of Peres's support of the settlers and saw it as an act of subversion designed to undermine his own position. From that point on it was difficult to halt the deterioration in their relationship.

Rabin's anger at Peres would burst out a few weeks later, in January 1976, during Rabin's trip to the United States. Rabin was visiting in order to participate in the U.S. bicentennial. He was warmly received by President Ford, who was pleased by the signing of the September 1, 1975, interim agreement. But when Rabin visited Congress, he was embarrassed by questions about Israel's request for sophisticated weapon systems, including ballistic missiles capable of carrying a nuclear warhead. The requests for arms were presented by Peres in December, then modified when Rabin and Peres realized, thanks to Congress's questions, that the Israeli list had been exaggerated. When Rabin met with a group of Israeli journalists at Blair House, he allowed himself to be openly critical and dismissive of both Peres and Prof. Yuval Neeman, Peres's advisor, who was thought to be responsible for preparing the list. Rabin said the list "contained some items that were more than superfluous; they bordered on the ludicrous."[11] His comments were widely reported in Israel and met with heated reactions and criticism. In his memoirs Rabin once again expressed regret for his style but not for the substance of his comments.

The personal tension between Rabin and Peres mounted, and in the spring of 1976 Rabin felt he had to deal with it as well as with the negative effects of the Sebastia affair. Rabin knew his position and authority were being severely challenged, and he decided to explain himself by giving another interview to Yoel Marcus. This time, the lessons learned in the 1974 interview were applied, and Marcus's article was attributed not to Rabin himself but to "an internal knowledgeable source." The title was "An internal knowledgeable source estimates the PM's views, authority, successes and failures."[12]

In the interview Rabin (or "the internal man") tried to play down the Sebastia issue. Places like Qadum were "not real settlements" and were not to determine Israel's future borders. It was therefore not an issue warranting a governmental or an intraparty crisis. As for concerns about his and his government's authority, he argued, there was no need to worry. When compared to the great Ben Gurion, who had to threaten several times to resign in order to get rid of his foreign minister, Moshe Sharett, or to the powerful Golda, who for five years had to tolerate Eban, a foreign minister she did not care for and whose policy was dictated by Dayan, Rabin's position was quite good. Rabin told Marcus he did not have to capitulate to his defense minister's *diktats* but nonetheless spent a large part of their conversation complaining about him. He regretted that the Knesset had not passed the proposed law authorizing the prime minister to fire members of his cabinet, and he made no secret of the fact that it was the minister of defense he had in mind.

Rabin's criticism of Gush Emunim in the interview was relatively mild compared to what he wrote about it in his memoirs and to his pronouncements in several off-the-record interviews in 1976 that were made public in 2015.[13] "I see in Gush Emunim," he said, "one of the gravest threats to the state of Israel. . . . It is not a settlement movement, it is a cancer in Israel's social and democratic fabric, a manifestation of an entity that takes the law into its own hands." In another off-the-record interview he described his despair at the situation forced upon him by Gush Emunim: "I do not believe one can exist over time if one does not want to get to apartheid with a million and a half Arabs inside a Jewish state. Over this I am willing to go to elections. . . . In a historical perspective one will think of what Israel dealt with in 1976? With some lousy place that has no significance; in a mystical debate around which Israel's existential problems are now focused. . . . What is a settlement? What kind of struggle is it? Qadum is an empty bag."[14]

It was characteristic of Rabin, as I've noted, that conflict and antagonism caused him to dig in and become blunt. His argument against Gush Emunim was threefold: first, that it represented a threat to Israeli democracy owing to its ideology and resort to violence; second, that its claim to be a new incarnation of the pioneers who settled the country and built the Israel of 1948 was a bogus one; and, third, that Israel's true problem was the demographic threat resulting from the continuing control over a million and a half Palestinians. The way out of the problem was a political settlement, and in order to get one Rabin was willing to go to a fresh election. This would turn out not to be a feasible option for Rabin in 1976. He was already on a collision course with Gush Emunim that would culminate tragically in 1995.

As might be expected, the May interview with Marcus brought matters to a head in the Labor Party. Peres responded angrily to the criticism of him and offered to resign. But neither Rabin nor Peres wanted to take their conflict to the edge. They met and agreed on a truce. Rabin gave Marcus another interview (in which he was again described as "the internal man") and put his earlier comments in a more positive context and softer light.[15] A crisis was averted, but the tension between Rabin and Peres remained stark and continued to undermine the government's standing and popularity.

ENTEBBE

Entebbe, Uganda's international airport, is the shorthand term commonly used to refer to one of the other major crises—and achievements—of Rabin's first term. On Saturday, June 26, 1976, two Palestinian and two German terrorists hijacked an Air France passenger plane on its way from Tel Aviv to Paris. The operation was staged by Wadie Haddad's Popular Front for the Liberation of Palestine–External Operations, a radical Palestinian group headquartered in Baghdad and operating in cooperation with such European terrorist groups as the German Bader-Meinhof Group. The plane was diverted first to Libya and landed finally at Entebbe, where the hijackers enjoyed the cooperation of the Ugandan dictator, Idi Amin. On board were 246 passengers, among them 105 Israelis and 12 crew members. The hijackers demanded the release of 53 prisoners, most of them Palestinians held in Israeli jails and some European terrorists held in their own countries.

Nearly a decade after June 1967 and the establishment of Israeli rule over the West Bank and the Gaza Strip, Israel had assembled a rich experience in dealing with a variety of terrorist acts. It had registered a number of spectacular successes as well as painful failures. In earlier cases of hostage taking in return for the release of prisoners, the policy was to subdue the hijackers rather than make a deal. In May 1974, in the final weeks of Meir's government—in the town of Ma'alot, near the Lebanese border—twenty-two schoolchildren were killed by their hijackers when the IDF stormed the school they had occupied. On Rabin's watch, in March 1975 eight civilians and three soldiers, including a senior officer, were killed when a Fath squad took over the seedy Savoy Hotel on Tel Aviv's beach. Negotiation was not an option, and the hotel was stormed in a costly operation. But in June 1976 a military operation thirty-eight hundred kilometers from Israel did not initially seem a viable option.

Rabin appointed a small team of cabinet members to help him navigate the crisis. All hopes of finding a diplomatic solution faded rapidly; years earlier Idi Amin had had a close relationship with Israel, but he had drifted away and was clearly supporting the hijackers. Pressure on the French government to pull its weight as the owner of Air France yielded no result. A reluctant Rabin authorized negotiations predicated on an agreement in principle to release jailed terrorists. It took three days for the IDF to start looking seriously at the idea, after all, of planning a military operation designed to release the hostages.

The difficulties of planning such an operation were daunting, to say the least. The hostages were being held in the old terminal at Entebbe, guarded by twelve terrorists and an external ring of Ugandan soldiers. The Israeli air force had cargo planes that could fly there, but they would have to land without alerting the guards and, assuming a successful operation, would have to refuel in order to fly back to Israel. There were, however, a number of redeeming aspects: an Israeli corporation had built the airport and was familiar with it; the non-Israeli passengers were released, and some of them could provide useful details; and Israel had a friendly relationship with Uganda's neighbor, Kenya.

By the middle of the week planning went into high gear. Rabin conducted a two-track policy: to negotiate with the hijackers and to explore the prospect of a rescue operation. The negotiation was conducted in earnest. It was another manifestation of Rabin's famous (to his detractors, notorious) caution. He would not authorize the rescue operation before he was absolutely certain it was likely to succeed. His rich military experience taught him that many things could go wrong, that the unexpected could and would happen. The stakes were very high: if the raiding force failed to surprise the captors, a large number of hostages could be killed. If a fundamental mishap occurred, Israel's finest commando soldiers would be in harm's way thousands of kilometers away. Rabin kept grilling the military, checking every detail. His spokesperson, Dan Pattir, wrote in his diary, "Yitzhak is navigating the crisis in its broadest scope. He feels that behind his back in the defense system complaints are spread that he is hesitating to authorize a military operation. But despite the damage to his image he sticks to his position: bring me only serious, practical proposals for a comprehensive military operation rather than 'pharmaceutical' (sic) ideas."[16]

It would take until Friday, July 2, in a meeting at the prime minister's Tel Aviv office for Rabin to feel that the IDF had a plan he could authorize. A dry run was conducted successfully at Sharm a-Sheikh at the southern tip of the Sinai Peninsula on Friday night. Four air force Hercules planes took off from there on Saturday morning, and the cabinet was convened at noon to officially approve the operation. There was still time to recall the planes in midair if they did not. Rabin composed, with his aides, a letter of resignation. He planned to take full responsibility and pay the price in the event of a failure. Fortunately, it proved to be a gallant but unnecessary act, as the operation was a spectacular success. The Israeli planes managed to land undetected among commercial flights. The Israeli commandos were detected by the Ugandan guards, but they were able to surprise the captors and kill them. The hostages were put aboard the planes and, after refueling in Kenya, landed safely in Israel. One Israeli officer, Yehonatan (Yoni) Netanyahu, was killed by Ugandan fire. He was the leader of one of the IDF's most prestigious commando units and commanded one of the raiding teams under the overall command of Dan Shomron, a future chief of staff of the IDF.

In short, the Entebbe raid was a great accomplishment. It was a complex operation executed perfectly, based on imaginative, meticulous planning and requiring collaboration between several branches of the defense establishment. It not only provided a successful ending to a difficult crisis but also restored much of the confidence and prestige Israel and the IDF had lost in the October War. Rabin had orchestrated the operation and obtained the tacit collaboration of both the opposition and the media, no small feat. But like so much else during his first tenure, this accomplishment too was marred by the bad relationship between the prime minister and the minister of defense. Once Peres became persuaded there was a military option, he pushed for it with his customary tenacity. This clashed with Rabin's deliberate, methodical caution. Nor did Peres relish the fact that Rabin was dealing directly with the military. The chief of staff during those years, Motta Gur, was close to Peres, and he and Peres, as his boss, resented Rabin's conduct. Rabin, in turn, felt that he was ultimately responsible and that a crisis like this was not the time for niceties and formalities.

The successful outcome of the operation also launched an ugly war among those claiming credit for it. Peres saw it as his own operation and presented it as such. He claimed to be the one who conceived of the military operation and pushed for it against Rabin's skepticism. This version of events was propagated by his effective supporters in the media. In 1991 he even published a book titled *Entebbe Diary*. A special bond was created between him and the Netanyahu family, who had lost their eldest son in the operation and incorporated it into their legacy (the late father's reputation as a great historian, Yoni's death in Entebbe, and, of course, Benjamin Netanyahu's long tenure as prime minister). Rabin responded to this version of events angrily. In his memoirs he is dismissive of Peres and his role during the crisis. Rabin asserted it was he who forced Peres to have the chief of staff of the IDF come to a cabinet meeting held three days after the hijacking. "The deplorable fact," he writes, "[was that] fifty-three hours after we learned of the hijacking [Peres] had yet to consult the Chief of Staff on possible military means of releasing the hostages."[17] In a normal state of affairs, the two approaches and the two narratives could be reconciled. It was up to the defense minister to push for a military operation, and it was up to the prime minister, as the repository of ultimate responsibility, to make sure the operation was highly likely to succeed before he agreed to it. And in a normal state of affairs there would be sufficient credit to go around for both of them. But by the summer of 1976 Rabin's and Peres's relationship had become so poisonous that such an equitable division of labor and credit was no longer possible. To their credit, though, both recognized the lines in the sand—despite the poisoned atmosphere, the actual conduct of the operation was not disrupted.

THE END OF RABIN'S FIRST TERM

The parliamentary elections of May 1977 marked a historic turning point. After twenty-nine years of Labor hegemony, power changed hands in Israel, and Menachem Begin and his Likud Party formed a right-wing government. The change was the culmination of Labor's decline after too many years in power. It was also, more specifically, a delayed reaction to the debacle of October 1973, namely, the intelligence failure and the military setbacks of the war's first days.

In retrospect it is easy to see the four main developments that facilitated the transition of May 1977 during the Rabin government's final months. The first and perhaps most important was a series of financial and political scandals that portrayed the Labor Party as a decaying entity, corrupted by decades of domination.

In February 1975 Michael Tzur, the former director general of the Ministry of Trade and Industry and the chairman of the refineries owned by the Israeli Corporation, was arrested, indicted, and convicted for stealing fourteen million dollars from the corporation's coffers. Tzur was close to Pinchas Sapir, the architect of Israel's rapid economic growth and industrialization in the 1960s. Sapir's system, as it was called, gave precedence to the country's economic development, often disregarding due process. Syphoning off money to party coffers was illegal but tolerated. Sapir and his underlings were honest men, but the culture they created was conducive to personal corruption. This case was the first indication that the system was no longer working properly. There was more to come.

In November 1976 Asher Yadlin, the chairman of the Trade Unions' Federation, Sick Fund (HMO), who was nominated by the cabinet to be the next governor of the Bank of Israel, was arrested for taking a bribe and was sentenced in February 1977 to a five-year jail term. During the same period, the press reported that Avraham Ofer, the minister of housing, was also suspected of taking a bribe. Ofer insisted he was innocent, fought to expedite the investigation, and finally committed suicide on January 3, 1977.

It was against this backdrop that Dan Margalit, the *Haaretz* correspondent in Washington, published a story in March 1977 that Leah Rabin, the prime minister's wife, kept an active bank account in Washington. This was a violation of Israel's foreign currency law at the time. It was not the first time Rabin's financial matters in Washington became a public issue. As early as May 1974 questions were raised in the Knesset about the lecture fees he was paid during his ambassadorship. Now rumors circulated about the bank account. Rabin was warned several times that journalists and political enemies were seeking to exploit this issue. The attorney general, Aharon Barak, dealt strictly with the Rabins: Leah was prosecuted and paid a large fine. Rabin felt it was improper to argue that the bank account was his wife's, and on April 7 he resigned the nomination as the Labor Party's candidate in the May 17 elections. He also suspended himself as prime minister. Peres became acting prime minister and the Labor Party's candidate in the Knesset elections.

The second important development in the Labor Party's fall from grace was the emergence of a serious challenger within the ranks of the old Israeli establishment. In 1974 a group of intellectuals led by Amnon Rubinstein, the dean of Tel Aviv University's Law School, launched a new movement named Shinui (Change). Its platform was simple: the Labor Party's evident decay and the debacle of 1973 called for a change. Rubinstein and his colleagues were well aware that a group of intellectuals could not win the elections. They needed a leader who could galvanize the public. Their choice was Yigael Yadin, the second chief of staff of the IDF and a well-known archaeologist at the Hebrew University. Yadin had been perceived for years as an Israeli De Gaulle, waiting for the call to return to the public arena and lead the country out of crisis. After several months of negotiations, in the second half of 1976 Rubinstein and Yadin agreed to collaborate. In November 1976 the two formed the Democratic Movement for Change (DMC). They were joined by two supporters: Meir Amit, a retired IDF general, former head of the Mossad, and the chairman of a large conglomerate, and Shmuel Tamir, a noted attorney who had rebelled against Begin in the Likud. The DMC offered an alternative to disenchanted traditional Labor voters who could not quite bring themselves to vote for Begin's Likud.

At the same time, this trend away from Labor was reinforced by the growing acceptance of Begin and the Likud as legitimate contenders. For decades Ben Gurion had successfully managed to portray Begin as an outcast, a danger to Israeli democracy. But this perception was fading. Eshkol treated Begin differently. For three years Begin and his party were part of the national unity government formed on the eve of the Six-Day War in June 1967 and were seen by the public as part of the establishment. The party itself was expanded by the union with the bourgeois General Zionists and lost some of its edge. It also became a magnet for the disaffected immigrants from Middle Eastern countries who saw Begin, himself a distinctive product of east European Jewry, as their champion—like them, an antithesis to the Labor establishment which absorbed them, integrated them, and, in their eyes, humiliated them in the 1950s. Many of these immigrants and their offspring have held a grudge against the Labor governments that, upon their arrival in Israel in the early fifties, put them in tents, sent them to remote development towns, and, worst of all, sprayed them with DDT.

The coalescence of a large right-wing bloc went hand in hand with what can be seen as the third development, a sharp decline in the Labor government's standing and popularity in Israeli public perception. Public opinion polls indicated unhappiness with both Rabin and Peres and with the government in general. The Israeli press, the influential *Haaretz* in particular, were critical of Rabin. Television was beginning to have an impact on public opinion. A popular satirical program, *Nikkuy Rosh* (Hebrew for "complete engine overhaul"), was merciless in poking fun at the prime minister and his government. The public was unhappy with the weak impact of the economic reforms, but the single most damaging aspect of the government's performance was the endless row between Rabin and Peres. Indeed, Peres contested Rabin's leadership of the party in the vote held in February 1977 when the party's center was convened to elect the candidate for the May 1977 general elections. Rabin barely won, with a tiny majority of forty. What Peres saw as proof of his own entitlement to the party's leadership, Rabin saw as the ultimate proof that Peres had never accepted the party's decision in 1974 and ever since, as a member of his cabinet, had consistently tried to undermine his position.

The fourth and final development that ushered in the Begin era was the end of the intimate cooperation between Rabin's government and the U.S. administration. This rupture was primarily the result of Carter's victory in November 1976, which ended Kissinger's dominance and replaced his incremental diplomacy with a quest for a comprehensive settlement of the Arab–Israeli conflict. The divergence between Washington and Jerusalem became apparent during Rabin's first visit with the new president in March 1977, but indications of the change had been apparent earlier.

In the latter half of 1975, after the interim agreement was signed, attention in the United States began to shift toward the Palestinian issue. In addition to the growing opposition to Kissinger's step-by-step diplomacy and the hearings of the House Committee on International Affairs on the Palestinian question, the Brookings Institution put together a study group to deal with the Arab–Israeli conflict. It was composed of foreign policy experts, Middle East experts, and Arab American and Jewish American leaders and was managed by a retired diplomat, Charles Yost. The report the group published in December 1975 recommended that the United States seek a comprehensive solution to the conflict and that the solution be based on Israeli withdrawal to the lines of June 1967 as well as on the establishment of a Palestinian state in return for contractual peace given by the Arabs to Israel.

The Brookings report may well have remained simply yet another report on the issue. But Carter won the November 1976 election, and two of the report's authors became influential members of his foreign policy team: Zbigniew Brzezinski became the national security advisor and William Quandt was put in charge of the Middle East at the National Security Council. The document was effectively adopted as a blueprint for Carter's Middle East policy. With Brzezinski's encouragement, Carter decided to launch his new policy toward the Arab–Israeli conflict early in his tenure. The new secretary of state, Cyrus Vance, was dispatched to the Middle East for a study tour in February;

in March Rabin arrived in Washington as the first Middle Eastern leader in a series to visit the U.S. capital in order to meet the new president and discuss his plans for moving forward in a new, ambitious peace process.

On March 6, 1977, Rabin met with the president in what was to be a very different meeting from those he had had as ambassador and as prime minister during Nixon's and Ford's tenures. Carter was pushing systematically for progress based on the Brookings report: a conference with the Arab states and the Palestinians; full Israeli withdrawal; and Palestinian statehood. Rabin stated his own view of a settlement: withdrawal from the bulk of the Sinai, with Israel retaining Sharm a-Sheikh and a corridor leading to it; territorial compromise with Jordan over the West Bank; no negotiations with the PLO; no Palestinian state; and no negotiations with Syria, who was, according to Rabin, not ready for a peace settlement. As the discussion continued, Rabin wrote later, "a warning light flashed in my mind, this was the gist of the Brookings report. . . . It seemed to me that Carter was set on the Brooking report and intended to sell it to me piecemeal."[18]

The meeting resulted in a stalemate, so Carter tried a different approach and invited Rabin to have a private discussion. Carter asked Rabin for his "real position." Rabin, typically, explained that he did not have two positions; what he had presented in the larger meeting was his real position. Carter then tried another ploy and invited Rabin to join him in the living quarters of the White House as he was going to tuck in his young daughter, Amy. Carter must have expected that such familiarity would soften Rabin up and lead him to become more accommodating. Rabin was unaffected by the gesture, and the visit ended on a very negative note.

Carter, Rabin, and their teams met for another hour the next morning, March 8. It was an almost hostile session, a sterile dialogue. Carter continued to push for a Geneva conference with PLO participation. He chided Rabin for failing to act "more aggressively" in order to take advantage of "the chance for peace" that in his view had "arrived" and "to forget about the past and about history" and adopt a fresh perspective. The settlements in the occupied territories "are illegal" and "the amount of territory to be kept ultimately by you will only . . . involve minor modifications." Carter also regretted the fact that "your position is now more inflexible than when Secretary Vance talked to you." Rabin, of course, argued back: "It was a mistake for the US to present its own position at the outset. If it did that, it could not act as an effective mediator. This was demonstrated in 1969 [when the Nixon administration issued the Rogers Plan]." The administration's position regarding the PLO was counterproductive and undermined the trend in the Arab world to assign a greater role to Jordan. On dealing with the PLO, Rabin said, "You have your position and we have ours."

An irritated Carter summed it up: "But you avoid being specific about boundaries and about the Palestinian issue for your own reasons. You also avoid being specific about Palestinian representation at Geneva. Well, I think we understand each other. We can move on."[19]

And move on he did. On March 16, while Rabin was still in the United States, Carter declared in a speech in Clinton, Massachusetts, that he supported the creation of a Palestinian homeland—a state with its own boundaries.

Rabin's visit to the United States in March 1977 took place while he was the prime minister of a transitional government. In December 1976 Rabin had dissolved his government and coalition and moved the elections to May 1977. The whole episode is known in Israeli political folklore as "the brilliant maneuver." On December 10, 1976, the first three F-15 fighter jets supplied by the United States arrived in Israel. It was a Friday, and the planes landed at dusk. In Jewish religious law, dusk is considered the beginning of the Sabbath. Rabin proceeded with the ceremony, and his NRP coalition partners abstained when a no-confidence vote was tabled at the Knesset. The government won the vote and Rabin could have moved on, but he decided to fire the NRP ministers, thereby triggering a governmental crisis and an early election set for May 1977. Rabin acted under the advice of his political confidants in the Labor Party. It was speculated that this was an attempt to stop the political decline of his government and to hold the next election before the new DMC had time to organize properly. Whatever the calculus, the "brilliant maneuver" backfired. The DMC did well in the May elections. The NRP, already on its way out of the historic partnership with Labor, was given further motivation to join the Likud, and subsequent events, including Rabin's resignation and the conflict with the Carter administration, further undermined the Labor Party's position on the eve of the May election.

As it turned out, Rabin had to step down in April 1977 and was not present to absorb the damage caused by the rift with the Carter administration. But the resignation was yet another blow to the Labor Party on the eve of the May 1977 elections. A party that had prided itself on the successful conduct of Israel's most important foreign relationship had to face the Israeli electorate against the backdrop of tension with Washington and a sharp turn in U.S. policy toward the Middle East and its relationship with Israel.

In the May 1977 elections the Labor Party lost nineteen seats and declined from fifty-one to thirty-two Members of the Knesset, while the Likud went from thirty-nine to forty-three. The Likud's victory was enhanced by the success of the DMC, which received fifteen seats. Labor was undoubtedly weakened by the transfer of some of its traditional votes to the DMC. Begin was able to form, first, a narrow government with the NRP (twelve seats) and other smaller parties, and then took the

DMC into his coalition. It was the first real transfer of power in Israeli politics after a Labor hegemony that had lasted ever since the 1930s in prestate Israel and the first elections held in the State of Israel in 1949.

5

————◆•◆•◆————

Fall and Rise, 1977–1992

FAILED LEADERS are rarely given a second chance. Rabin was to be an exception. By responding to adversity with tenacity, taking full advantage of his skills, and acquiring the political toolbox he had so glaringly lacked during his first term as prime minister, Rabin would first reestablish a leadership position for himself in the Labor Party and then go on to build a strong persona in the Israeli public mind as "Mr. Security." What Rabin lacked in charisma he compensated for with his authority, directness, and integrity. A six-year tenure as a popular, authoritative minister of defense would be the perfect platform for regaining the leadership of the Labor Party and the premiership.

But all of this seemed very remote in May 1977. In the fifty-four years of Rabin's public career as a soldier, diplomat, and political leader, the years 1977–80 represented the lowest ebb. His term as prime minister ended in disgrace; he watched as his rival Peres replaced him and his party was voted out of power; and he was blamed by many for the electoral defeat of May 1977.

In the aftermath of May 1977 Rabin made two major decisions: first, to remain in politics as a member of the Knesset, and, second, to settle the score with Peres, whom he held at least partly responsible for his fall and largely for the difficulties he had throughout his tenure as prime minister. In the May 1977 elections Rabin asked to be given the number 20 on the Labor Party's list of 120 names—the same number he had been given in the 1973 elections. It was a clear signal: Rabin was distancing himself from the party's leadership but staying in the game. He did not particularly enjoy the role of Knesset member but soon enough was drawn into more significant activity. Surprisingly, public opinion polls revealed that he was quite popular with the Israeli public. He was not deeply hurt by the "dollar account" affair, in fact was even given credit for his willingness to share the responsibility with his wife. He was, however, less popular with his colleagues in the Labor Party leadership and apparatus, who did hold him responsible, at least in part, for the 1977 defeat. A pattern was thus established that remained relevant for the next decade: Rabin was popular with the public, more so than Peres was, while Peres dominated the party's institutions.

This pattern was temporarily disrupted by the publication of the Hebrew version of Rabin's memoirs in early August 1979. Most of the book was a standard, fairly detailed memoir, but the chapters dealing with Rabin's first tenure and his relationship with Peres were a bitter tirade. He accused Peres of undermining him, of leaking sensitive information, of turning the press and public opinion against him. Rabin used rough language, accusing Peres of playing into the hands of the radical settlers by supporting their project and calling Peres "an indefatigable intriguer." Rabin was not known as a particularly eloquent person, but over the years he did coin a number of memorable phrases, and this was to be one of them. It raised a storm of protest. Many Labor Party members and supporters who were not necessarily hostile to Rabin or friendly to Peres felt Rabin had seriously damaged the party by his vitriolic attacks on its leader. On August 12 the Labor Party's Bureau met to discuss the issue. Some of the participants argued that Rabin should be censured, but Peres, wary of direct confrontations, decided against it. Retaliation took a different form. In September several letters to the editor were sent to two Israeli newspapers, *Haaretz* and *Davar.* They were critical of Rabin, supportive of Peres, and, to discredit Rabin, included a false quotation from the diaries of a former prime minister, Sharett, casting Rabin in a negative light. Sharett's aspersions were directed at the young Sharon, and the forger replaced Sharon's name with that of Rabin. It was a crude, clumsy act; it took little effort to show that the passage from Sharett's diary was false and that the signatories were all employees of the Fogel advertising firm, an agency employed by the Labor Party. Rabin filed a complaint with the party's auditor, who conducted a thorough investigation and recommended that the party terminate its relationship with the Fogel agency and rebuked the party's spokesperson, Yossi Beilin.

November 1980 was another low point for Rabin. In 1979 Alon announced he was challenging Peres in the December 1980 Labor Party primaries. In February Alon died suddenly of a heart attack. Rabin was persuaded by Alon's widow and friends to step into his shoes and run against Peres on behalf of their wing of the party. It was a mistake, a premature decision, as Rabin had yet to recover from the events of 1977 and the fallout from the publication of his memoirs. But Rabin's rivals took no chances. In November 1980, a month before the primaries, they planted a story in the French weekly *L'Express* that Betzalel Mizrahi, a suspected leader of Israel's organized crime, had paid the fine imposed on Leah Rabin in 1977. It was another crass, ugly move and patently false. The French journal was sued by Rabin and wasted no time in issuing an apology and paying damages. Nonetheless, the challenge to Peres would end in a humiliating defeat for Rabin, who received less than 30 percent of the vote. This phase in Rabin's career coincided with a difficult time in the life of his daughter Dalia. Her husband had been wounded during his military service in the Sinai, and they subsequently divorced. Rabin and Leah spent much of their time during these years helping their daughter and spending long hours with her two children. Rabin's soft side as a family man, a father closely attached to his children and grandchildren, was manifested during this period. The warm relationship between him and his grandchildren was sadly highlighted during his funeral in 1995 when his granddaughter, Noa, delivered the ceremony's most moving eulogy.

It took several more months before Rabin's relations with Peres began to take a reasonable course again. In anticipation of the 1981 parliamentary elections Peres announced that, should he win, his candidate for minister of defense would be Haim Bar-Lev. In late 1980 and early 1981 Begin was afflicted by depression and was trailing in the polls. But as the elections drew near, he recovered. The destruction of the Iraqi nuclear installation in May 1981, ordered by him, boosted his campaign. Peres began to pay closer attention to public opinion polls that indicated that designating Rabin as his prospective minister of defense would make a notable difference. Peres replaced Bar-Lev with Rabin, but this move did not change the course of events. Begin won by a narrow margin, but he was elected.

Peres and Rabin both realized that they were bound together and that it was in their best interest to overcome personal antagonism and collaborate in the leadership of the Labor Party, with Rabin accepting the number two position. Although they did not grow fond of each other, they began tentatively to get past their differences and forge a way of working together.

In 1982 a new channel of communication between the two emerged, thanks to Giora Eini. Eini was a lawyer in the Trade Union Federation and had a good relationship with Peres, whom he met through the party. In 1982 Rabin filed a complaint that his supporters in the Trade Unions' Federation were being discriminated against. Eini managed to reassure Rabin that they were not and then established a comfortable relationship with him. Seeing a possible way to help the two headstrong men work together, Eini managed to arrange a meeting between the two in Peres's office. Over the next thirteen years Eini established and maintained a channel of communication between the men as a mediator and messenger. Eini was reliable and discreet and did not seek personal gain. Rabin and Peres lived close to one another; in those pre-cellphone days, Eini could be seen calling from a pay phone in the street, speaking to either Peres or Rabin after meeting with one of them. He continued to perform this role as intermediator through Rabin's last day on November 1995.

As a senior member of the opposition party, Rabin was forced to respond to policies and decisions made by Prime Minister Begin rather than formulating his own. Between 1977 and 1979 he had to watch passively as Begin made peace with Sadat. Rabin felt, correctly, that much of the credit belonged to him owing to the interim agreement of 1975, which was an essential step. Later in 1981, as the autonomy negotiations—a product of the peace treaty with Egypt—foundered and the Lebanese crisis loomed large, Rabin's commentary and criticism became more significant. He became a popular analyst and commentator on Israeli and Middle Eastern issues. It proved to be an excellent way to keep his name in the news and rebuild his reputation and authority. Most notably, Rabin was dispatched by the large Israeli newspaper *Yediot Aharonot* to meet with major international figures. The journalist Eitan Haber, who later became Rabin's aide and speechwriter, traveled with Rabin and published the text of his conversations with these leaders, first in the newspaper and then in book form.

The policy pursued by Rabin in the Lebanese crisis of 1976, that is, offering humanitarian and limited military support to the Christian side but refusing to be drawn into the Lebanese civil war, was altered by Begin's government. The increasing challenge posed by the PLO in South Lebanon, Begin's romantic ambition to turn the Jewish state into the savior of Lebanon's beleaguered Christians, the Mossad's fascination with the prospect of a strategic alliance with the Maronite community, and, starting in 1981, Sharon's influence as Begin's defense minister all worked to draw Israel into a deepening involvement with Lebanon. In 1981 two confrontations—the first with Syria, in concert with Israel's Maronite allies, over the town of Zahle; the second an artillery duel with the PLO—ended in a draw. During the confrontation over Zahle, the Syrians moved their Soviet-made ground-to-air missiles forward, and in the artillery duel with the PLO across the Israeli–Lebanese border Israel failed to achieve a clear-cut decision. Rabin was worried by the drift of Israel's new policies; specifically, he was concerned that under Begin Israel was slowly being drawn into massive involvement in the Lebanese civil war and to a full-blown military confrontation with Syria. In August 1981 he issued a far-sighted warning:

> In my view the Israeli aims with regard to Lebanon should be . . . a central government that will grow gradually stronger and will be able to govern the country and at a later stage will lead to a Syrian departure from Lebanon. These aims will only be accomplished if the central government in Lebanon is reinforced by the implementation of the Shtura Agreements [yet another attempt to end the Lebanese civil war]. . . . Any attempt to set more radical aims could lead to an Israeli failure. This has already been proven by the fighting around Zahle. . . . Had Israel given greater support to

the radical Christian line it would have found itself involved in a war with Syria in Lebanon. Israel has no interest in such a war and cannot expect to emerge from it with political gains. Therefore, with regard to Lebanon's future, we should continue to strengthen the Christians on the basis of the principle set by the government that I had the honor of heading: to help them help themselves keeping sight of the (essentially political) solution predicated on Christian military and economic sustainability and support for the unity of the Lebanese state.[1]

On June 5, 1982, Begin's government took exactly the path Rabin had warned against. Begin won a second term in 1981 and gave the defense portfolio to Sharon. Sharon had conceived of a grandiose scheme to transform Israel's position in the Middle East by invading Lebanon in collaboration with the Phalangist Lebanese Forces militia, destroying the PLO's infrastructure in South Lebanon and Beirut, and installing Israel's ally, Bashir Jumayyil, as Lebanon's new president. Bashir was the son of Pierre Jumayyil, the founder of the Maronite-Christian Phalangist Party, who founded the Lebanese Forces militia. The goal was for Israel to then have a peace treaty and a strategic alliance with its northern neighbor. Furthermore, Jumayyil and his cohorts were planning to push a large part of Lebanon's Palestinian community across the border to Syria. From there, it was assumed, they would be further pushed into Jordan, where the influx would help turn the Hashemite Kingdom of Jordan into a Palestinian state.

By the end of 1981 Begin realized that he had been wrong to assume Sadat was willing to make a separate peace with him and help him push the Palestinian issue to the sidelines. The talks on the autonomy plan for the Palestinians envisaged by the Camp David agreement (the 1978 prelude to the 1979 Israeli–Egyptian peace treaty) were going nowhere, and the artillery exchange with the PLO across the Lebanese border in 1981 ended in the embarrassing draw mentioned above. Begin was now ready to adopt Sharon's grandiose plan. The assassination attempt on Israel's ambassador to London, Shlomo Argov, was a trigger for Operation Peace for the Galilee, launched on June 5, 1982. This was the starting point of a tragic and costly adventure that would not end until 2000 and whose long-term consequences are still felt in Lebanon and Israel.

The First Lebanon War, as it eventually came to be known, was deceptively described by the government as a limited military operation designed to destroy and push back the PLO's Katyusha rocket launchers beyond their forty-kilometer range. Its more ambitious goals were not revealed until later, when the Israeli public discovered it had been unknowingly engaged in an outright war with ambitious aims. Israel's Lebanese allies did not implement their part of the joint plan with an attack in Beirut. Consequently, the IDF had to fight its way to the outskirts of Beirut and lay siege to the city. Sharon did manage to have the Lebanese parliament elect his ally, Bashir Jumayyil, as Lebanon's new president on August 31, 1982. It seemed for a moment that Sharon's grandiose plan was working, but in short order his house of cards collapsed. Jumayyil was assassinated, probably by Syria's emissaries, on September 14, and two days later the Lebanese Forces perpetrated a massacre in the Palestinian refugee camps of Sabra and Shatila. This sparked the largest protest rally in Israel's history, staged in Tel Aviv. A judicial commission of inquiry was formed, which forced Sharon out of the Defense Ministry. Yasser Arafat, the chairman of the PLO, and his troops were sent from Lebanon to Tunisia, but after Jumayyil's assassination Israel ended up without a Lebanese ally. Begin was overcome by the turn of events and, incapacitated by severe depression, finally resigned and was replaced by Yitzhak Shamir.

Critical as Rabin and the Labor Party were of Begin's and Sharon's war, once the war was launched Rabin was faced with a dual dilemma: he was a political dove and a military hawk. As former chief of staff he believed that once the IDF found itself in a conflict—let alone a war—it was imperative to win it. It would have also been awkward for a mainstream opposition party to criticize a war or a major military operation while it was still unfolding. Furthermore, at some point it seemed that the Lebanese adventure might end successfully. Rabin had to juggle his statements according to the war's ebb and flow. He failed once. On July 4, 1982, Sharon, his former advisor and protégé, invited him to visit the troops besieging Beirut. Rabin's advice was "to tighten the siege of Beirut." The statement, misguided in its own right, was made in the presence of journalists and was widely quoted and criticized in Israel and abroad.

MINISTER OF DEFENSE, 1984–1990

By 1983 it was clear Israel's adventure in Lebanon was a failure, tainted even more by the massacre carried out by Israel's Lebanese allies in Sabra and Shatila. Amin Jumayyil, Bashir's older brother, now elected to the presidency, distanced himself from Israel. Whatever hopes Israel had left regarding its alliance with the Lebanese Forces and the Maronite community were fading. Shiite terrorists allied with Iran and Syria staged massive suicide attacks against American and French forces who were sent to Lebanon in an effort to stabilize the situation. Another suicide attack destroyed the U.S. embassy in Beirut. Israel did sign a peace treaty of sorts with Lebanon, but it proved to be a worthless piece of paper. Moshe Arens replaced Sharon as minister of defense and oversaw the withdrawal of the IDF from the outskirts of Beirut to the Awali River line south of the city. The one achievement Begin's government could point to was the departure of Arafat and his troops from Lebanon to Tunisia. The halo of peace with Egypt was marred by the failed reckless adventure in Lebanon.

The elections of July 1984 were held in the shadow of the Lebanon War. But angry as the Israeli public was at the architects of that war, Labor, under Peres, still did not win a sufficient majority to form the new government. Even against the backdrop of the Likud's debacle in Lebanon and spiraling inflation and with the uncharismatic Shamir as its leader, the Likud somewhat amazingly managed to get forty-one seats in the Knesset, with Labor at forty-four. This small edge did not suffice for Peres to form a government since the Orthodox parties and some small right-wing factions tended to support the Likud. Several important new patterns in Israeli politics were now detectable: the Israeli public had drifted to the right, and Labor had a hard time forming a ruling coalition even with a plurality of the votes. One of the Labor Party's major problems, evident in the 1977 elections, has remained the alienation of the "Mizrahi" electorate, Jews from Middle Eastern countries and their offspring. To them, as we have seen, Labor represented the Ashkenazi east European establishment that had absorbed them and humiliated them in the 1950s and remained what they considered the establishment long after it had lost its political power. The Likud, by contrast, represented the antiestablishment (even when in power), national security, and a tough stance toward the Arabs. Within this context, Peres was seen as the epitome of Labor.

A third failure to win power in an election made it evident that there was a problem with Peres's leadership. Yet in 1984 Rabin did not contest Peres's supremacy. Their relationship underwent a curious twist when Yitzhak Navon, the popular former president of Israel, was about to throw his hat in the ring, seriously considering contesting the leadership against his friend Peres. After some hesitation Rabin decided to keep his partnership with Peres against the new potential challenger, and Navon withdrew. As Navon tells it in his memoirs, he invited Rabin to a meeting in order to persuade him to join him as his number two. Navon asked Rabin whether he was going along with Peres, and Rabin replied, "Yes, listen, the Party does not want a contest." To which Navon replied, "Yitzhak, but you know and you also say that the surveys show that with Peres we will not win and if I am at the head of the list, we could win. Let us go together, we need to think about the good of the state and how to topple the Likud." Rabin responded with polite assertiveness, "Look, the Party does not want any additional contest. I reached a settlement with Shimon and there is calm in the Party."[2]

To break the deadlock between the Likud and Labor produced by the 1984 elections, a novel arrangement was introduced into Israeli politics: a national unity government based on rotation. It was agreed that Peres would serve as prime minister for the first two years of a four-year term, while Shamir would serve as foreign minister. Rabin was given the Defense Ministry for the full four years. The agreement went on to give a highly detailed division of labor and positions, including the Washington and UN ambassadorships. Contrary to many expectations, the government survived the four years and functioned quite well. It dealt successfully with the immediate consequences and residue of the Lebanon War, first and foremost the need to withdraw the IDF further south, and was able to reduce the spiraling inflation that threatened to destroy the Israeli economy. The government was in practice actually not divided into two but into three. As minister of defense, Rabin had his own fiefdom. When he was prime minister, Rabin had been annoyed by the huge power invested in the Ministry of Defense, held by Peres, but now, as minister of defense himself, he could fully enjoy this power. In fact, Rabin flourished in this new incarnation. Defense was his métier, he enjoyed the company and the work, and he was relatively removed from politics. He no longer had to serve as an analyst or commentator; the media were eager to interview him and quote him formally in this capacity. Indeed, during the six years of the two national unity governments, the Ministry of Defense was referred to jokingly as "the Tel Aviv government." Rabin was in full control of the huge defense establishment and, as a member of the trilateral "Prime Ministers' Club" (alongside Shamir and Peres), his status, not to mention his influence, was not inferior to theirs. His relationship with Peres at this time was reasonable, and with Shamir it was quite good.

The Prime Ministers' Club did have to deal with two scandals that threatened the stability of the unity government. One was the "Bus Line 300" scandal in the final period of Shamir's government in April 1984. Two Palestinian hijackers of an Israeli bus were killed by officers of the General Security Service (GSS). The killing itself, but, even more, the efforts to cover it up and the ensuing damage to the GSS and the Israeli legal system, developed into a lengthy and nasty political affair. Although the act had taken place under Shamir's government, Peres and Rabin had to deal with its potential destructiveness in regard to the very foundations of Israel's democracy and legal system and the stability of their government. In 1985 another scandal erupted when Jonathan Pollard, an employee of the U.S. Naval Intelligence, was arrested by the FBI for spying for Israel. Pollard had been recruited to spy for Israel by a cadet branch of Israel's intelligence community during Sharon's tenure as minister of defense. This was a terrible mistake. Its ramifications via-à-vis American–Israeli relations and the stability of the government were far reaching. The national unity government responded to the demands presented by the administration of President Ronald Reagan and managed to bring the crisis in its relationship with Washington under control. Pollard was sentenced to a lengthy prison term, and until his release in 2015 his case remained an irritant in American–Israeli relations. Here, too, the cooperation among the three members of the club proved to be very effective.

In addition to advancing the normal busy agenda of a minister of defense, Rabin had to deal with four major issues during this time: the partial withdrawal from Lebanon, the First Intifada, the cancellation of the Lavi project, and the effort to revive the autonomy plan for the West Bank and the Gaza Strip.

The Partial Withdrawal from Lebanon

As minister of defense in the national unity government, Rabin was in charge of Israel's policy in Lebanon. The Likud government's policy in the aftermath of the war had been neither coherent nor effective. Israel confronted a weak, unfriendly Lebanese president in Amin Jumayyil; an increasingly confident Syrian regime seeking to obliterate any residue of the 1982 war; a United States reeling from the devastating attacks on its embassy in Beirut and the marines' barracks, as well as a host of contending local forces in the southern part of the country, north of the Israeli border. Formally, Israel's position in Lebanon and its relationship with its government were regulated by the May 1983 so-called peace agreement, but that agreement remained a dead letter, and Hafez al-Asad was determined to annul it. After Sharon's forced departure from the Ministry of Defense, his successor, Moshe Arens, withdrew the IDF from the vicinity of Beirut southward, to a line running more or less along the Awali River. Staying within that line made no sense. The IDF was harassed and attacked, and Arens and the IDF leadership saw no point in staying. But Arens could not get Prime Minister Shamir and a majority of the Likud ministers to support further withdrawal. Sharon was still influential at the time, and he was clinging to any shred of what could be claimed as an achievement produced by the war. Israel insisted that all foreign forces, namely, the Syrian army, should withdraw from Lebanon as a condition for its own departure, while trying at the same time to come to an agreement with Jumayyil's administration. Neither policy had any prospect of being implemented. Syria had no intention of pulling its troops out, and, to boot, its Iranian allies were building up their presence in and influence on the Shiite community.

Rabin's initial effort to clean up this mess was aimed at coming to an indirect understanding with Syria through the United States. It was modeled after the successful red line policy of 1976, according to which Israel agreed to a Syrian military presence in Lebanon as long as Syria kept its distance from the area of the Israeli border. The American diplomat Richard Murphy tried to implement this plan for Rabin but was rebuffed by Asad. The Syrian president, having overcome the initial debacle of 1982, felt confident and empowered. He now spoke of achieving "strategic parity" with Israel and had no intention of easing Israel's predicament in Lebanon. Rabin then decided that Israel's only option was a unilateral withdrawal. In January 1985, with the support of Shamir and two other Likud ministers, he obtained the cabinet's approval for a phased unilateral withdrawal that was to be implemented over six months. Israel would protect its northern border by keeping a ten-kilometer-deep security zone and by supporting an enhanced local militia, the South Lebanese Army, commanded by the former Lebanese army general Antoine Lahad. North of the security zone, the UN's peacekeeping force, UNIFIL, created in 1978, was to continue its mission.

The IDF's withdrawal to this new line was implemented by June 1985. It was not a complete withdrawal, and Israel's direct and indirect presence in the security zone would remain a difficult problem until 2000. In the immediate aftermath of 1985 the full scope of the lingering problem was not yet apparent. Two Shiite groups—Amal, linked to Syria, and Hezbollah, an arm of the Iranian regime—as well as a number of Palestinian groups were vying for control and were primarily preoccupied with building their position and influence. The South Lebanese

Army was incapable of standing on its own feet and had to be reinforced by IDF presence in the security zone. Israel had to deal with harassment and casualties, but the problem seemed to be manageable.

Limited as Israel's casualties in South Lebanon were at the time, Rabin was extremely sensitive to every loss of life in the IDF. As he had been when he was chief of staff of the IDF, Rabin was in command of the minutest details of Israel's redeployment in Lebanon and insisted on going out to the field to supervise the deployment of the IDF units. And as he did in the fifties and sixties, he spent hours with the junior officers and the rank-and-file soldiers, thus gaining command of the reality on the ground without losing sight of the big picture. When casualties were sustained by the IDF in Lebanon, Rabin would take public responsibility for them. He appeared on television and stated that as minister of defense he took full responsibility for the event. These were not the calculated acts of a clever politician but a genuine reflection of Rabin's concept of his role. Rabin was in the prime of his life, and his virile looks, his gravelly voice, and the ever-present cigarette in his hand all contributed to his authoritative image. This resonated well with the Israeli public and played a major part in building Rabin's image as a straightforward, credible leader. His leadership would soon be tested by the outbreak of the First Intifada.

Rabin and the First Intifada

The events set in motion by the First Intifada, or spontaneous uprising (as the Arabic term *intifada* implies), were to be the cause of a radical change in Rabin's outlook and policy, and they shifted the future course of Israeli politics. When the intifada broke out, Rabin was on a visit to the United States, and it caught him by surprise. Like most of his colleagues in Israel's political and defense establishments, Rabin had come to believe, after twenty years of relative calm in the West Bank and Gaza, that the status quo could be maintained. The Fath and other Palestinian groups had tried to roil the Palestinian population through their attacks, but the bulk of the people did not rise. The spontaneous uprising in December 1987 thus surprised Israel and also, in fact, the PLO leadership and was not seen at first as marking a dramatic change. In sharp contrast to terrorist acts the PLO had tried to initiate in earlier years, the intifada manifested itself through demonstrations and rioting by civilians, including women and children. Rabin, in the middle of his working visit to the United States, did not feel the need to cut short his visit. He would be criticized for this error of judgment.

Once back in Israel, Rabin's initial response once again reflected his tendency to think and act as a military hawk and a political dove. The hawkishness came first. Rabin believed that security challenges must be defeated, and he ordered a tough policy predicated on the use of force to subdue the uprising. He was accused of having told the IDF soldiers "to break the bones" of the demonstrators, but this is not accurate. The story originated in a meeting Rabin had with IDF soldiers on a hilltop near Ramallah shortly after his return from the United States. As was his habit, Rabin, not wanting to manage the confrontation with the Palestinians from his desk, went out to the field. The soldiers, who had been ordered not to shoot, complained they were powerless and humiliated by their inability to deal with the demonstrators, women and children included, who pelted them with stones, beat them, and spat on them. Rabin told them that rather than stand idle they should storm the demonstrators and use force and sticks if necessary. True or not, the story and the order attributed to Rabin haunted him for years. The IDF's judge advocate at the time, Amnon Strashnov, describes how Rabin made a personal statement in the Knesset on July 11, 1990, according to which the decision to shift to the use of force while seeking to avoid the use of live fire was his, "and I, as the minister of defense at that time, carry full responsibility for it in the context of the guidelines I issued to the forces. According to the best of my memory I never said that bones should be broken, the guidelines that were issued from my office to the IDF commanders were clear." Strashnov questions the clarity of Rabin's instructions and implies they were sufficiently ambiguous for some officers to understand they were allowed to use excessive force.[3] But even if Rabin did not make that explicit statement, he clearly was the author of a policy that sought to defeat the intifada through the use of force while minimizing the use of firearms. He pursued this policy long after he had reached the conclusion that there was only one way to deal with the intifada, and that was through a political solution. As he saw it, the violent challenge had to be defeated before a political process was launched or it would be perceived as an Israeli defeat. Subsequently there were several cases of abuse, and several officers and soldiers were brought to trial.

Within a few weeks of its outbreak, Rabin understood that the intifada was driven by deep currents and powerful forces and represented a sharp turn in Israeli–Palestinian relations. For twenty years Israeli society had lived with the occupation of the West Bank and the Gaza Strip because it had limited impact on most Israelis. There was resistance and there were acts of terror, but most Israelis could and did conveniently turn a blind eye to these events. A popular rebellion and the new brand of semiviolent resistance represented a new challenge. Israel would now have to suppress resistance via civilian opposition, and Israelis would have to watch their children, IDF soldiers, chasing after teenagers in Nablus and Ramallah who were pelting them with stones. Such a scenario was unacceptable to many. New thinking, a different approach, and possibly new policies were called for.

One manifestation of this groundswell of imperative change was an unusual gathering convened by Rabin a few weeks after the outbreak of the intifada. In attendance were army generals, current and past officers of the Civil Administration in the West Bank and Gaza, and specialists in Arab affairs and the Middle East from both government service and academia. Rabin wanted to hear what these experts had to say about the intifada and the policy Israel should pursue. The most weighty presentation was made by the Middle East historian, Prof. Shimon Shamir, whose prepared text put Israel's dilemma vis-à-vis the intifada in the context of the experience of other Western societies who had dealt with popular insurrections in territories under their control. Shamir showed how, in practically all cases, efforts to crush the resistance by force failed, and a political settlement had to be resorted to. The analysis was thorough, eloquent, and hardly surprising. The surprising fact was the appearance in Shamir's office the next day of an emissary sent by Rabin, who wanted the text. Another emissary was sent by General Ehud Barak. The text was widely distributed within Israel's defense and security establishments. The Israeli effort to crush the intifada continued, but a lesson had registered in Rabin's mind. A year later he stated that "the solution can only be a political one." The statement was a harbinger of an impending change. By 1988 Rabin was seeking to give new life to the idea of Palestinian autonomy that had been raised by Begin a decade earlier at the Camp David negotiations.

The Cancellation of the Lavi Project

One of the main issues—and controversies—of Rabin's tenure concerned the Lavi Project, the effort to produce an advanced fighter jet in Israel, an idea born in the late 1970s. The Likud politician Moshe Arens, an aeronautical engineer by profession, was its chief promoter. In 1978 he led the Knesset's Foreign and Defense Affairs Committee to recommend the project. In 1980 Ezer Weizman, the former commander of the Israeli air force and minister of defense at the time, made the decision to go ahead. The project underwent several major changes during the next few years, becoming more ambitious and more costly. When Arens became minister of defense in 1983, he was well placed to promote the project. He was able to secure American support, and the Reagan administration agreed to provide a number of advanced technologies and financing for research and development.

But in 1984 the landscape changed. Rabin became the minister of defense in the national unity government. Since the 1950s, as we have seen, he had been consistent in preferring first-class weapons systems bought off the shelf abroad (preferably in the United States) over local, self-produced projects. His predilection was reinforced by economic realities as part of the government's herculean effort to fight the economic crisis. Rabin cut the defense budget and saw no reason to incur the costs of an increasingly expensive project. His was not a unilateral decision: part of the air force's leadership also argued that the quality of the U.S.-made F15 and F16 was better, and they did not wish to sacrifice quality for the sake of Israel's technological development. Other ranking IDF officers were concerned that the investment in the project would lead to further cuts in the defense budget. Most important, the Pentagon came out against the project, seeing no reason for the United States to help finance a fighter plane that could conceivably compete with U.S. products in the international defense market.

In December 1986 the first prototype of the Lavi jet performed a test flight. But the debate and controversy grew fiercer and uglier. The project's proponents were influential, and they marshaled powerful arguments: The project employed thousands of engineers and technicians, and terminating it would lead to massive firing and eventually, they argued, to the migration of first-class manpower and know-how. In addition to those directly employed in the project, Israel Aircraft Industries employed a very large workforce that was well organized as a political lobby. Arens and other proponents of the new jet maintained that Israel's future as a scientific and technological power was at stake.

As the Pentagon's pressure mounted, Rabin made his final decision, and in August 1987 he persuaded the cabinet to vote with him to terminate the project. Ironically, Peres, the godfather of Israel's defense industries, voted with Rabin. The controversy, however, lingered. The project's supporters continued to contend that ending it was a terrible mistake, that Israeli technology had suffered a deadly blow, that know-how produced in Israel had percolated into other countries. Eventually, however, it became clear that the thousands of engineers who were let go at the end of the 1980s applied their expertise elsewhere in Israel, contributing to the subsequent flourishing of the Israeli high tech industry. In sum, Rabin demonstrated his ability to make an incisive decision and put an end to a controversy that had afflicted the Israeli defense establishment for several years.

The Effort to Revive the Autonomy Plan and the End of the Unity Government

As the 1980s drew to a close, the notion of unity began to fray. Surprising many who either did not believe Peres would actually hand power over to Shamir or actively advised him not to, Peres lived up to his commitment in October 1986. He may have done it simply because it was the right thing to do or perhaps because he was hoping this would establish his credibility with the Israeli public once and for all. Roles were reversed, and he became minister of foreign affairs. Now that the two main initial tasks of the unity government, that is, extricating Israel from most of its involvement in Lebanon and stabilizing the economy, had been accomplished, Peres devoted his attention and energies to the revival of the Israeli–Arab peace process.

Peres underwent a transformation. In the mid-1970s he was the hawkish minister of defense in Rabin's cabinet who supported the establishment of settlements in Samaria. He now became an advocate of peace, willing to back the concessions that peacemaking required. This put him on a collision course with Shamir, the new prime minister, who was committed to the territorial status quo and opposed to any concession. Rabin, by his own predilection and owing to the new political landscape, occupied the centrist middle ground.

Peres's main peacemaking effort was invested in Hussein. During the early months of 1987 Peres met with little success. The king was not enthusiastic, and insisted that a Jordanian–Israeli negotiation be conducted only within the framework of an international conference. Because his claim to the West Bank had been nullified by the Arab summit in 1974, this would give him cover against the charge that he was conducting an illegitimate separate negotiation with Israel. From an Israeli perspective this was a major obstacle. An international conference meant Soviet and Syrian participation, a radicalization of Arab positions through the dynamics of the Arab collective, and, of course, prominence given to the Palestinian issue and the question of Palestinian representation. In April 1987 Peres had a breakthrough. At a meeting in London the king agreed to define the international conference in such terms that in practice it would be a thin, harmless cover for a direct Israeli–Jordanian negotiation. An international conference modeled after the Geneva conference of December 1973 would be convened, but the real negotiations would be conducted between Israel and a Jordanian–Palestinian delegation. A short paper known hence as the London Agreement was signed.

It was a major breakthrough, but there was one cardinal

problem. The whole move had been conducted by the foreign minister without consulting or informing the prime minister. When Peres returned to Israel and updated Shamir, who was not given a copy of the paper, the prime minister was furious. He objected to both the substance and procedure of the London Agreement. King Hussein insisted that the endorsement and support of the United States were an essential condition. Shamir dispatched his confidant, Arens, to see U.S. Secretary of State George Schultz to express his opposition. Schultz wanted to see progress in the peace process, but he declined to proceed with the foreign minister in the face of the prime minister's veto. The London Agreement was dead, and the relationship between Peres and Shamir irreparable. Rabin, meanwhile, gave Peres mild support but failed to share either his initial enthusiasm or his subsequent frustration and anger. Rabin was supportive of the idea that the Palestinian issue should be resolved through an agreement with Jordan, but he was critical of the fact that Peres, as foreign minister, confronted the prime minister with a fait accompli and was also doubtful that the London Agreement was viable.

The outbreak of the First Intifada in December 1987 increased the pressure to move on in a peace process. Schultz, a friend of Israel, launched an initiative in March 1988 that called for negotiations between Israel and a Jordanian–Palestinian delegation on an autonomy agreement, to be followed by negotiations on a permanent status solution. It may not have been acceptable to the prospective Arab participants and the Arab consensus but was in any case rejected by Shamir. In late 1988, in preparation for the transition from the Reagan to the George H. W. Bush administration, Schultz started a low-level dialogue with the PLO in Tunis. The message was clear: if he himself failed to start an Israeli–Palestinian negotiation, he was at least determined to facilitate the task for his successors. His successor as secretary of state was James Baker, and Baker and President Bush were eager to revive the Israeli–Arab peace process, but consultations held within the new administration pointed to huge difficulties confronting any such effort.

One of the difficulties was the domestic political change in Israel. In the November 1988 elections, the Likud, led by Shamir, won forty seats, while Labor, led by Peres, was down to thirty-nine. A second unity government was formed, this time without rotation. Rabin kept the defense portfolio, and Peres was shifted from foreign affairs to the Ministry of Finance. Arens became the new foreign minister. Parity was replaced by a tenuous Likud hegemony. But Washington's policy makers identified hopeful signs. One of them was a tentative attempt by Shamir's government to initiate new negotiations with the Palestinians during the transition from the Reagan to the Bush administration. Shamir and his advisors were trying to preempt a pro-Arab shift by an administration they perceived to be dominated by Texas Republicans who leaned toward Arab oil interests. In 1989 Shamir presented Baker with what Baker, in his memoirs, called "a murky four-point plan" for holding elections in the West Bank and Gaza. In 1989, as Baker and his team were trying to put more flesh on Shamir's ideas and find a formula acceptable to both Israelis and Arabs, Baker presented his own "five-point plan."

Two of the most thorny issues in the give-and-take between the Bush administration and the Israeli government had to do with the participation in the elections of Palestinians from outside the occupied territories and with the residents of East Jerusalem, viewed by Israel as part of its sovereign territory. The administration's chief partner on the Israeli side was Rabin. Having concluded that the intifada could not be quashed and needed to be settled through negotiations, he was willing to invest serious efforts in bringing about talks. Rabin's cooperation with the administration was carried out under the radar. He would sometimes go to the U.S. ambassador's residence north of Tel Aviv to speak to Dennis Ross, Baker's director of policy planning, on the State Department's secure line. The State Department, in turn, used a code name for Rabin, who was called in its cables and memoranda "the man who smokes." Rabin devised a solution to the issue of Palestinian participation from outside the territories: allow a Palestinian deportee to come back to the West Bank and thus become a negotiator "from outside." This was actually accepted by the Palestinians.

Typically for the convoluted politics of this supposed unity period, Foreign Minister Arens found out about this development only when he went to Washington on a visit. The U.S. ambassador to Israel at the time, William Brown, offered a vivid account of the whole episode:

> I had a secure phone at home in a special vault in my residence. I would invite Rabin over for drinks, which he never refused. We would have a glass of this or that, would go upstairs to this special vault and I would then bring out and key in the special phone. Having made telephonic contact with Dennis Ross I would then turn over the secure phone to Rabin and he and Dennis would conduct a conversation. I didn't involve myself in these conversations.

Brown had to tread softly in dealing separately with Shamir, Rabin, Peres, and Arens. He described his meeting with Arens after yet another difficult phone call:

> As I said goodnight to Arens he said "I suppose now that you are going over to see Rabin." I said "That's right, Moshe." Then I went to see Rabin under instructions. By now it was well after midnight. I reviewed the points in the Baker–Arens conversation as Dennis Ross had given them to me as well as the points that I had made to Moshe Arens. Rabin just sat there in his home soaking it in. I'll tell you that at times in this process I thought that I was dealing with about four different Israeli governments. . . . Rabin made it very clear to

me that he was reporting to Prime Minister Shamir. He said: "I want you and Washington to know that I am not playing games here. I am telling Shamir what's going on."[4]

At the end of the day, Rabin and Peres discovered that Shamir and his party were not willing to move ahead. And when Shamir was willing to show some flexibility, the hard-line opposition within the Likud succeeded in blocking him.

A speech delivered by Rabin on March 26, 1989, sheds light on Rabin's view that the Palestinian problem should be addressed through an implementation of the autonomy plan envisaged in the Camp David accords signed by Begin; that Israel's interlocutors should be local leaders in the West Bank and Gaza rather than the PLO; and that the Labor Party should push for the implementation of this policy despite the opposition of its Likud partners in the national unity government:

> We and the Likud are essentially different in one thing: The final goal, the final status solution, between the complete land of Israel and a Jewish Democratic state, no control over a million and a half Palestinians. . . . What do the basic principles, that I fully accept, say? Opposition to a Palestinian state between Israel and Jordan. Therefore, no negotiation with the PLO. . . . I am not sure that if elections take place in half a year, we will do better than in the previous elections. . . . It therefore seems to me that we should come up with a proposal, that I have presented. . . . I believe it can also be agreed and coordinated with the US. . . . The policy should be based on the following phases: Restoration of calm, elections, negotiation over a transitional period of five years and no later than three years a final status negotiation begins. . . . This move must be predicated on the Camp David accords. . . . The second thing is to continue with the policy of using force against the violence. . . . The third thing, coordination with the US. . . . And what if the Likud does not accept it? . . . Of course, we can leave the government.

And what will happen? An extreme right-wing government will be formed, Likud and the Orthodox. And what will happen after three years? What happened in the settlements during the last years will be multiplied.[5]

As time went on, the Labor Party and Peres, more than Rabin, grew increasingly restless. Shamir's unwillingness to respond to Baker's five points was but one manifestation of the government's drift to the right. By early 1990, while the controversy over the peace process and the relationship with Washington was coming to a head, Peres was convinced he could tilt the ultra-Orthodox parties and possibly additional Knesset members to support him in order to form an alternative coalition. In March 1990 Shamir's majority rejected outright Baker's latest compromise formulation, and Peres became persuaded he had secured the requisite parliamentary support to form his own government. Shamir was aware of Peres's activities and fired him. The Labor ministers then resigned as a bloc. Rabin, meanwhile, was dubious about Peres's move. It was one of those moments that revealed the differences between the two men. Peres was bold, even adventurous, while Rabin's feet were solidly planted on the ground. Furthermore, Rabin felt comfortable with Shamir, sometimes more so than with Peres. He tried unsuccessfully to mediate between Peres and Shamir. Yet, however unhappy he was with the course of events, he joined his colleagues in the Labor Party alongside Peres. Peres was now engaged in a herculean and ultimately fruitless effort to bring the ultra-Orthodox and a small faction of potential dissenters in the Likud into his coalition. Rabin, convinced that Peres's efforts were futile, went along halfheartedly until the final collapse in April 1990 of what Rabin later described as "the smelly exercise"—another of his contributions to the Israeli political lexicon.

The events of March 1990 proved to be a turning point in

two respects. Shamir was now the prime minister of a pure right-wing government. He was also outflanked on the right by Sharon and several other ultra-hawkish Likud leaders. There was no prospect of peace negotiations, and the construction of new settlements in the West Bank was expedited. The tension with the Bush administration turned into an open rift. The rupture was temporarily obscured by the need to close ranks after the invasion of Kuwait by the Iraqi president Saddam Hussein and through the First Gulf War but then came to a head again when Israel asked the Bush administration for loan guarantees to help with the absorption of the massive wave of immigration from the former Soviet Union. The administration declined, sparing no effort to demonstrate its unhappiness with the Shamir government and its policies. Secretary of State Baker went so far as to announce on television the phone number of the White House exchange so that Israel would know where to call "when it became serious about peace." He also banned Benjamin Netanyahu, at that time the deputy foreign minister, from entering the State Department building after Netanyahu publicly criticized the administration. This acrimony was political poison: the Israeli public still judged a political leader's performance by his ability to get along with the U.S. president. Bush and Baker were deliberately and effectively chipping away at Shamir's standing in Israel.

Meanwhile, the Rabin–Peres rivalry was once again rearing its head. For the past nine years Rabin had accepted Peres's seniority, and their relationship was somewhat reasonable. Since 1980 Rabin had had his own camp in the Labor Party, one which grew in scope during the next decade. He was quite happy with his position as minister of defense. The crisis of March and April 1990, however, led to his losing that position, and he blamed Peres for an unnecessary and doomed clash with Shamir. According to the late Gad Yaacobi, a Labor minister in the unity government, Rabin said to Peres during a meeting on May 3, "I am sick and tired of your gimmicks. The truth should be spoken. I knew that the whole thing would lead [us] to opposition, and I said so. I tried to save us from this embarrassment by retracting the firing and the resignation, and you prevented it."[6] Rabin was now ready to challenge Peres. Later that day he announced in a television interview, "There will be more than one candidate for prime minister, and I will be one of them."[7]

The failure of Peres's bid in March–April 1990 spelled the end of his leadership in the Labor Party. Having failed to win power in four elections since 1977 and having exposed his party to the risks of an ill-conceived political gamble, he was now seen by many party members and activists as incapable of bringing the party back to power. Support was shifting to Rabin, who seemed capable of winning. He was the authoritative, popular minister of defense for six years, and it was widely understood that only a centrist candidate with strong security credentials could overcome the Israeli public's evident refusal to accept the Labor brand. Rabin was now ready to return to the ring.

And yet it would still take almost two years for Rabin to receive his party's nomination, in the 1992 parliamentary elections. He made the mistake of taking Peres on at the party center in July 1990 in a premature move. The party's rank and file were shifting their support to Rabin, but Peres still controlled the party apparatus. He won the vote by 54 percent to 46 percent and remained the party chairman. Over the course of 1991, however, the tide shifted. Rabin, in his new incarnation as Mr. Security and popular for his authoritative style and for his credibility, was the only candidate who could swing a sufficient number of votes from the center and the soft right in order to bring Labor back to power.

Although essential, this shift did not guarantee Rabin as Labor's candidate in the 1992 elections. But a crucial development took place: the party passed a resolution to elect a candidate in primaries rather than through the party's center. This enabled Rabin to circumvent Peres's hold over the party apparatus and capitalize on the support of the rank and file. Races run by two other candidates also helped Rabin's cause: Israel Keisar received some 20 percent of the vote, many of which votes would have gone to Peres. This enabled Rabin to win slightly over the 40 percent minimum needed to guarantee election in the first round. And thus, in February 1992, Rabin became the Labor Party's candidate for prime minister.

THE 1992 ELECTIONS

The Labor Party's strategy in the 1992 elections was twofold. First, it was run practically as a personal campaign by Rabin as candidate for prime minister. This tactic was designed to exploit Rabin's popular persona and to underplay the role of the party itself. At this point it was well understood that a large part of the Israeli electorate was reluctant to vote for Labor, and it was hoped it would be easier for that segment to vote "Labor under Rabin." The security activist profile of the party's leadership was underlined, and members of its left wing were pushed back during the campaign. Rabin's platform combined his security credentials with a vision of breaking the political–diplomatic deadlock and renewing a deliberate movement toward peace. The second important theme in the campaign was the need to repair the relationship with the United States. Rabin, a former successful ambassador to Washington, was exceedingly well qualified to accomplish this task.

Even with all these advantages Rabin barely won the elections. His list won forty-four seats, the left-wing Meretz Party twelve, and the Arab parties five. This gave Rabin the requisite number for blocking the formation of a government by Shamir. Since Israeli–Arab parties were not (and still are not) candidates for joining a governing coalition, Rabin had in fact, at that point, a coalition of fifty-six, but the support of the five Arab members gave him the majority of sixty-one. This was an important fact because it enabled the ultra-Orthodox Shas Party to join the coalition. Shas was founded in 1982 as an ultra-Orthodox, Sephardic party, and in 1984 made its first run for the Knesset. It was to all intents and purposes a right-wing party even though its spiritual leader, Ovadia Yosef, a rabbi, and its political leader, Aryeh Deri, were actually supportive of moving forward in the peace process. Shas would not join the coalition before it had the requisite number of votes, but once it did, it joined. By joining the coalition Shas gave it a broader base, but its participation was tenuous and could not be relied upon over time. Rabin thus began his tenure determined to make critical choices, choices resting on slender political foundations.

During this second tenure of Rabin, his relationship with Peres transformed for the better even though the rivalry and dislike persisted. On Election Day, June 23, 1992, Rabin waited in his hotel room for the final results to arrive. His aides persuaded him to avoid at all cost the embarrassment of declaring victory prematurely. Watching television in his hotel room, he could see Peres celebrating downstairs with a crowd of party activists. Rabin's famous temper manifested itself when he came downstairs. Red-faced and angry, he stated, "I will navigate." It took some time for Rabin to digest the fact that he would have to offer Peres a major ministry as well as the de facto number two position. But Rabin started his second term guided by several lessons from his first, problematic, term; one of them was the need to avoid a repetition of the destructive bickering with Peres. Peres was unquestionably there, and thus a working relationship had to be crafted. Rabin kept for himself the Defense portfolio, and Peres was assigned the Foreign Ministry. In the division of labor between the prime minister and the foreign minister, the former kept responsibility for managing the bilateral negotiations in the peace process and the relationship with the United States. Peres was given responsibility for the less important multilateral track of the peace process. But this division of labor would soon change, when, during the first few months of Rabin's second term, Peres and his men created the Oslo channel and moved to the center of the peace process.

6

Rabin's Peace Policy, 1992–1995

On July 26, 1994, Prime Minister Rabin and King Hussein spoke to a joint session of the U.S. Congress, and on July 30 they signed an agreement in Washington ending the state of war between Jordan and Israel. It was an interim step leading the way to a full-fledged peace treaty, which was signed on October 26, 1994. Jordan thus became the second Arab state after Egypt to sign a full peace treaty with Israel. In his speech to Congress, Rabin said, "I, Yitzhak Rabin, military ID number 30743, Lieutenant General retired, a soldier in the IDF and in the army of peace. I who have sent troops into the fire and soldiers into their death am saying to you, the King of Jordan, and saying to you, American friends: We are launching today a war that has no killed and wounded, no blood and suffering, the war for peace."

In earlier years Rabin was not an orator, not even a first-rate public speaker. But in his second tenure his collaboration with his bureau chief and speechwriter Eitan Haber produced several memorable speeches. This was one of them. Despite the rhetorical hyperbole with which Rabin himself felt visibly uncomfortable, his statement reflected two profound truths. To Rabin, making peace at this point—having reached the peak of his career and as he approached the end of his life—was a natural extension of his early career as a soldier. There had been a time for war, and finally there was a time to make peace. To the Israeli public it was crucial that the peace process of the 1990s be led by a former chief of staff of the IDF and a minister of defense. Israelis were anxious and dubious about the peace process that began in 1993, and they were willing to go along with it only under the leadership of a prime minister they trusted deeply and who instilled in them a sense of security while these concessions were made.

There was, by this time, nothing controversial about making peace with Jordan. Israel and Jordan had fought in the past, at times ferociously, but King Hussein and Hashemite Jordan were seen in the 1990s as potential allies and peace partners. Israel now saw Jordan as the friendly part of the Israeli–Jordanian–Palestinian triangle and as a trusted protector of its longest land border. Furthermore, the concessions made to persuade Jordan to sign the peace treaty were minor and painless: Israel returned to Jordan land it had taken over in the south and was allowed, in return, to lease its cultivated part. But in order to be able to make this landmark peace with Jordan—to turn more than twenty years of clandestine contacts with King Hussein into fruitful and official peace negotiations—the far more controversial Oslo Accords had to have been made a year earlier. Only when the leadership of the Palestinian National Movement signed its agreement with Israel and went, with Israel, through a process of mutual recognition, did the king of Jordan have the legitimacy and the urgency to make his own peace with Israel.

The Oslo Accords and the Oslo process they produced were the defining events of Rabin's second tenure as Israel's prime minister. He paid for them with his life, but they turned him into an international statesman, a leader who could make bold decisions, go against his own grain, and carry his public with him.

THE ROAD TO OSLO

When Rabin introduced his government on July 13, 1992, it was not at all apparent how far he was willing to go in the peace process. In his speech to the Knesset that day he spoke about changing Israel's national agenda. He was determined to put an end to what he saw as the mortgaging of Israel's resources and future to the settlement project in the West Bank and Gaza— the settlement campaign, as he saw it, was draining Israel's economic resources and undermining its international position— and to instead divert resources committed previously by the Likud governments to this project to new investments: in infrastructure to prepare Israel for the twenty-first century, in absorbing the massive waves of immigration from the former Soviet Union, and in repairing Israel's relationship with the United States. He had also promised, during his election campaign, to conclude an autonomy agreement with the Palestinians within nine months. In his speech Rabin asked, "Should a national priority be given to huge investments in the territories or to fighting unemployment? To education? . . . In the current reality, there are only two options: either a serious effort will be made to make peace with security . . . or that we will forever live by the sword."

Rabin had reservations about the Madrid process he had inherited, launched by the Bush–Baker administration in October 1991 in the aftermath of the First Gulf War. The United States was then at the height of its influence in the Middle East, having defeated Saddam Hussein, liberated Kuwait, and saved Saudi Arabia from an Iraqi invasion. The Soviet Union had just collapsed, and the United States was the world's only superpower. Bush and Baker decided to convert these assets into a fresh effort to resolve the Arab–Israeli conflict at a Madrid peace conference and the ensuing Madrid process. Three tracks of direct negotiations were established: between Israel and Syria, Israel and Lebanon, and Israel and a joint Jordanian–Palestinian delegation. The PLO, weakened by its miscalculated gamble on Saddam Hussein, had to settle on a subordinate position within the Jordanian–Palestinian delegation. The Palestinian component of the delegations was composed of residents of the West Bank and Gaza and included no PLO activists. In addition to the direct negotiating tracks, five working groups dealing with such issues as regional security, environment, and refugees were constructed.

Rabin's reservations were based on the fact that he felt it was wrong to predicate an Arab–Israeli peace process on a negotiation between Israel and the Arab collective. As we have seen, since his first experience with Israeli–Arab diplomacy in 1949 and on subsequent occasions, he had learned that a peace conference attended by the Arab collective tended to be radicalized by the most extreme Arab participant. It was much better, he felt, for Israel to negotiate separately with individual Arab states. But there was no point in trying to rattle or alter the Madrid framework right at the outset, so Rabin resigned himself to starting his own peace process under its guise.

In the aftermath of the Madrid conference, the Shamir government's delegations met in late 1991 and early 1992 several times with their Arab counterparts in Washington. There was no progress on any of the tracks, and negotiations were suspended in anticipation of the Israeli elections of 1992. Rabin retained the original heads of two delegations—Elyakim Rubinstein as chief negotiator with Jordan and the Palestinians, and

Uri Lubrani as chief negotiator with Lebanon. He replaced Yossi Ben Aharon, the director general of Shamir's office, who had been the chief negotiator with Syria, and appointed me to that position. I was a historian of modern Syria at Tel Aviv University, the former head of the country's leading research institute on Middle Eastern affairs, and the rector (provost) of Tel Aviv University. I had a friendly but superficial social and professional acquaintance with Rabin. A close and deep relationship would develop between us rapidly through our work together. It was characteristic of Rabin that when he was appointed to a new position he brought with him a handful of his own people and tended to work with the old team unless there was a compelling reason to introduce changes. In this case, he felt that Ben Aharon, a close associate of Prime Minister Shamir and a well-known hawk, could not continue in his role as chief negotiator with Syria. Rabin wanted to send a message that he took these negotiations seriously.

It was clear from the start that Rabin intended to make meaningful headway in the peace process. He felt that he had not been given a rare second chance just to spend several more years sitting in the prime minister's chair and that changing Israel's relationship with its Arab environment would be his most effective way of having an impact. Rabin believed the main threats to Israel's national security lay in the Middle East's eastern flank, in Iran and Iraq, and he saw an opportunity to transform Israel's relationship with its immediate neighbors in order to deal with the graver challenges from the East.

In the conversation we had at his home when my appointment was made, in July 1993, Rabin indicated to me he was willing to go a long distance in the negotiations with Syria. He told me that during Baker's last visit to the region in his capacity as secretary of state Hafez al-Asad had told him he was willing to sign a peace agreement with Israel similar to that signed in 1979 by Sadat and that the Bush administration was ready to underwrite an Israeli–Syrian peace. Rabin told me that my mission was to find out through the negotiations whether this was in fact feasible. It was an interesting and significant moment. During his campaign in 1992 Rabin had stated that Israel must not give up the Golan Heights. And yet an Israeli–Syrian peace agreement modeled after the one with Egypt would entail full withdrawal for full peace. In the relationship between a leader and his negotiator, not everything is spelled out; some things are left to be understood. By telling me my main task was to find out whether the settlement envisaged by Baker was feasible, Rabin was in effect saying he was willing to go the distance if it turned out there would be a Syrian partner in the journey.

At that point Rabin had not yet allocated a priority to either the Syrian or the Palestinian track of the peace process. There was a clear advantage to the Syrian track. The Israeli–Syrian conflict was simpler than the Israeli–Palestinian one, essentially a territorial conflict over the Golan Heights rather than a national conflict. Syria was a state with a powerful, authoritative regime led by a president who had the reputation and the record of a tough negotiator who kept the agreements he made. The Palestinians were a nonstate actor under the leadership of a man (Yasser Arafat) whose persona and credibility had yet to be deciphered by the Israeli leadership. Lebanon was a Syrian client, and King Hussein would not move before any actions he might take were legitimized by an earlier agreement by either Syria or the Palestinians. At that early phase in the summer of 1992 Rabin did not make a choice between the Syrian or the Palestinian track. His delegations had to restart the negotiations before he could determine the prospects of either track.

In the division of labor between Rabin and his foreign minister, Peres, Rabin took charge of the direct negotiations and assigned the multilateral working groups to his partner and rival. Rabin followed the bilateral negotiations closely. He expected to be consulted on such sensitive issues as territory and security but did not seek to micromanage. For several months progress in the Washington talks was slow. The Palestinian delegation was clearly receiving its instructions from Arafat and the PLO in Tunis. The Palestinians' supposed bona fides were a convenient pretense, as if Israel was not negotiating with the PLO, but the negotiations nonetheless went nowhere. Some progress was made in the Israeli–Syrian negotiations. Some of Rabin's statements and the initial speech I made indicated that Israel was willing to make unspecified concessions in order to achieve peace with Syria, with phrases like "the depth of withdrawal will reflect the depth of peace." The atmosphere in the negotiations was transformed from the open hostility of the Shamir days to a businesslike demeanor. The Syrian delegation put on the table a concept paper regarding the peace. It was a curious paper, speaking about peace but not mentioning the word "Israel" even once. Couched in very vague terms, it still represented a measure of progress in that the term "peace" was introduced into the Syrian official vocabulary. But that measure of progress was far from a breakthrough. The main obstacle was that Syria demanded that Israel commit to full withdrawal from the Golan *before* entering into any concrete, detailed discussion of the peace Syria was willing to offer in return for such withdrawal.

The Washington talks were disrupted in December 1992 with an early indication of the severe disruptive impact terrorism was to have on Rabin's peace policy. An Israeli Border Police officer was abducted and killed by Hamas. Hamas (an acronym for the Islamic Resistance Movement), the Palestinian branch of the Egyptian Muslim Brotherhood, became active in Palestinian politics in December 1987, at the time of the outbreak of the First Intifada, and presented itself as an Islamist alternative to the secular PLO. In 1989 it began to sponsor a variety of terrorist activities. Rabin was determined to put an end to those terrorist activities by the radical measure of expelling the bulk of their cadre, about four hundred Hamas activists, to South Lebanon. In the end it proved to be an erroneous, costly decision. By February 1993 Israel had to admit the deportees back as a condition for the renewal of the Washington peace talks. The Hamas activists returned to the West Bank and Gaza, and the period they spent together in South Lebanon in fact made a major contribution to the organization's consolidation.

In March 1993 Rabin came to Washington for his first working meeting with President Bill Clinton. It was not their first meeting. Rabin had met Clinton and his deputy, Al Gore, in August 1992, during the presidential election campaign, but it was a formal, not a particularly cordial, meeting. A warm, cordial relationship began to develop between Rabin and Clinton during their second meeting. Rabin was impressed by Clinton's quick grasp of matters and his political intuition, by the charisma and graciousness he exuded, and by his evident care for Israel. Clinton saw Rabin as an older, mature, confident, and authoritative statesman, a soldier who now wanted to make peace, and a leader who was willing to upset conventions, and he appreciated his openness and directness. Rabin had clearly been transformed in this role, and what was once his awkward bluntness was turning into captivating candor. It is difficult to envisage the developments of the following three years without keeping sight of the personal relationship between these two men. About two years after that meeting, in May 1995, when the two leaders appeared together at a meeting of AIPAC, Clinton described their meeting in the following terms: "When we first met, as I have said over and over again, he was looking at me and I was looking at him and he was sort of sizing me up and I already knew he was bigger than life."[1]

Rabin and the Clinton administration had similar views of the peace process. The administration's vision was formulated under the heading of "dual containment" and envisaged a containment of both Iran and Iraq, while the core area of the Middle East would be stabilized by Arab–Israeli peacemaking. Since Rabin was willing to make significant concessions in order to achieve the progress he had in mind, the relationship between him and the Clinton administration was tension-free. There would be tactical disagreements, but these were dwarfed by the larger common vision and by the warm relationship between the two leaders.

During the March meeting between the two men, Clinton expressed his administration's clear preference for the Syrian track. The U.S. team knew Rabin wanted to move on one track at a time. Politically he could cope with the opposition to either a Syrian or a Palestinian deal, but not with both. Rabin, in turn, skillfully expressed his willingness to go a long way in order to achieve peace with Syria but evaded a clear commitment to full withdrawal.

The meeting began with Clinton briefly presenting the dual containment concept underlying his administration's policy in the peace process, then moving on to say that, according to his secretary of state, Warren Christopher, there were better prospects on the Syrian track. Rabin responded at some length. During the course of this meeting as well as at other meetings between Rabin and Clinton and most of his meetings with Secretary of State Christopher, there was a one-on-one part, but in practice "one-on-one" meant "two-on-two" since the meeting was also attended by two note takers. I was fortunate to be the Israeli note taker during these meetings and witnessed many dramatic moments. Following is the gist of Rabin's statement according to my notes:

> Undoubtedly (said Rabin), the two keys to progress are Syria and the Palestinians. Strategically Syria is more important, but in terms of the country's daily life there is also great importance to a Palestinian deal. With the Palestinians the problem is both political and emotional. The problem with

Syria is this: there is a leader and there is a capacity to make
decisions, but in a democracy like Israel public support must
be mobilized for painful concessions. . . . There are two
components here: 1) what does peace mean? 2) the peace
[with Syria] must stand on its own feet, namely not a separate peace but one that does not depend on other tracks. I
therefore do not use the term "full withdrawal"; it would not
be advisable for any Israeli [leader] to say that. It is impossible to conclude an agreement with Syria without meetings
by leaders. It cannot be left to a relatively low level. . . . We
will not be able to have real progress before I and the public
will be persuaded with regard to all the important points I
mentioned and I will add to them security. The mood in Israel is difficult due to the terror and this has its own impact.
I prefer implementation in stages. We give tangibles and receive paper and words. We live in a region devoid of democracy. What happens if we make concessions today and Asad
will not be there tomorrow? We say to the public that we are
aware of conditions in the neighborhood, but without risks
there is no peace.

Clinton then made another attempt to get Rabin to say he
was ready for a full withdrawal from the Golan. Rabin evaded
again. He agreed that the Syrians would not agree to a full peace
without a full withdrawal, but it would not be wise for any Israeli to say that for the record before we understand that they
will accept our conditions. "Therefore," said Rabin, "I would
not want for the time being to go beyond what I have said."
Clinton pushed on: if Syria would respond regarding the definition of peace, there would be a U.S. peacekeeping force and
guarantees for the stability of the agreement, as was the case in
Camp David. Would that suffice to change Israeli public opinion? Rabin was not enthusiastic about U.S. peacekeepers on
the Golan: "We have always prided ourselves on the fact that
we have never asked that an American soldier will risk his life
for Israel. It is an element of strength in our relationship. The

Israeli public would prefer partial withdrawal over full withdrawal supported by an American force. I will say frankly, the issue depends on the Israeli public's view of Syria's peace intentions." Rabin attributed great importance to getting Asad to engage in public diplomacy. In his view, the peace he would be making with Syria would be, to a great extent, modeled on the peace Begin made with Egypt. Begin's task had been easier. He had the benefit of dealing with Sadat, who intuitively understood he had to help Begin by persuading the Israeli public that Egypt ceased to be an enemy. Asad, by contrast, did not understand the role of media in Western democracies and was adamant in his refusal to reach out to the Israeli public. Rabin's comment led Clinton to ask what Syrian conduct would change the Israeli public's perception. Rabin's response: Asad appearing on television in front of his own people, Syria's behavior in Lebanon, and, first and foremost, public acts. Not a journey to Jerusalem but public acts.

Rabin then mentioned that he might have to submit an agreement with Syria to a referendum. Clinton wanted to know what the timing of such a referendum would be. Rabin's response: between the initialing of the agreement and the final signing. But, he repeated, there is no chance for a referendum before we can present the terms of peace. "I myself went to the Golan and was not received with flowers." Clinton replied, "This is the price of leadership."

Rabin replied, "I am seventy-one. I have seen many wars and their price and I am willing to take risks for peace. There is a certain period of time before fundamentalism peaks and before Iran obtains weapons of mass destruction and missiles. Many ask me what is the point of making peace in the inner circle while the external circle behaves the way Iran does. My answer is that making peace in the immediate circle will reduce the risk in the external one. For Israel it is also important to preserve the Hashemite regime in Jordan."

Toward the close of the meeting, Rabin shared with Clinton an idea he had already raised with Secretary of State Christopher and National Security Advisor Tony Lake. He wanted the United States to propose that Faisal Husseini be invited to join the Palestinian delegation to the Washington talks. Husseini was a respectable, fairly independent leader in East Jerusalem, a scion of one of the most prominent Palestinian families. Curiously, his father, Abdul Qader Husseini, had been the commander of the Palestinian irregulars who fought against Rabin's soldiers on the road to Jerusalem in 1948 and was killed in action. Rabin explained that Husseini represented the last chance that a local leader could stand up to Arafat and put substance into the Washington talks. He was the only local leader in the West Bank and Gaza who possessed both the public standing and courage to act independently of the PLO. Having annexed East Jerusalem in the aftermath of the Six-Day War, Israel refused to negotiate with Palestinian representatives who lived in East Jerusalem. In 1989, as minister of defense, when Rabin was trying to promote the idea of negotiating autonomy with local leaders rather than with the PLO, he got around this issue by including in the Palestinian delegations residents of East Jerusalem who had a second address in the West Bank. Rabin was willing to do the same with Husseini in 1993. He was also fully aware of the informal negotiation with the PLO in Oslo he had authorized in February, but at this point Rabin still viewed the Oslo channel as an exploratory exercise and the Washington talks as the main avenue. Characteristically, Rabin was willing to explore several options in parallel before making his final decision.

The issue of the PLO's participation was raised in another interesting meeting Rabin had during the March visit. He met for a breakfast discussion with the U.S. peace team. The peace team was composed of the group of diplomats who conducted Washington's policy in the peace process and included the assistant secretary of state, Edward Djerejian, the director of policy planning in the State Department and former U.S. ambassador to Israel, Sam Lewis, the president's assistant for Middle Eastern affairs in the National Security Council, Martin Indyk, the two State Department officers, Daniel Kurtzer and Aaron Miller, and Dennis Ross, who was at that point believed to be on his way out of the administration. It was most unusual for the prime minister of a foreign country to have an informal seminar with a group of diplomats and analysts, but Rabin was very comfortable in that setting. Issues of rank and seniority never bothered him, and he conducted himself as one analyst among many. He learned a lot during such conversations and the impact of them was huge. The free conversation with the U.S. peace team, mutatis mutandis, was of the same kind. Toward the end of the discussion, Sam Lewis said directly to Rabin that the inescapable conclusion from the prime minister's analysis of the Israeli–Palestinian negotiations was that Israel had to talk to the PLO. Rabin smiled enigmatically. Few in the room knew Rabin was already negotiating indirectly with the PLO.

While Rabin was in the United States a wave of terrorist stabbings by Palestinians began unfolding in Israel. Having learned his lesson when he failed to return to Israel in December 1987 during the First Intifada, Rabin interrupted his visit and immediately flew back to Israel. It was a powerful reminder of the importance of terrorism in the ultimate failure of the peace process of the 1990s.

But the visit had nonetheless forged important understandings between the United States and Israel and prompted the Clinton administration to try to move forward. In the spring of 1993, as a direct follow-up to the Clinton–Rabin discussion in March, the United States began to invest a special effort in trying to break the deadlock in the Israeli–Syrian negotiations. Christopher met with Foreign Minister Farouk al-Shara in

Vienna and tried in vain to persuade him—and, through him, President Asad—to adopt a more flexible attitude. Later, the assistant secretary of state, Ambassador Djerejian, flew in a U.S. military plane on a secret mission to Damascus in order to meet with Asad himself. Djerejian had been a successful ambassador in Damascus and played an important role, alongside Secretary Baker, in persuading Asad to participate in the Madrid conference. But he, too, failed to move Asad, who continued to insist that Israel must commit to full withdrawal from the Golan before he would spell out his concept of peace.

The ongoing war between Israel and Hezbollah in South Lebanon and across the Lebanese–Israeli border added another important dimension of the trilateral relationship between Israel, the United States, and Syria. In the late 1980s Hezbollah became the dominant actor in the south of the country when, with Iranian and Syrian help, they defeated Amal in the struggle for hegemony over the Shiite community in Lebanon. Hezbollah was a peculiar entity: a political movement, a guerilla force, a terrorist organization, and an arm of the Iranian regime all at once. In the early 1990s it escalated its attacks on the IDF soldiers posted in South Lebanon as reinforcements for the South Lebanese Army, which could not stand up to Hezbollah on its own. Every so often Hezbollah would also fire Katyusha rockets into northern Israel. Rabin's (indirect) interlocutor for dealing with Hezbollah was Damascus. It was characteristic of Asad, who believed in negotiating from a position of strength and exploiting every asset he had, that he combined negotiations with Israel with support for Hezbollah's attacks on Israel. If Israel was sensitive to casualties, that was all the more reason to escalate the pressure in South Lebanon. The Israeli view of Asad's behavior was quite different. As Rabin explained to Clinton in March, Asad's conduct in Lebanon reinforced his negative image with the Israeli public and was a significant obstacle to an Israeli–Syrian deal.

THE OSLO PROCESS

The Oslo process began in December 1992 as a classic track-two exercise in diplomacy and culminated eight months later, in August 1993, in a formal agreement between Israel and the PLO. The Oslo process was produced by the convergence of three strands: the activism of Yossi Beilin, Peres's deputy foreign minister; the quest of Terje Larsen, the head of the Norwegian Institute for Applied Social Science Research, to facilitate Israeli–Palestinian contact and negotiations; and the PLO's willingness to enter the peace process with Israel.

The process began with a meeting in London between Yair Hirschfeld, an Israeli academic and a Beilin associate, with Ahmad Qurei' (Abu Alaa'), one of the PLO's senior leaders. The meeting took place shortly before the abrogation of an Israeli law forbidding contacts with the PLO. Hirschfeld then traveled to Oslo, with Beilin's permission accompanied by another Israeli academic, Ron Pundak, for a meeting with Abu Alaa' and two of his PLO colleagues. The early discussions focused on the implementation of the autonomy plan through Israeli withdrawal from Gaza, economic cooperation, and, at Beilin's insistence, the formulation of a Declaration of Principles defining Israeli–Palestinian relations during the interim period.

Beilin took some time before he updated Peres in January. Peres, in turn, took some time before he updated Rabin in February. To Peres's and Beilin's surprise, Rabin gave them the green light to continue. Rabin was concerned by the lack of progress in the Washington talks and in his pragmatic way was willing to experiment with what came to be known as the Oslo track. He was fully aware of the significance of dealing with the PLO, albeit through an informal channel. He was also aware of the fact that Peres was now entering the mainstream of the peace process through the Oslo channel, returning from the corner to which he had been relegated in the early days of the Rabin government. The Oslo channel was kept in strict secrecy. Rabin did not update even his closest aides, and the Clinton administration was updated by reports given to Daniel Kurtzer, a member of the U.S. peace team, by Beilin as well as by the Norwegian government. There were additional meetings in February and March to discuss the declaration of principles. In May, Rabin agreed to have Uri Savir, by then the director general of the Foreign Ministry, join the Oslo talks. Oslo was thus transformed from an informal channel to a formal one. Rabin was still determined to keep the Washington talks as his main channel, but in the absence of progress in Washington he was assigning a greater role to the Oslo channel. Savir's counterpart was Abu Alaa'. In June the Foreign Ministry invited Joel Singer from Washington to review the Declaration of Principles that Pundak and Hirschfeld had prepared together with their Palestinian counterparts during the preceding months. Singer was an interesting choice for the task. He was a retired colonel in the IDF, former head of the International Department in the Military Advocate General's Office, and was employed as a lawyer in a Washington law firm. He had broad experience in Arab–Israeli negotiations (with Egypt and Lebanon) in the late 1970s and 1980s. Rabin trusted former officers of the IDF and was pleased by Singer's coming on board.

In June 1998 Singer published in *Haaretz* a review of Savir's account of the 1990s peace process.[2] It is worth quoting at some length because of Singer's important role in the Oslo process and his unexpected critique of its conduct:

> The Oslo Agreement draft was written with an unprofessional hand. The ideas included in it seemed to me to be partly good, but some of them tended too much to the Palestinian side. I appreciated Peres, Beilin and their assistants, but I was concerned that their enthusiasm with the very fact that an agreement had been reached with the PLO might

obscure for them its downside. I was not particularly impressed by their stories of the chemistry that prevailed in the Oslo talks and believed that in addition to chemistry there was also need for physics. Namely, to anchor in clearly in the agreement the protection of Israeli interests. I therefore decided to warn them in a very blunt fashion against signing the agreement. . . . At the end of the meeting I was persuaded that I will no longer see "the Oslo group." But I found out that I was wrong. At about the same time, Rabin instructed Peres in writing to stop the Oslo contacts since he too formed a negative impression of the agreement. Peres invited me back to Israel and this time summoned me together with Beilin to a conversation with Rabin. Finally, after Peres suggested to add me to the Oslo team, Rabin agreed to allow the team to start a formal negotiation with the PLO provided I prepare for his approval a draft of the agreement in the spirit of his instructions. Pure logic required that the work be restarted, but to my concern, I was instructed to accept the existing draft as a premise and to introduce in it only mandatory minimal corrections. The Foreign Ministry's people explained to me that since the negotiations have been under way for six months, and the Palestinians expect that the agreement will be signed within one or two additional meetings. The whole Oslo Accord could unravel if I tried to introduce far-reaching amendments. Despite all my efforts to minimize the corrections, the PLO representatives in Oslo were shocked when I presented them, because I took away from them all the achievements they were able to extricate from their Israeli interlocutors.[3]

As Singer indicated, in June Rabin became displeased with the course taken by the Oslo talks. He was not reassured about the seriousness of the Palestinian negotiators and was worried that the Oslo channel could neutralize the Washington talks he was determined to keep going. He instructed Peres in writing on June 6 to suspend them. Rabin wrote as follows to Peres:

The contacts known as the "Oslo contacts" in the present situation constitute a danger to the continuation of the peace negotiations. . . . The Tunis people are the extremist elements among the Palestinians who want a peace process and prevent the more moderate elements from progressing in the negotiations with us. . . . It is possible that the Tunis people intend to torpedo any prospect of reaching a real negotiation in Washington and to force us to speak only to them, which would present a danger to the peace negotiations with Syria, Lebanon and Jordan. . . . I ask to stop the contacts until further clarification.[4]

He changed his mind on June 10 when Singer came back from Oslo and reassured Rabin of the seriousness of the Palestinian delegation and approved a renewal of the Oslo track. Rabin went along with Peres and his team when he realized Oslo was turning out to be a more promising alternative to the Washington talks, but he remained ambivalent about making a deal with the PLO and suspicious of Peres. Rabin was being updated on the Oslo talks in weekly meetings held on Friday mornings in the Ministry of Defense, but he was not sure he was told about every detail in the negotiations. And he knew perfectly well that an agreement reached in Oslo would boost Peres's position by bringing him from the margins to the center of the peace process. Rabin was also worried by the prospect that a decision to end the Oslo process would lead Peres to challenge him in the Labor Party by presenting himself as the champion of peace and Rabin as an obstacle.

Rabin's ambivalence played out in real ways. For one thing, he authorized two of his confidants to explore alternative channels to Oslo. One was Haim Ramon, the minister of health and an influential Labor Party leader. Ramon built a channel with the Israeli Arab politician Ahmad Tibi, who was working closely with the PLO's leadership. Both Rabin and Mahmoud Abbas (Abu Mazen) used the Ramon–Tibi channel in order to check on their partners/rivals. Rabin wanted to verify Peres's account of the Oslo negotiations while Abu Mazen was testing reports by Abu Alaa'. In any event, Arafat did not allow any alternative channel to develop, as he expected Oslo to provide him with the best possible outcome.

Another effort was also embarked upon through Ephraim Sneh, a retired senior IDF officer and Labor Party politician. In May 1993 Sneh persuaded Rabin that the way to break the deadlock in the Washington talks was to recognize the PLO conditionally after six months of no terrorist attacks in the West Bank and Gaza; to initiate a series of gestures and confidence-building measures in the West Bank and Gaza; to hold elections for a Palestinian parliament; and to turn over control of the Gaza Strip as a model to be applied later in the West Bank. The transition from one phase to the next would depend on successful implementation.

The plan was predicated on a mutual modification of the Declaration of Principles proposed to the parties by the United States in May as part of the Washington talks. On June 7 Sneh flew to London equipped with detailed instructions from Rabin in order to negotiate the text of a Declaration of Principles with Nabil Shaath, a senior PLO official. Having completed their task on June 9, Sneh and Shaath flew home to report to Rabin and Arafat. Rabin shared with Sneh an intelligence report which stated that Arafat was apparently determined to avoid any alternative to Oslo—wherein he expected to achieve more in return for less in the way of commitments. A few days later Rabin told Sneh that Peres was irritated by the attempt to open an alternative channel and that his people rebuked Abu Mazen for wanting to meet Sneh as Rabin's personal emissary. Rabin, Sneh wrote in his book, now "understood that Oslo was the only game in town."[5]

Rabin continued to keep the Oslo channel a secret from his closest aides, including his chief negotiator with the Palestinians in the Washington talks, Elyakim Rubinstein. It is hardly surprising that several of these aides became harsh critics of the Oslo process. The secrecy was designed in part to protect the negotiation from leaks, but it also reflected Rabin's ambivalence toward Oslo. Rabin was ambivalent by nature and certainly so with regard to an agreement representing such a sharp departure from his own public position, standing on uncertain foundations, and managed by his greatest competitor. He also continued to keep his American partners only partially briefed with regard to the Oslo channel. Beilin's briefings of Kurtzer were then suspended and were only renewed in late July as the negotiations in Oslo were about to yield an agreement. This too was in part because of Rabin's ambivalence, but it was also a reflection of his belief that the United States should not become a mediator in Arab–Israeli negotiations. To him, the optimal scenario was a discreet, direct Israeli–Arab negotiation, with the United States called in at a late stage to become an underwriter and to help clear the final hurdles. A U.S. endorsement and subsequent role were, for Rabin, a sine qua non. He told Peres that his own ultimate endorsement of the agreement was subject to Washington's endorsement.

The Oslo negotiations proceeded in June and July through ups and downs. An agreement began to take shape. It was quite different from the product of the early negotiations during the first months of 1993. The main change was the introduction of the notion of mutual recognition between Israel and the PLO. The agreement was predicated on the autonomy concept of the late 1970s but took it much further. An autonomous Palestinian Authority (PA) would be established in Gaza with a foothold in Jericho in the West Bank, as an indication that the agreement was not limited to Gaza. The territory under autonomy in the West Bank would be extended in phases over time. The duration of the agreement would be five years, at the end of which final status negotiations would lead to a final agreement. Arafat and his men would be allowed to return from Tunis and take charge of the new PA. For Rabin and Peres the most difficult but potentially most promising element of the agreement was the mutual recognition and new partnership with the PLO. Recognition by the Palestinian national movement was a key to ending the core conflict with the Palestinians and to transformation of Israel's relationship with the larger Arab and Muslim worlds. But could Arafat be trusted?

There were positive benefits to the transitional nature of the agreements; no settlements had to be removed for the time being. But five years would pass and the tough issues of a final status agreement would then have to be faced. The term "Palestinian State" was not mentioned in the agreement, but the Israeli leadership knew that the PLO wanted statehood and that a fully autonomous PA in the West Bank and Gaza was a major step on the road to statehood.

Meanwhile, during the spring of 1993 there was a serious escalation in the fighting with Hezbollah in the security zone in South Lebanon and in rocket launching by Hezbollah into northern Israel. In late July Rabin decided on a major military operation in South Lebanon. It was given the name Operation Accountability and consisted of attacks on Hezbollah strongholds and a deliberate effort to drive large numbers of civilians northward toward Beirut, on the (erroneous) assumption that this would create popular pressure on Lebanon's central government to assert its sovereignty and restrain Hezbollah's activities. By the end of July Rabin concluded that the operation had run its course; there were no further gains to be made. Rabin asked the Clinton administration to use its good offices with Asad to negotiate a cease-fire under terms that would provide stability in South Lebanon. This was done by Secretary of State Christopher and Dennis Ross (who stayed on and became the head of the U.S. peace team), along with Christopher's Syrian counterpart Farouk al-Shara. It was a performance of sorts;

al-Shara would claim that, of course, Syria had no influence over Hezbollah, but somehow he did manage to work out the cease-fire agreement. Christopher and Ross did the initial work for the agreement on the phone and then flew to the region in August 1993 to finalize the deal.

THE AUGUST 1993 TURNING POINT

When they left for the Middle East, the secretary of state and his team did not realize their visit would become a crucial turning point in the history of the peace process. Rabin decided the time had come to make crucial decisions. He knew that without a painful decision on either the Syrian or Palestinian track there would be no breakthrough in the peace process; he was determined to make one happen. In private conversations with confidants Rabin expressed concern over the Israeli public's and the IDF's ability to shoulder the price of a long-term, seemingly endless conflict. He was worried by the Israeli public's response to the Iraqi missile attacks in 1991, when a large number of Tel Aviv residents left the city for the relative safety of Jerusalem, and by the IDF's mediocre performance in the Lebanon War of 1982. If conditions in 1993 might enable Israel to transform its relationship with the Arab world, it should seize this opportunity. Rabin also felt pressure in the narrower sense of political time. He had committed to deliver an autonomy agreement with the Palestinians within nine months. Furthermore, his coalition was fraying. Aryeh Deri, the leader of Shas, was facing criminal charges for corruption; Shas would probably leave the Labor-led coalition. It was much better to make the requisite concessions with a right-wing Orthodox party as part of the coalition than with a center-left government relying on the votes of the Israeli Arab members of the Knesset, anathema to the Israeli Right.

Christopher's trip was constructed so as to enable him and

his team to meet first with Rabin, to listen to his position and questions, and then proceed to Damascus in order to get Asad's responses. Christopher landed in Cairo on August 1 in order to brief and consult with Egypt's president, Husni Mubarak, an important partner of U.S. policy in the region, and in Israel on August 2 for a meeting with Rabin and his team at the prime minister's office in Jerusalem on the morning of the third. The full meeting was preceded by the traditional small meeting with the two principals and their note takers (in this case, Ross and me). The one-on-one earlier meeting is normally a brief affair, but not in this case. Rabin went directly to the heart of the matter: he could make a significant move on one track of the peace process; he preferred it to be the Syrian–Lebanese track and to offer the Palestinians a limited deal, such as Gaza first, without Jericho. With regard to Syria and Lebanon there were two options. One was Lebanon first, namely, an early deal with Syria's Lebanese client to be followed by an Israeli–Syrian agreement, but he doubted that would be acceptable to Damascus. However—and this was the dramatic moment in the meeting—he asked Christopher to explore with Asad the idea that if his own demand was met (namely, full withdrawal from the Golan), would Syria be ready (a) to sign a peace treaty with Israel that was not linked to progress on other tracks; (b) for a *real* peace, including normalization, diplomatic relations, and all the other paraphernalia of real peace; and (c) to offer elements of this peace prior to the full implementation of complete withdrawal. Rabin told Christopher that he envisaged the whole process as being completed over five years and that, given the fact that Israel was being asked to give tangibles in return for intangibles, he in turn wanted tangible proofs of peace before going through a significant withdrawal. His vision was inspired by the Egyptian–Israeli precedent set when Sadat had agreed to the establishment of embassies after the completion of the first phase of withdrawal.

In addition to the three questions to be put to Asad, Rabin raised four other points. First, he expected U.S. participation in the postsettlement security regime. Second, Rabin emphasized that he was speaking of "an assumption" (namely, a hypothetical statement, not a commitment). Third, he emphasized the strict confidentiality of this exercise and repeatedly told Christopher that his deposit was to stay in the secretary's pocket and must not be "put on the table." Finally, Rabin told Christopher that a referendum would have to be held in Israel before he could sign an agreement with Syria based on full withdrawal.

Rabin and Christopher discussed these issues for a time, clarifying and examining the issues involved. Christopher wanted to know whether Jericho (giving the PLO a foothold in the West Bank in addition to Gaza) would be part of the concomitant "limited agreement" with the Palestinians that Rabin had in mind; this was clearly an echo of the parallel negotiations going on with the Palestinians, which the secretary of state was familiar with, at least in general terms. Rabin's answer was that in the event of an agreement with Syria, the agreement with the Palestinians would have to be limited to Gaza, but should the first agreement be made with the Palestinians, both Gaza and Jericho would be included.[6]

As we made the short walk from Rabin's office to the conference room in which Rabin's and Christopher's aides were impatiently waiting, I said to Ross that I could hear the wings of history in the room. I knew Rabin had just given Christopher the keys to an Israeli–Syrian peace deal. Rabin's gambit was exceptionally bold. His willingness to deposit with the U.S. secretary of state a hypothetical, conditional willingness to withdraw from the Golan Heights was as dramatic as his willingness to negotiate with the PLO. He had in the past been opposed to getting down from the Golan and said so explicitly during his election campaign. As the former commander of the IDF's Northern Command and as chief of staff in the years leading to the Six-Day War, he was both professionally and emotionally engaged in the security of the upper Galilee. He had a strong constituency in that part of the country and on the Golan Heights, where many of the settlers were Labor voters. Rabin was clearly providing Christopher with a key to a Syrian–Israeli settlement and told him expressly that such a settlement would result in a downgrading of the deal that was about to be made in Oslo. Rabin also knew that Peres would not react kindly to such a turn of events, but, with a Syrian deal at hand, Rabin could ward off a Peres challenge in the party. Rabin preferred this "Syria first" option but, faced with possibly futile negotiations with Asad, he chose to go to Oslo.

Before he made a final commitment to Oslo, Rabin was attempting to find out whether there was a Syrian alternative. Had it turned out that there was, he would have been willing to pay the requisite price to secure it. Having made the fundamental decision that a massive concession would have to be made in order to mount the peace process on a meaningful track—either dealing with the PLO or getting off the Golan Heights—Rabin was ready to commit to either.

Rabin now had to wait to discover whether there was a Syrian option. Christopher and his team flew to Damascus with the deposit on August 4 and came back on the fifth. Rabin was deeply disappointed by the response. Asad was willing to offer formal contractual peace for full withdrawal and was, in principle, willing to view the agreement as "standing on its own two feet." However, then came a long list of "ifs and buts." Most significantly, Asad did not accept Rabin's demand that the agreement be implemented in a fashion that would offer Israel a large measure of normalization at the outset for a limited withdrawal. Nor did he accept a five-year time frame, offering instead a six-month period for implementing the agreement. Christopher and Ross saw Asad's response as positive in that he accepted "the basic equation," but Rabin had a very different view of the matter. Asad's response on the issue of linkage to the other tracks, while positive in principle, was not clear. Rabin knew that Syria would insist on full linkage to the Lebanese track and understood that Asad needed a measure of progress with the Palestinians in order to legitimize his own move, but it was not clear what that measure was. Asad agreed to a full-fledged peace, but he told Christopher he had difficulties with the very term "normalization." He rejected Rabin's idea of establishing a direct, discreet channel; the most he agreed to were meetings between his chief negotiator, Muwaffaq Allaf, his Washington ambassador Walid Muallem, and me, also to be attended by an American representative. The whole issue of security arrangements was not discussed in any detail (at least as reported to us by Christopher and Ross), and Rabin's insistence that without meaningful Syrian investment in public diplomacy he would lack the political basis for moving on fell on deaf ears.

Based on Christopher's and Ross's account, Rabin understood that his deposit had not in fact been kept in the secretary's so-called pocket during the meeting with Asad but instead had been laid squarely on the table. As might be expected in response to such a tactic, Asad, while offering a positive response in principle, started the bargaining process. Rabin had padded his position in anticipation of such a bargaining process, but he felt the rug had been pulled out from under him. He was also surprised to hear from Christopher that he and his team were flying back to the United States for their summer vacation. Did that leave him with a Syrian option or not?

Rabin's ultimate decision was that there was not a Syrian option. It was not an easy decision. Asad had given a positive response "in principle," and the secretary of state felt it was adequate. A decision by Rabin to abandon the Syrian option and proceed with the Oslo negotiations was bound to anger the administration. It was also a full commitment to a scenario Rabin was ambivalent about. Yet the option of abandoning Oslo for a lengthy, arduous, and possibly futile negotiation with Asad on the Syrian track seemed even less attractive. And an open rift with Peres caused by abandoning the Oslo option and replacing it with a limited agreement with the Palestinians as a corollary to a Syrian deal would probably be more painful than Christopher's pique. Had Rabin been able to display a breakthrough with Syria, he could have overcome Peres's wrath and potential challenge, but Asad's response and Christopher's decision to depart immediately for the States left him with nothing to show. There was another advantage to the Oslo option: it was an interim agreement, and the toughest decisions could be delayed for five years. In a deal with Syria, the most painful choices would have to be made up front. Rabin ended up deciding to give the green light to conclude the Oslo negotiations and forsook a Syrian track. But he insisted that Washington's endorsement of the Oslo negotiations would have to be secured before the deal could be formally made.

Rabin's American partners were indeed angered by this choice. They felt used and misled. As they saw it, they had been given a deposit (which they tended to refer to as a "commitment"), conveyed it, and came back with a response they saw as positive. Whatever they were given by Rabin, they saw themselves as having made a commitment to Syria. But their anger was soon brought under control. For one thing, given the overall excellent nature of the relationship between the Clinton administration and Rabin's government, an incident of this magnitude could be easily contained. More important, they realized the enormous potential of the mutual recognition between Israel and Palestinian nationalism, and the establishment of an autonomous Palestinian entity, that was at the core of the Oslo Accords. Clinton and his team preferred the Syrian option, but they knew they were nonetheless being handed a breakthrough that earlier administrations had sought and failed to achieve. The Clinton administration's perspective is described in a book by Martin Indyk, who was a staunch supporter of the Syria first policy and unhappily (and incorrectly) came to the conclusion that Rabin had intended all along to go for the Palestinian deal and used the United States vis-à-vis Syria in order to improve its terms. Indyk wrote, "We thought we had an agreement of the way forward—a common effort to achieve peace with Syria first, based on full Israeli withdrawal from the Golan. It was typical of our naiveté that we never expected Rabin would use US influence for his own purposes. The problem in this case was a failure of coordination, not too much of it. Clinton had promised Rabin not to surprise him but had failed to make clear that in return the United States expected not to be surprised by Israel. Coordination needed to be a two-way street."[7]

On August 19 the Oslo Accords were initialed secretly during a visit to Oslo by Peres. The next step was getting Washington's endorsement. Peres and his Norwegian colleague, Ian Holst, flew to Point Mugu, a U.S. Marine Corps base near Santa Barbara, California, to meet with Christopher, who was vacationing at his country home. I flew to Santa Barbara a day earlier to oversee the preparations for their arrival. They were accompanied by a small team of advisors. Peres was anxious and nervous. He was afraid his negative experience with Schultz in 1987 might be repeated. But this was not to be the case with Christopher. He and his team listened to an exposition of the agreement given by Singer. Christopher then excused himself and went to call Clinton. He came back to say the United States decided to endorse the agreement. It was soon decided that the United States would become an active partner and would host the signing ceremony on the White House lawn on September 13.

The festive signing at the White House would be preceded

by a crisis in Rabin's relationship with Peres. The original intention was for the ceremony to be held at the level of foreign ministers, that is, Christopher, Peres, and Abu Mazen. But as the date drew nearer, two developments began to shift that plan. One was Clinton's preference to play a personal role in what was about to be a major international event and a success for his administration. In Israel, some of Rabin's aides were pressuring him to travel to Washington and take part in the ceremony. Rabin was not particularly eager to meet Arafat and shake hands with him, but he understood that if the ceremony and the agreement were to mark the transformation of Israel's relationship with the Palestinians he should be front and center at that event. And there was the inevitable issue of his relationship with Peres: should he relinquish center stage to Peres? or should he occupy it himself? Rabin's final decision to travel to Washington was made practically at the last minute, overnight on Friday, September 10. Peres was surprised and offended by Rabin's decision and by hearing about it on the radio. Furious, Peres, on Saturday morning, gave an interview at his official apartment in Jerusalem to two prominent Israeli journalists, Nahum Barnea and Shimon Shiffer, and spoke angrily about the way Rabin had treated him. He told them emphatically he was not going to Washington. During the interview Peres twice asked the reporters to leave the room so that he could make sensitive phone calls. Neither he nor the journalists realized that the tape recorder they left on the table was voice-activated, and part of these sensitive phone calls was recorded. One of the journalists was Giora Einy. This is how Einy's role as a go-between was discovered and eventually reported by Barnea. The banner headline of their newspaper, *Yediot Acharonot*, on Sunday morning announced Peres's decision not to go to Washington. In the end, however, Peres did go to Washington after all, as second in command. The newspaper was published about the time Peres landed alongside Rabin at Andrews Air Force Base.

Rabin's performance at the signing ceremony illustrated the importance of his personal role in selling the revolutionary shift in the country's policy toward the Palestinians to the Israeli public. Rabin, not previously known as an orator, delivered a powerful speech. He also found the perfect demeanor for dealing with Arafat. He shook his hand, but his discomfort was evident. His facial expression and body language reflected his uneasiness. For an Israeli public who had to absorb Arafat's transformation from a rabid and unacceptable enemy into a partner in a peace process, Rabin found the perfect pitch.

1994: INITIAL DIFFICULTIES AND THE PEAK OF THE PEACE PROCESS

The breakthrough on the Oslo Accords and the euphoria generated by the signing ceremony on the White House lawn were followed by several difficult months during which long, complex negotiations were conducted over implementation. Arrangements had to be agreed upon on Arafat's arrival with his soldiers from Tunis for a division of labor regarding security, for the relationship between an emerging PA and the Israeli settlements in the West Bank and the Gaza Strip, on border crossing to Jordan, and on economic issues. Rabin appointed General Amnon Shahak, the deputy chief of staff of the IDF, to negotiate most of these issues with Nabil Shaath, appointed by Arafat. The economic issues were assigned to the minister of finance, Avraham (Baiga) Shochat. On April 29 the Paris Protocol, governing the economic relationship between the PA and Israel, was signed; the implementation agreement was signed in Cairo on May 4, 1994. The signing ceremony in Cairo was marred when Arafat refused to sign and was eventually coaxed by President Mubarak to do so. It was an early indication of the difficulties that lay ahead.

The main negotiation, conducted between Shahak and Shaath in Taba, in the Sinai, was long and arduous. It dealt with a host of practical arrangements and minute details—for example, the precise makeup of the checkpoints into and out of the PA—between two parties that had until recently been bitter enemies. Israel had to trust its former enemies to look after its own security against potential terrorist acts. It took time for the two sides to develop the requisite mutual confidence. In 1994 terrorism's deadly influence was added to the scene. A Jewish fanatic, Baruch Goldstein, massacred twenty-eight Muslim worshipers on February 25 in the Tomb of the Patriarchs in Hebron. Hamas launched its first two deadly suicide bombings in two Israeli towns, Afula and Hadera, on April 6 and 13. It was only in May 1994, when the implementation agreement of the Oslo Accords was signed in Cairo and King Hussein finally decided to move toward peace with Israel, that the tide began to turn toward true peace.

Another difficulty was Washington's pressure to move swiftly to negotiate an Israeli–Syrian deal, the administration's original preference. Rabin preferred to move on with Jordan, which promised to be an easier deal requiring limited concessions. But it took King Hussein some time to absorb the shock of Israel's deal with the PLO and then to reach the conclusion that his best choice was to join the process fully. The Clinton administration did not, of course, oppose an Israeli–Jordanian peace deal (an important progression in its own right), but wanted it to come after, not before, the Syrian deal. They felt beholden to Asad because, in the administration's view, he had responded positively to Rabin's deposit. Asad, needless to say, was upset with the Oslo Accords. For one thing, he saw himself as the senior partner among the Arab parties negotiating with Israel. From his perspective, a breakthrough should happen in his negotiations, not on the Palestinian track. Asad never trusted Arafat and felt betrayed by him. Ironically, the issue of linkage had now been removed from the Israeli–Syrian agenda. Asad was free of any commitment to the Palestinians and was focused on Syria and Lebanon. Asad responded to the administration's request, refrained from denouncing the Israeli–Palestinian agreement, and sent his ambassador to Washington to take part in the signing ceremony.

Rabin, in turn, was worried by the Clinton administration's eagerness to mollify Asad and to expedite progress on the Syrian–Israeli track. On the eve of the Washington signing ceremony Clinton had a thirty-minute-long phone call with Asad and shared his enthusiasm with the *New York Times*'s influential columnist Thomas Friedman: "Each successive day that the agreement builds up in strength, I think that this enables the government in Israel to engage with Syria. I personally believe that it is a lot more important than this piece of land on the Golan Heights or anything else."[8]

In the coming months the administration's efforts to push forward on the Israeli–Syrian track and its pressure on a reluctant Rabin continued. The United States continued to hold the view that an Israeli–Syrian agreement was key to a strategic change in the entire region and to a comprehensive Arab–Israeli peace. A disappointed Asad could easily upset the apple cart. Rabin's perspective was quite different. As he saw it, he had just concluded a very controversial agreement with the PLO and needed to give it time to work and to let the Israeli public digest it before proceeding with Syria. He had given Asad a chance, and Asad failed to use it.

In January 1994 Clinton traveled to Geneva to meet with Asad to discuss both the substance of the prospective Israeli–Syrian deal and the public diplomacy Rabin saw as crucial. Rabin had repeatedly told Clinton, Christopher, and their team that without a real effort by Asad to persuade the Israeli public that Asad wanted real peace, he, Rabin, would not be able to garner support for a Syrian deal. He knew Asad was not Sadat, and a gesture comparable to Sadat's voyage to Jerusalem could not be expected of him, but there was so much he *could* do, like speak to his people explicitly about peace with Israel, invite Israeli journalists to Syria, help clarify the fate of the Israeli soldiers missing in action since the 1982 war in Lebanon. Clinton and the U.S. peace team tried hard to persuade Asad to reach out to the Israeli public during their joint press conference. But it was Clinton who had to take the initiative and to state in Asad's name that Asad had made his strategic decision to make peace with Israel. These results were mixed at best. Rabin was not impressed by Asad's cautious, yet positive statement and Clinton's evident effort to upgrade his message. When Ross and Indyk flew from Geneva to Jerusalem to brief Rabin on the meeting, he was cold and dismissive.

Rabin did promise the administration to renew the Israeli–Syrian negotiation as soon as the new relationship with the Palestinians was consolidated. His preference, however, was to expedite the Israeli–Jordanian negotiation. King Hussein had been surprised and angered by the Oslo Accords. Jordan's abandonment of its claim to and role in the West Bank was never complete. Given the more than 50 percent of Palestinians who lived in the East Bank, the king and the Hashemite regime's political elite were fully aware of the repercussions of any major political development in the West Bank on the kingdom's future. The emergence of the autonomous PA in the West Bank and the Gaza Strip was seen by them as a potential threat to their stability. But there were other, countervailing considerations. The signing of the Israeli–Palestinian agreement and the mutual recognition between Israel and the PLO paved the way for Jordan to make its own deal. And, unhappy as they were with the Israeli–Palestinian agreement, they realized that the rules of the game had changed; it would be preferable for Jordan to participate in the game and influence its course rather than watch it from the sidelines.

Jordan began to move forward at a deliberate pace. On September 14, 1993, the heads of the Israeli and Jordanian delegations to the Washington talks, Elyakim Rubinstein and Abdul Salam Majali, signed a Common Agenda that had actually been agreed upon earlier. The agenda represented modest progress and was important in displaying that Israeli–Jordanian relations were moving forward as well. On October 1 Crown Prince Hassan and Foreign Minister Peres met openly at the White House. That meeting was followed by two more. In early October Rabin traveled to Jordan to meet with the king in an effort to restore the relationship. Since it had to a large extent been predicated on common opposition to the PLO, their relationship had now to be redefined. The second meeting took place when Peres, with Rabin's approval, traveled to Jordan on November 2 for a meeting with King Hussein. A road map for Israeli–Jordanian peacemaking was outlined, and the notion of Middle Eastern economic conferences attended by Israel, heretofore impossible, was put on the agenda.

But Peres, who conducted himself impressively during his meeting with the king, couldn't resist the urge to assume credit for the unfolding progress with Jordan. Peres was on a roll after the Oslo Accords. He was the architect of the agreement, and he asked for and received a lot of credit for the breakthrough. The balance between him and Rabin shifted in his favor, and he was pushing ahead. Peres made no secret of his supposed secret meeting with the king, and in short order the media reported it. The king was incensed and told Rabin that if he wanted to move forward with Jordan, he would have to keep Peres out of the picture. Rabin was quite happy to do so. Here was an opportunity to retake the initiative in leading the peace process. He deposited responsibility for the Jordan negotiations with Ephraim Halevi, a senior Mossad operative who had a close personal relationship with King Hussein, and Rubinstein. Rubinstein was miffed by the fact that he was kept in the dark about the Oslo channel while he was negotiating in Washington, but as a loyal civil servant he avoided public comment and agreed to continue as negotiator with Jordan. General Danny Yatom, Rabin's military assistant, and Eitan Haber, his bureau director, worked with Halevi and Rubinstein.

The issue of Syria first versus Jordan first would come up repeatedly in the give-and-take between Rabin and Peres and their U.S. counterparts. Rabin was fully aware of the administration's preference for a Syrian deal and for the sense of obligation they had to Asad, but he made it clear his priority was to move first on Jordan. His argument was simple: an Israeli–Jordanian peace agreement would be painless because the territorial concessions required of Israel would be minor. By coming to an agreement on a peace treaty with Jordan, Rabin would be able to present a major, uncontroversial achievement to the Israeli public. Against the backdrop of the bitter criticism of the Oslo Accords by the Israeli right wing, a Jordan pact would be a major political asset for his government. The turning point for King Hussein was the signing of the Israeli–Palestinian implementation agreement on May 4. Up to that point he was not certain the agreement was a done deal—but on May 4 it became one. On May 28 the king and Rabin met in London and laid the foundations for a breakthrough.

While the negotiation had been conducted directly between Israel and Jordan, the king now wanted to involve the United States. This was his opportunity to normalize his position in Washington, where many were still critical of his conduct during the First Gulf War, when he was perceived as an ally of Saddam. King Hussein also wanted debt relief from the United States, so he informed the administration he was ready to take a major step with Israel short of full peace. After a brief give-and-take, on July 25 the Washington Declaration ending the state of war between Jordan and Israel was signed on the White House lawn. It took another three months to complete the negotiations for a peace treaty that was signed in the border area between Israel and Jordan, north of Eilat, on October 26, 1994. President Clinton and a U.S. delegation flew in for the ceremony. After the proceedings, Clinton went on to Amman and Damascus. The trip to Damascus was intended to mollify Asad, who had now been left out for the second time. A visit to Damascus, however, raised a political difficulty in Washington. How could a president visit a country that appeared on the State Department's list of states sponsoring terrorism? A solution was found in a press conference to be held at the end of the visit, in which Asad would be asked a question by an American journalist regarding terrorism and would use the opportunity to specify his distance from it. But, as happened several times when it came to dealing with the media, the U.S. hope of transforming Asad and his regime into effective partners ended in failure and embarrassment. Asad was indeed asked about terrorism but instead of denouncing it he insisted that "one man's terrorist was another man's freedom fighter." The incident led to a rare, private incident between Clinton and Rabin. When Clinton came to Jerusalem, he stayed at the King David Hotel. Rabin went to see him in his suite; Indyk and I attended as note takers. Rabin first took Clinton out on the balcony overlooking the walls of the Old City and told him about one of the formative events of his life: the failure to take the Old City in 1948. Back in the room, Clinton asked Rabin to help him deal with the embarrassment in Damascus by stating in their press conference, the next day, that everything was fine with the press conference in Damascus. Rabin, typically, said he could not do that since it was not true. A red-faced Clinton stood up and said he was leaving immediately. Rabin then quickly changed his mind and undertook to accommodate him. The next day at the press conference Rabin spoke positively about Clinton's visit to Damascus.

During these weeks, progress continued on other tracks. In

May, Arafat, his entourage, and his militia came from Tunis and began to exert their control in the PA in Gaza and Jericho. In late April Rabin lived up to his commitment to Secretary of State Christopher and invited him to come to the region to renew the Israeli–Syrian negotiation. The secretary of state traveled first to Damascus, and when he arrived in Jerusalem he had bad news: Asad now insisted that "full withdrawal" meant withdrawal to the lines of June 4, 1967, rather than to the 1923 international boundary established between Mandatory Syria and Mandatory Palestine. The difference in square kilometers was not large, but the symbolic meaning and the issue of sovereignty over Lake Tiberias were important. The main motivation for Asad's demand was that he wanted to do better than Sadat. If Sadat had gotten back the whole of the Sinai, Asad wanted more. Christopher was aware of the flimsy ground for Asad's demand, but from the perspective of a superpower the difference between the two lines seemed negligible. He expected Rabin to agree to extend his original deposit so as to refer to the lines of June 4.

Rabin agonized over this dilemma for several weeks. The lines of June 4, 1967, gave Syria direct access to Lake Tiberias, Israel's most important water reservoir. From Rabin's point of view, Asad's demand was illegitimate and would make the concessions involved in an Israeli–Syrian deal even more controversial than they were already. He finally authorized Christopher to tell Asad that "his impression" was that Rabin accepted his demand. Asad then agreed to upgrade the format of the negotiation. An "ambassadors' channel" was established between the Syrian ambassador in Washington, Walid Muallem, and me. When Asad insisted we meet only in the presence of an American diplomat, we were joined by Ross and Indyk. The meetings went well. Muallem wanted to make a deal, particularly with Washington, and a lot of ground was covered. I then reached the conclusion that we would not be able to crack the difficult security issues without high-level military meetings. It took additional American pressure on Asad before he agreed to dispatch the chief of staff of the Syrian army, Hikmat Shihabi, to meet with an Israeli counterpart. Rabin dispatched Ehud Barak, who was to end his term as the IDF's chief of staff at the end of December.

Rabin wanted the chief of staffs' meeting to be kept secret. Publicizing it would create the impression in Israel that a Syrian–Israeli breakthrough was imminent and would galvanize the opposition. But the Syrians chose to leak the meeting, probably to give the impression that Syria was moving toward regaining the Golan. This played into the hands of the swelling movement in Israel against withdrawal from the Golan. The volume of protest and opposition in Israel was, in fact, not warranted by the limited degree of progress in the actual Israeli–Syrian negotiations. The Golan settlers had successfully orchestrated a popular campaign under the banner "The people stand for the Golan." In June 1974 a movement called the Third Way was established. It was composed mostly of Labor members and supporters who were critical of what they saw as Rabin's drift to the left on both the Syrian and Palestinian fronts. But they were primarily focused on their opposition to withdrawal from the Golan. Rabin was personally hurt when several of his Palmach friends and IDF colleagues joined the movement. They were critical of his policy, but they were also personally offended by the fact that as he rose in the political ranks, he distanced himself from his friends and spent his social life with a new circle of friends or, rather, acquaintances. The political challenge was exacerbated when two Labor members of the Knesset joined the movement as well. Rabin's coalition was now hanging by a thread. In September 1994 the Golan settlers tried to pass the Golan Entrenchment Law in the Knesset. This would have required a special majority both to repeal the Knesset's 1981 law that had applied Israeli law to the Golan and to approve the referendum Rabin had promised in the event of an agreement with Syria, including a withdrawal from the Golan. Rabin was fortunately able to quash this effort by mobilizing sufficient votes in the Knesset.

The difficulties with the PA and the deadly impact of terrorist attacks were fortunately overshadowed by the expanding normalization of Israel's relationship with the Arabs of the Gulf and North Africa. A second Middle Eastern Economic Conference was held, with the participation of a large Israeli delegation, this time in Jordan. Ever since 1948 one of the chief weapons used by the Arab world against Israel after the military defeat was the denial of normalcy, by exercising a direct and an indirect boycott. The sight of Middle Eastern economic conferences in which Israeli and Arab officials and business people rubbed shoulders with one another was an impressive manifestation of the success of the peace process of the 1990s.

CONTRADICTORY TRENDS IN 1995

The peace process in 1995 resembled that of 1993. Israel was negotiating with both Syria and the Palestinians; there were difficulties on both tracks. Rabin played one track against the other and ended up making a second major deal with the Palestinians, leaving Asad angry on the sidelines. But this end result was not purely the outcome of clever manipulation by Rabin. Asad proved to be an exceedingly difficult negotiating partner, one who ultimately led Rabin to conclude he was not interested in a deal or, more charitably, not sufficiently interested to make a traditional negotiation work.

The Israeli–Palestinian negotiations that led to the Oslo II agreement were centered on the extension of the PA's sway over additional parts of the West Bank beyond the original area in and around Jericho. The lengthy, extremely challenging negotiations led to the creation of Areas A, B, and C in the West

Bank. Area A comprised the West Bank's main cities; the bulk of the population in that area were to be under the PA's full control. Area B would be under the authority's civilian control but under Israeli military control. Area C, a large, sparsely populated part of the West Bank, would remain under Israeli control.

The agreement, signed at the White House on September 24, 1995, was a very critical step on the road to a final status Israeli–Palestinian agreement. According to the original Oslo Accords, final status negotiations were to be completed within five years of the conclusion of the implementation agreement that was signed in May 1994. Both supporters and opponents of the Israeli–Palestinian peace process understood the magnitude and implications of Oslo II. The opposition in Israel to signing such an agreement reached a new, unprecedented level, one that would have lethal consequences.

The Syrian track, in turn, now reached a dead end. In the aftermath of the Barak–Shihabi meeting, Asad insisted that prior to another meeting "the principles of the security arrangements" be agreed upon and that they be "on equal footing." While Rabin argued that the security arrangements should compensate Israel for getting off the high ground, Asad argued that Syria was the threatened party. It took months of linguistic exercises before a compromise formula was devised. Asad authorized Shihabi to travel to meet with the IDF's new chief of staff, Amnon Shahak, in late June 1995. The meeting went well, but when Shihabi returned to Damascus Asad once again decided it was not a good meeting. It was at that point Rabin decided that Asad was not really interested in coming to an agreement. Asad was now railing at the format of the peace process. High-level Syrian–Israeli meetings that failed to produce real progress served to legitimize the normalization of Arab–Israeli relations, he claimed. Asad felt that Rabin had outmaneuvered him. His fullest criticism of the peace process was made in an interview he gave to the Egyptian newspaper *Al-Ahram* on October 11: "The Israelis are seeking to exploit these processes by exercising pressure on the other parties. Oslo created pressure on Jordan, and Jordan and Palestine created pressure on others [namely, Syria]. . . . We are in the peace process but we do not collaborate in the effort to exercise pressure on us."

Asad's criticism was shared by prominent Arab intellectuals, who coined the term *taharwul* ("racing") to denounce those Arabs who hastened to recognize Israel and deal with her. Asad also found an unexpected ally in Cairo. Egypt had reached a peace deal with Israel in 1979 but kept it as a "cold peace" because of the failure to implement the Palestinian component. Now that Israel and the PA were moving forward, Egypt could, in theory, have thawed its relations with Israel. But this failed to happen. Egypt also saw Israel as a competitor for regional hegemony and was worried that Arab–Israeli normalization would catapult Israel into a hegemonic position. The large Israeli delegation that went to the first regional economic conference in Casablanca, Morocco, served to feed this anxiety. Egypt chose to use the nuclear issue to slow normalization down. Cairo had traditionally been a foe of Israel's nuclear program, and it now came out forcefully against Washington's effort to get the Non-Proliferation Treaty, which was about to expire in 1995, extended. Cairo insisted that Israel be forced to join the treaty.

On October 5, 1995, during a special session of the Knesset convened to ratify Oslo II, Rabin delivered a particularly significant speech explaining the essence of the agreement and charting his road map for the next phases of Israel's relationship with the Palestinians. Calling the agreement "a significant breakthrough in the resolution of the Palestinian–Israeli conflict and in the effort to put an end to decades of terror and blood," Rabin proceeded to describe his view of the permanent solution:

We see the permanent solution in the framework of the State of Israel that will retain most of the territory of the land of Israel as it was under the British Mandate and alongside it a Palestinian entity that will be home to most of the Palestinian inhabitants who live in the Gaza Strip and in the area of the West Bank. We want this entity to be less than a state that will manage independently the lives of the Palestinians under its authority. The borders of the State of Israel at the time of the permanent solution will be beyond the lines that existed before the Six-Day War. We will not return to the lines of June 4, 1967.

Rabin went on to mention the areas to be added to Israel's territory in the final status agreement: Greater Jerusalem, a security border in the Jordan Valley broadly defined, several specific areas near Jerusalem east of the Green Line, and "Jewish settlement blocks." He explained that his government chose the option of a Jewish state over that of Greater Israel. The Palestinians, Rabin said, "did not in the past and do not in the present constitute an existential threat to the state of Israel." The main threat to the implementation of the peace process with the Palestinians was presented by the Palestinian terrorist organizations. The PLO under Arafat ceased to engage in terror but the PA was required to do much more than it had been doing against the terrorist organizations.

Rabin described in detail the arrangements in areas A, B, and C and the process of redeployment and further redeployment by the IDF. It was a phased process designed to enable Israel to scrutinize the PA's performance. He expressed his disappointment with the PA's failure thus far to modify the Palestinian National Charter and stated that "the changes required in the Palestinian charter will be an important and serious criterion as to the further implementation of the whole agreement." Rabin surveyed in detail the other aspects of the agreement and concluded on a cautious note: "We possibly open today a new phase in the history of the Jewish people and the State of Israel. We know the prospects, we know the risks." Rabin thanked the large Israeli team that had negotiated the agreement and, specifically, Peres. This graciousness was the manifestation of a new phase in their relationship. In June, Peres committed in writing not to challenge Rabin's leadership. Rabin accepted him as his second in command, and both agreed on the way forward.

7

—◆◆◆◆—

Politics, Policy, Incitement, and Assassination,
1992–1995

Rabin's genuine desire to make a difference in his second
term was a tall order for a government that rested on a slim
majority. With Shas in the coalition, it held a minimal majority
of sixty-two seats. The Arab members could be counted on to
support the peace process, but Shas was an uncertain partner.
Shas's spiritual leader, Rabbi Ovadia Yosef, had issued a ruling
stating it was permissible to give up parts of the Land of Israel
in order to save Jewish lives. In other words, he assigned priority to the sanctity of life over the sanctity of the land—in stark
contrast to Gush Emunim's doctrine, which gives precedence
to the Land of Israel over the State of Israel and to some extent
over its people. But the rank and file of Shas and the bulk of its
voters were hawkish, and at the end of the day its support of the
peace process was bound to be tenuous. Rabin also had to worry
about both the right and left wings of the forty-four members
of the Knesset of his own party, whose support could not be

taken for granted. In other words, undivided, constant attention and effort were required to guarantee the government's survival.

The Rabin government's slim majority proved sufficient to make and implement bold decisions, but a ceaseless effort had to be invested in order to guarantee a parliamentary majority. One reason for the sense of urgency in the weeks prior to the conclusion of the Oslo Accords was the criminal investigation of Aryeh Deri. Deri, the Shas Party's lay political leader, was suspected of engaging in corruption and was eventually convicted on that charge. It seemed likely his arraignment would take his party out of the coalition. When the Oslo Accords were voted on in the Knesset, they were, in fact, approved by a majority of sixty-one to fifty with eight abstentions and one absence. The Shas members abstained, as did three Likud members who decided "to give Oslo a chance." In September Shas left the coalition.

The Oslo Accords and their sequels had a contradictory effect on the Israeli public and the political system. The underlying tension between left- and right-leaning political groups was exacerbated by the substantial leap forward in the peace process. Supporters of the accords were galvanized by the breakthrough with the Palestinians, the prospect of a further one with Syria, the peace with Jordan, the dramatic improvement in Israel's international standing, and other critical manifestations of normalization in Israel's relationship with the larger Arab world, such as the participation of a large Israeli delegation at the economic conference in Casablanca in October 1994. This segment of the Israeli public felt Rabin was leading the country toward a transformation of its regional and international position, from the all-too-familiar state of siege to a normal existence. The right wing and its supporters, on the other hand, were horrified by the concessions made in Oslo and likely to be made in future agreements. But the greatest damage to the Israeli public's support of the peace process was caused by the series of terrorist attacks by Hamas and the Islamic Jihad that were launched in Israel's cities and towns starting in April 1994. To get a sense of the escalation, one needs to compare the one minor terrorist attack in 1993 to the five deadly attacks in 1994 and another five in 1995. Thirty-eight Israelis were killed in 1994 and forty in 1995. The psychological impact was horrendous. Festive signing ceremonies and the sight of Israel's flag hoisted in Gulf and North African Arab countries were one thing; the prospect of being killed on a bus in the middle of an Israeli town was quite another. The right wing's charges that depositing Israel's security into the hands of Arafat and his PA was a reckless act resonated for many. Two terms and slogans convey the sense of the bitter debate over these issues at the time. One was the term "victims of peace," used sarcastically by right-wing critics. The other was "do not give them guns," a line taken from a poem written by Israel's national poet, Nathan Alterman, in the 1930s and used by critics of the Oslo Accords to underline the fact that part of the responsibility for Israel's security was now in Palestinian hands.

The opposition to the peace process and the political challenge to Rabin's majority increased in 1995, fed by two sources. One was the growing opposition toward an Israeli–Syrian deal involving withdrawal from the Golan. It was led by the Golan settlers, who had considerable support in the country as well as inside the Labor Party, and by the new movement called the Third Way. In July 1995 a bill was presented in the Knesset requiring a special majority in a Knesset vote on withdrawal from the Golan. Rabin's political lieutenants were able to pull away two members of the Knesset from the right-wing Tzomet Party. The result was a tie: sixty to sixty. The motion did not pass, but it was an unmistakable indication of the fragility of Rabin's parliamentary majority.

Much more ominous was the agitation of the West Bank settlers and the right wing in general in anticipation of the signing of the Oslo II agreement. They knew the agreement would represent major progress toward turning the Oslo Accords into a new reality, placing Arafat and the PA in control of a core area of the West Bank. The incitement against Rabin's government and Rabin personally began to reach a new and dangerous level. The struggle against an Israeli–Syrian deal moved from the Knesset into the streets and city squares.

It is impossible to separate the Oslo process from the complex relationship between Rabin and Peres. The Oslo Accords had illustrated what the two men could achieve when they worked together. Peres brought bold initiative, and Rabin the careful scrutiny and ability to bring along the Israeli public. But Peres's and Rabin's old rivalry, temporarily set aside in their collaboration during the early part of Rabin's second tenure, was awakened when Peres tried to exploit his post-Oslo popularity and standing by taking charge of a second track of bilateral negotiations with Jordan. Rabin put an end to that and took charge of the negotiations. After the signing of the non-belligerency agreement with Jordan in July 1994, Rabin humiliated Peres by railing against him in front of several Israeli journalists. In December 1994 Rabin and Peres were awarded the Nobel Peace Prize together with Arafat. The Nobel committee was smart enough to split the prize, thus keeping the competition behind the scenes. But on the whole Rabin and Peres understood and accepted the fact that they were bound inextricably, and they learned to live and work together. In June 1995 they formalized their understanding when Peres undertook to accept Rabin's leadership and Rabin accepted Peres as his number two. This personal understanding was buttressed by a larger agreement going forward, as manifested in the signing of Oslo II.

DOMESTIC POLICIES

Rabin's second tenure in 1992–95 is and will be remembered primarily for its peace policy, but his was also a government that pursued vigorous domestic policies, part of Rabin's promise to reorder the national priorities. It was a period of rapid economic expansion. Early in his tenure Rabin traveled to the United States and reached an agreement with the Bush administration to release the $10 billion in loan guarantees that had been denied to Shamir's government. Rabin also made a quick decision to stop construction in the settlements. It was a political statement with economic repercussions: the funds raised through the loan guarantees and those saved by the stoppage of construction in the settlements were invested in new priorities. The education budget grew by 70 percent; a massive investment was made in new roads—most important, the Cross Israel Highway—bridges, and exchanges; the higher education system was expanded; and new public colleges offered greater access to higher education. The budget of the chief scientist in the Ministry of Trade and Industry was increased so as to enable larger investment in research and development. A major investment fund, *Yozma*, or "Initiative," was started as a governmental enterprise and subsequently privatized. Both measures played a central role in the development of Israel's high-tech industries.

As the peace process accelerated, a sense of optimism about the country's future grew in Israel and abroad. Foreign investment grew dramatically. Multinational corporations like Volkswagen and Nestlé invested in the Israeli economy. In less than four years foreign investment grew from $180 million per annum to nearly $6 billion. Israel's economy grew at an annual rate of 6 percent (except in 1993, owing to the moratorium on construction in the settlements).

Rabin's minister of finance, Avraham (Baiga) Shochat, was

an important political ally and aide, but the issue of unemployment was a bone of contention between them. Rabin attached great importance to fighting the unemployment rate, which in 1992 stood at eleven percent, and demanded that Shochat initiate state-sponsored projects in order to reduce it. Shochat and his "treasury boys" shared Rabin's vision but insisted on sponsoring projects that had at least some added value. In any event, unemployment was brought down to 6.5 percent, despite the need to integrate into the workforce the recent wave of immigrants from the former Soviet Union. Related to the issue of unemployment was the pressure exerted by Treasury to open the Israeli economy and markets to the world. They saw no value in protecting low-tech textile and plywood plants and argued that opening these sectors of the economy to competitive imports would reduce the cost of living and force Israel's industry to upscale its products. As someone who grew up inside Israel's Labor movement, Rabin felt it was part of his heritage to protect workers. But Rabin was also influenced by his American period and understood the need to integrate Israel's economy into the global system.

Rabin's second tenure is viewed by Israel's Arab minority as a golden period. He was not initially well received by this constituency, who remembered him as the aggressive minister of defense who employed an iron fist in the First Intifada. But as prime minister, Rabin directed considerable resources to the Arab sector. Child allowances for Arab families were equated to those in the Jewish sector (politically, this was balanced by increasing the allocation to IDF soldiers at the end of their mandatory service). Money to the Arab sector was allocated directly or indirectly through the education budget and by investments in infrastructure in Arab areas, including the construction of roads and the extension of electricity networks.

CHRONICLE OF AN ASSASSINATION FORETOLD

Sometime toward the end of 1994 Yehoshafat Harkabi, a retired professor at the Hebrew University, a former director of Israel's military intelligence, and one of the country's most prominent public intellectuals, issued a prophetic, gloomy forecast as he observed the agitation against Rabin and his policy by the parliamentary and extraparliamentary opposition: "The internal debate will be horrendous, there will be attempted assassinations, Rabin will not die a natural death, the country will be affected by a terrible shock. Some will say we were not mistaken, Rabin was guilty of being soft-hearted."[1]

The French Jewish journalist Victor Cygielman wrote an article for *Le Nouvelle Observateur* that was published on November 2, 1995, just two days before Rabin was assassinated. In it he described a series of violent acts, extreme forms of incitement, and ominous ceremonies perpetrated by radical right wingers: Rabin was denounced as a traitor, implicitly and then explicitly; radical rabbis pronounced him guilty of acts warranting death or killing; he was shown in placards wearing an SS uniform or Arab headgear and portrayed in acts amounting to incantatory prefiguration. Cygielman concluded that "the stage has been prepared for Rabin's assassination, and an actual attempt is just a question of time."[2] Indeed, hindsight was hardly necessary in order to notice the course of events that led to Rabin's assassination. After the signing of the Oslo Accords, these events unfolded in several stages: legitimate political opposition; illegitimate political opposition; discrediting and delegitimizing the government and its leader; dehumanization of the political rival; symbolic conduct and ritual murder; violent political conduct and actual assassination.[3]

The opposition to Rabin's government in 1993 was led by Benjamin Netanyahu, who was elected to the Likud's leadership after the 1992 elections. The opposition, like the Israeli public, was surprised and shocked by the signing of the Oslo Accords, and it took some time for it to organize itself and bring to bear effective, legitimate opposition to the government's policy. The Likud itself felt weak and joined a larger coalition that spanned Israel's right wing, a coalition managed by an entity called the joint staff and, later, Mathe Ma'amatz (Hebrew for "effort staff"). It was composed of the Yesha Council, the organization of West Bank and Gaza settlers, the Likud and three other right-wing parties, and various representatives of the religious parties and extraparliamentary groups. The main role was played by the Yesha Council. The coordination between the Yesha Council and the Likud was managed by two Likud activists, Tzahi Hanegbi and Reuven Tzadok. The joint staff organized demonstrations, marches, vigils, and media work. In 1994 legitimate opposition was transformed into a series of acts seeking to delegitimize the government and its policies, including violent unauthorized demonstrations, disruption of events organized by the government or attended by Rabin, and blocking of roads. The loose structure of the joint staff enabled its leaders to cooperate with groups like the supporters of Meir Kahane, a radical Orthodox American Jew who had imported his ultranationalist movement and ideology from the United States to Israel, while maintaining plausible deniability.

It was obvious at this stage that the government and the opposition were on a collision course. Rabin was determined to implement the Oslo Accords and to move on as the peace process unfolded. The settlers' movement was determined to obstruct it. From their perspective, the Oslo Accords threatened not only the country's safety and existence but also the settlement project, in which their lives and identity were invested. Their opposition derived from a profound religious belief in the sanctity of the land and an absolute rejection of the Palestinian claim to it. As we have seen, in Gush Emunim's worldview and in the theology of their rabbis the Land of Israel is superior to the State of Israel, and no Israeli government has the authority to give away any part of it. Any government willing to do that was, by definition, illegitimate. As early as the 1970s Rabin had expressed his view of the settlers' political movement as a "cancerous entity." In 1984 the so-called Jewish Underground, composed of radical settlers, was exposed. Its members had tried to assassinate several West Bank mayors, and the more radical among them plotted to blow up the al-Aqsa Mosque on Temple Mount. The members of the underground came from the ranks of the settlers but broke ranks with mainstream settlers by taking the logic and policies a few steps further. They were arrested, convicted, and sent to jail, but in 1988 they were pardoned as a by-product of the coalition agreements that enabled Yitzhak Shamir to form his government. The pardon was indicative of a tolerant attitude toward Gush Emunim by the more moderate right wing and even by some elements in the Labor Party who viewed them as latter-day pioneers. The Gush leaders excelled at manipulating the governmental and political systems and in bending the law, taking full advantage of the political system's unwillingness to confront them. Money was funneled to them by right-wing Israeli governments, and all governments were either passive or helpless when new settlements were created and existing ones expanded. In 1993 they saw the Oslo Accords as the most dangerous threat ever to their project, and they were clearly willing to go a long way to obstruct them. Rabin agreed, reluctantly, to have one meeting with the settlers to try to reach a mutual understanding. The meeting failed, and the effort to engage in dialogue was discontinued.

In late 1993 the settlers' council launched a campaign seeking to "break the spirit" of Rabin. Their model was Begin's collapse in the aftermath of the First Lebanon War in 1983.[4] When that failed, the campaign against Rabin escalated. He was now denounced as a traitor. He was depicted in placards wearing

Arab headgear. Later, analogies to the Holocaust were introduced into the public discourse. Rabin's government was nicknamed Judenrat, the derogatory name for Jews who collaborated with the Nazis. The campaign was further radicalized under the impact of the Hamas suicide bombings. On October 19, 1994, twenty-two Israelis were killed and dozens wounded when a bus on Dizengoff Street in Tel Aviv exploded. The leader of the opposition, Netanyahu, went to the site and, standing before the television cameras, blamed Rabin for the tragedy: "The PM chose to prefer Arafat and the welfare of Gaza's residents at the expense of the inhabitants of Israel." But this tactic was to backfire. Netanyahu was severely criticized for breaking the code of conduct of mainstream Israeli politics, by which casualties, military or civilian, must not be exploited for political purposes. He continued to criticize and denounce Rabin and the government but refrained from showing up at the sites of terrorist incidents.

The incitement against Rabin, however, grew in leaps and bounds, both in amount and in actions. An unlicensed right-wing radio station, Channel 7, which broadcast from a point outside Israel's territorial waters, used the harshest language and terminology. Rabin was denounced as being bizarre and as a traitor, a murderer, and a drunk.[5] The settlers' publication *Nekuda* (A Point) wrote in July 1995 that Rabin "acts like a dictator . . . is reckless . . . is sick."[6] A right-wing psychologist published a "report" on Rabin's psychological state in which he determined him to be "a schizoid, detached from reality." Rabin's former friend Sharon joined the fray, also borrowing terminology taken from the Holocaust and Stalin's crimes. Sharon called Rabin's government "an insane government that shrinks Israel to Auschwitz borders, a reckless government, submissive, confused, treacherous, insane."[7] Rabin's colleague from the Palmach Rehavam Ze'evi competed with Sharon in his verbal assault on the prime minister.

In early summer of 1995 a new element was introduced into the picture when a movement called Zo Artzenu (This is our country) tried to stop the Oslo process through civil disobedience. It was headed by a settler called Moshe Feiglin, whose parents had come to Israel from Australia. Many of his associates had immigrated to Israel from the United States and France. Zo Artzenu was a well-financed, organized movement that managed to wreak havoc in Israel by blocking roads and intersections but failed to prevent Oslo II from being signed. Feiglin eventually joined the Likud, registering a large number of settlers and other radical right wingers for the Likud primaries and thus playing an important role in the Likud's drift to the right.

As early as 1994 extremist rabbis in the West Bank settlements and in the United States introduced two radical terms into the right wing's radical discourse: the "Law of the Pursuer" (Din Rodef) and the "Law of the Informer" (Din Moser). Both laws were adopted from the long history of the Jews in the diaspora and under foreign rule, and both sanctioned the killing of a Jew who either pursued or prosecuted other Jews or informed on them to gentile authorities. This project was handled carefully. The group of rabbis who tinkered with the two terms knew full well they could be charged with illegal activity and incitement to murder and therefore were cautious and evasive in using the terms. They were eventually shamed by a moderate rabbi in the settlements, Yoel Ben-Nun, who, feeling the shock of Rabin's assassination, demanded that either the national religious movement or the state investigate the use of these terms by several rabbis. Ben-Nun paid a personal price for acting against the members of his own milieu (he was practically ostracized by the settler community in the West Bank where he resides), and his campaign ended up being a futile one, but he shed much light on this pernicious activity that helped lay the moral foundation for an assassination "legitimized" by a supposed religious authority.

In January 1995 a letter was sent from the Har Bracha settlement in Samaria to forty Orthodox rabbis in Israel, the United States, Belgium, and Canada. The rabbis were asked to respond to two questions: In light of the Oslo Accords, were the prime minister of Israel and the members of his cabinet "pursuers" according to Jewish law? And should they therefore be warned that their punishment had been set? The letter was initiated by a team of three rabbis headed by the radical Eliezer Melamed, who was at the time the rabbi of a small yeshiva on Mount Bracha near Nablus. Of the forty rabbis, eleven responded. Two confirmed that the Law of the Pursuer did apply to Rabin; seven offered ambivalent replies; and two harshly criticized the writers of the letter for mixing Jewish law with politics. One of them warned, "You are playing with fire."[8]

In the atmosphere of those days it was not peculiar for radical rabbis in Samaria to try to involve diaspora rabbis in their campaign. The parliamentary opposition had already taken its campaign against the Oslo Accords and the prospect of an Israeli–Syrian agreement to the United States. This campaign was orchestrated by David Bar-Ilan, a former concert pianist and an associate of Netanyahu. Bar-Ilan tried to build opposition to the peace process in the U.S. Jewish community as well as among American Christian fundamentalists and right-wing elements. Bar-Ilan and his team fanned opposition to territorial concessions in the West Bank (the Holy Land, the Land of Israel, to Christian fundamentalists) and in the Golan. An Israeli–Syrian peace deal, they argued, would require the positioning of U.S. peacekeepers on the Golan and would place them in harm's way. Some radical Orthodox rabbis in the United States, not lagging far behind their West Bank colleagues, were opposed to and denounced any territorial concession in the Land of Israel. Rabbi Abraham Hecht, of Brooklyn, New York, stated in September 1995 that "he who gives away parts of the Land of Israel, he who kills him first is rewarded, but I was not since he is still alive." Rabbi Kurtz, the Chabad leader in Florida, decreed on October 15, 1995, that "Rabin qualifies as an enemy and therefore is subject to the rule act swiftly to kill the person who comes to kill you."[9]

In the summer of 1995 the incitement and denunciation of Rabin were transformed into a direct call for the killing of the prime minister. It took just a few months for these calls to be heard and translated into an actual assassination.

THE CHAIN OF EVENTS

In the chain of events leading up to Rabin's assassination three episodes that were harbingers of its imminence stand out. In March 1994, near the town of Ra'anana, north of Tel Aviv, a protest march against Rabin's government was organized by Kahane Hai, the movement founded by Rabbi Kahane. Netanyahu was seen marching in front of a coffin inscribed with the words "Zionism's murderer." Marching ahead of Netanyahu was a person carrying a gallows. This was an extreme example of incantatory prefiguration. When asked about his participation in the event, Netanyahu claimed he "just happened to pass by" and was not aware of the coffin and the gallows.[10]

On October 5, the day of the Knesset vote on Oslo II, the Likud organized a mass rally in Zion Square in Jerusalem; one hundred thousand people attended. The Likud's leadership stood on the balcony of a local hotel while flags of the State of Israel, the Likud Party, and Kahane Hai were hoisted by the crowd, alongside placards of Rabin dressed in an SS uniform. The rally turned into a mob scene at this point, and the crowd began chanting "Death to Rabin!" At some point the image of Rabin in SS uniform was screened on the wall behind the people who were speaking. The speakers harangued the crowd with inflammatory speeches, warning of the dangers inherent in the Oslo Accords and blasting the government that signed it.

Netanyahu gave a speech that emphasized the non-Jewish character of the government's majority—the fact that it relied on
Arab Israeli votes. A moderate Likud leader David Levi was
booed when he left the rally in disgust. Other moderate Likud
leaders like Dan Meridor left. The crowd was ecstatic and violent. The chief complaint against Netanyahu was not, in fact,
that his speech was objectionable but that by failing to tell the
galvanized crowd its conduct was not acceptable, he legitimized
it. The mayhem of the mob continued near the Knesset. Rabin's
car was attacked and vandalized. The Labor minister Fouad
Ben Eliezer was attacked by the mob on his way to the Knesset.
Once inside the building, he found Netanyahu and said to him,
"You must restrain your people or else it will end in murder.
They just tried to murder me now." Netanyahu responded with
an embarrassed smile, and Ben Eliezer continued, "I suggest you
wipe the smile off your face. Your people are crazy. If someone
will be murdered, you will be responsible."[11]

On September 10, 1995, Rabin went to a gathering held
by the Association of Immigrants from the United States and
Canada at the Wingate Institute, near Tel Aviv. Present at the
meeting were many right-wing extremists, as some of the immigrants tended to be. One of them, Rabbi Natan Ophir, employed by the Hebrew University, came very close to Rabin,
assaulting him verbally and fighting with his bodyguards. It
was a clear indication of the inefficacy of Rabin's protection.

The only thing it took to convert all of this explosive potential into an actual assassination was one man. That man was
Yigal Amir. At the time Amir was a twenty-four-year-old law
student at Bar-Ilan University, an institution with a national
religious orientation. Born to Orthodox parents who came to
Israel from Yemen, he lived in Herzliyya, just north of Tel Aviv.
Amir's early life and education reflected the blurring of the
distinction between Haredi (ultra-Orthodox) and national religious Judaism. Having received a traditional religious educa-

tion, he completed his military service in a combat unit and was then admitted to Bar Ilan to study law and computer science. Amir was a true believer, a headstrong fanatic who became associated with and influenced by the most radical advocates of messianic attachment to the Land of Israel. He frequented right-wing demonstrations, organized weekend trips to West Bank settlements, and soon came to the attention of the Jewish Division of the GSS, or Shabak, Israel's domestic security service. Amir fraternized with, among others, Avishai Raviv, the GSS's controversial agent provocateur, who operated inside the radical right-wing's hard core. Raviv was the only agent the GSS was able to plant inside this group. In order to build and maintain his credibility, he initiated and participated in unlawful activities. His problematic conduct has since been exploited by radical right wingers, who, since November 1995, have propagated a series of conspiracy theories holding that the GSS was responsible for Rabin's assassination.

Amir decided to kill Rabin in September 1993, after watching the signing ceremony of the Oslo Accords on the White House lawn. It took two years for this initial decision to mature into a resolute determination to act and for the opportunity to present itself. On three occasions Amir took his gun to a site where Rabin was expected to be present and for various reasons did not try his luck. A peace rally to take place in Tel Aviv on November 4, 1995, in a major square next to City Hall was to be addressed by Rabin. It seemed the perfect opportunity for Amir. The rally was a success, attended by a huge crowd of supporters. The size of the crowd, the enthusiasm, the support and warmth directed toward Rabin during the rally were pleasing to the beleaguered prime minister. After giving a short speech, a happy Rabin accompanied by a cheerful Peres prepared to leave the rally and began descending a short flight of stairs separating the balcony of the City Hall building overlooking the large square (now called Rabin Square) from their cars. Half-way down the stairs Rabin told Peres he was going back to the podium on the balcony to thank the organizers more appropriately. Peres decided to proceed to his car. At the bottom of the stairs, in theory "a sterile area," sat Amir, armed with his pistol. A video clip filmed from across the street by an amateur who lived nearby shows Amir's face as he appears to be pondering a dilemma: he could kill Peres, but then he would not be able to kill Rabin. Rabin was the key, the leader who could make Oslo work. Amir spared Peres. A few minutes later, he seized the opportunity and fired three bullets into the back of the practically unprotected Rabin.

How could a man like Yigal Amir, known to the GSS, get close enough to the prime minister of Israel to assassinate him? Israel is a country deeply familiar with terrorism and violence and well versed in security measures. Amir's success can be explained by the impact of a mindset, by a series of accidents and near misses, and by sheer incompetence. There was a pervasive mindset at the time, shared by Rabin himself, that the danger of an attempt on the prime minister's life lay only in the Arab/ Palestinian side—the belief was that "a Jew will not kill a Jew." Despite the rabid incitement of Rabin's Jewish opponents and critics, no one felt they would actually try to kill him. Some had tried to correct this erroneous mindset. In the spring of 1995 and later that summer the head of the Jewish Division of the GSS warned against the danger of an assassination attempt directed at Rabin and specifically that it could be perpetrated from within the "green line" (Israel in the pre–June 1967 boundaries) and not by a settler. The warning was unfortunately not translated into action by the GSS unit in charge of VIP security. Rabin himself refused to wear a protective vest, preferred not to use the armored Cadillac purchased for his security, and insisted on attending mass events and mingling with the public, as he had always chosen to do.

Amir had come very close to being exposed. He had told his brother Hagai about his plan. In addition, he had a small circle of friends at Bar Ilan University who had a vague sense of what he was plotting. His supposed plan was to collect weapons and train himself in how to shoot them in order to fire at Palestinian targets in the West Bank. In addition to Hagai, two members of Amir's circle, Dror Adani and Margalit Harshefi, were sentenced to serve time in jail for failing to report Amir when they became involved in these activities and even heard Amir talk about killing Rabin. The collusion would almost come to light owing to a sergeant by the name of Shlomi Halevi, who served in the intelligence department of the IDF's Central Command. Halevi's girlfriend, who was a member of Amir's close circle, told him about the talk between Adani and Amir. Halevi was torn between his sense of duty to report it and the need, as he saw it, to protect his friends. The compromise solution Halevi devised was to tell his superiors he had overheard a conversation in the toilet of Tel Aviv's central bus station that referred to "a smallish Yemenite with curly black hair from Herzeliyya who plans to assassinate the prime minister." Amir's name was registered in the GSS's portfolio at the time, but this information was far too vague and not seriously pursued as a lead. Raviv, the GSS's agent provocateur, knew Amir well but did not alert his control officers to the severity of the challenge he represented.

It is difficult to explain the series of oversights and failures by the VIP security unit of the GSS, whose director, among others, was immediately sacked after the event. The neglect began with the failure to increase Rabin's protection in 1995, when the handwriting was on the wall, and ended with many other failures, including not securing a real sterile area on the way to Rabin's car, not shooting Amir after he fired the first bullet, and not throwing Rabin to the ground and covering him, the most elementary of measures of personal protection.

THE AFTERMATH

More than twenty years later, the aftermath of Rabin's assassination has been sharply framed by the May 1996 parliamentary elections that brought Netanyahu to power. The six months separating Rabin's assassination from the transfer of power to the head of the opposition, who had sought to undermine Rabin and his policies, form a single unit of time that fully endowed the assassination with its short-term impact. The transfer of power magnified the assassination's impact as a landmark in Israel's drift to the right and swift, at least temporary, departure from the peace policy crafted by Rabin. It was a bitter irony that Rabin would be replaced by an opposition leader who, while not taking a direct part in the incitement against him, had not exactly distanced himself from it either. The failure of the center and left establishment to take the country through real soul-searching after the national trauma of November 4, 1995, also contributed to this course of events and eventually allowed the radical right and the settlers and their allies in Israel to remain entrenched, regroup, and get a stranglehold on the country's politics and policies.

These tectonic shifts were not immediately apparent. The country was in a state of shock, seized by grief. There was a pervasive sense of crisis and danger, of a potential civil war. The mainstream right wing went into a defensive and apologetic mode. Netanyahu's main effort at the time was to distance himself from the radical right and the circles associated with the assassination. The religious Zionist camp in Israel and the settlements did some examining of their conscience—in some cases genuine, in some cases affected. The center left was torn between wanting to punish the camp associated with the assassin, and a fear of a civil war and the sense that closing ranks and seeking national unity was the right thing to do.

But in the immediate wake left by the atrocity, the country

was unquestionably grief-stricken and in deep mourning. Rabin's body lay in repose in front of the Knesset. Tens of thousands of people came from across the country to bid him farewell. Almost everything in Rabin's life and career happened late, and that was true of the public's emotional attachment to him. In his prime, Rabin commanded respect from the public but not its love. During his last hours he was overtaken by the warmth he sensed in Tel Aviv's city's square. After the assassination, the warmth turned into an emotional swell of love, adoration, and a profound sense of loss. Thousands of young men and women kept vigil near the assassination site and near his home, holding candles: the "candles generation," as they came to be known. They mourned his death and sensed that the country's progression toward a better future was halted.

Rabin's funeral was an impressive event. Seventy-eight countries were represented, a huge number for a country used to standing alone. Two Arab heads of state attended: King Hussein of Jordan, Rabin's good friend, and President Mubarak of Egypt. Egypt had been at peace with Israel since 1979, but an Egyptian president had not been in Israel since Sadat's historic journey in November 1977, a symptom of the cold peace between the two countries. The massive international attendance reflected Rabin's stature and was also part of an effort to help Peres stay on the peace track. Of the eulogies delivered at the ceremony, President Clinton's eloquent and emotional tribute—with the proverbial "Shalom Haver" ("Good-bye, my friend")—stood out, as did that of Rabin's granddaughter, Noa, whose speech emphasized the personal warmth of a leader who had always been seen as tough and authoritative.

Overshadowed by these emotional heights were the actual decisions and measures taken in order to set the country, its politics, and its policies on a stable course. Peres replaced Rabin as prime minister and made three major, interrelated decisions at the outset of his term: not to hold a snap election in the aftermath of the assassination; to pursue a swift settlement with Syria as his main effort in the peace process; and to seek accommodation with the moderate wing of religious Zionism. A snap election probably would have given Peres a massive victory and reinforced his position as an elected prime minister. Instead, he decided to keep the original date of the next parliamentary election, scheduled for October 1996. Peres clearly wanted to be elected on his own terms rather than as Rabin's avenger. He sought to close ranks rather than settle accounts with the radical right wing and its softer supporters. The decision to keep the October date for the parliamentary election implied that Peres expected to make a major move in the peace process and to predicate his election campaign on that achievement. The election would become a referendum on the new agreement. Such an agreement could be made with either Syria or the PA.

These decisions were soon implemented through policies. A commission headed by Justice Meir Shamgar, former president of the Supreme Court, was charged with investigating the security failures surrounding Rabin's assassination. The commission was specifically asked by the government not to deal with the incitement or the political background of the assassination and instead focus on the security aspects. In keeping with this approach, Rabbi Yehuda Amital, a highly respected moderate religious Zionist leader, was invited to join the cabinet. The Israeli–Syrian negotiations were renewed, with Peres and the Clinton administration seeking a rapid breakthrough. But by the winter of 1996 things began to turn sour. The renewed Israeli–Syrian negotiations proceeded slowly; Asad was in no hurry to conclude an agreement with a prime minister who needed to be reelected in October 1996. When Peres realized he was not likely to reach an agreement with Syria in time for the October elections, he decided to move them up to May 1996. An angry Asad, upset by the de-facto suspension of the negotiations, allowed—or perhaps encouraged—Hezbollah to renew its firing of rockets into northern Israel, baiting Peres into launching the Grapes of Wrath operation against Hezbollah bases in South Lebanon in April 1996. It was not a particularly successful operation, and it ended tragically when a stray Israeli artillery shell killed a group of civilian refugees in the village of Kufr Kana. This was preceded by a wave of suicide attacks by Hamas in Jerusalem and Tel Aviv. Fifty-nine Israelis were killed in one week.

The chain of tragic events exacted a high political price. Peres, who was leading in the polls against Netanyahu by a large majority just a few weeks earlier, lost most of his support. Jewish voters were angered by the wave of terrorist attacks, while Arab Israeli voters were estranged by the Kufr Kana incident. Peres's and the Labor Party's campaign was badly run. To cite one example, the television debate between Peres and Netanyahu that ended up boosting Netanyahu's support was poorly prepared by Labor's team. In May Netanyahu and the Likud won the elections, and Israel started its march away from Rabin's way.

Epilogue

Soon after the twentieth anniversary of Rabin's assassination, on October 26, 2015, Benjamin Netanyahu spoke before the Foreign and Defense Affairs Committee of the Knesset. Netanyahu said of Rabin, "These days there is talk of what would have happened had this or that man remained. . . . This is irrelevant; we will forever live by the sword."[1] Netanyahu was clearly upset by the wave of nostalgia for Rabin generated by the anniversary of the assassination, which included a series of feature films and documentaries, television programs, books, press articles, and a major rally with President Clinton as the main speaker. This nostalgia was implicitly and even occasionally explicitly critical of Netanyahu. Netanyahu is currently well entrenched in power, in his third consecutive term and fourth in office, with no serious challenger in sight. But he is aware of the malaise affecting a significant part of the Israeli public: malaise produced by unhappiness with a leader who thrives on keeping the status quo, avoiding major decisions—a master of political survival who has failed to demonstrate a Rabin-like statesmanship in coping with Israel's underlying problems.

Netanyahu's statement in fact perfectly embodies the clash of narratives over Rabin's legacy, heritage, and memory. One such narrative is the debate over Yigal Amir's impact on the Israeli–Arab peace process of the 1990s. What would have happened if Amir had never made his fateful decision to assassinate Rabin? It could be argued that the assassin's bullets killed not just Rabin but also the peace process he led. This narrative resonates mostly with left-of-center liberal opinion in Israel and abroad, which contends that had Rabin not been killed he would have won the elections scheduled for October 1996 and would have reached an agreement with Arafat in the final status negotiations scheduled to conclude by May 1999. This view was articulated most eloquently by the *New York Times* columnist Thomas Friedman in an article titled "Foreign Affairs; . . . And One Man Voted Twice." Netanyahu, on the other hand, articulated a point of view held by the Israeli Right in which the peace process was bound to fail in any event because Arafat was not a genuine peace partner and had his own red lines he never intended to cross; at the moment of truth the negotiations would founder. The Israeli–Palestinian conflict, according to this view, is a hopeless, endless national conflict.

So which narrative is more plausible? Dealing with these opposing points of view is an exercise in counterfactual history. The assumption that Rabin would have won the 1996 elections is quite realistic, but that he would have come to an agreement with Arafat is less so. Rabin was critical of Arafat's failure to live up fully to his commitments and especially of his failure to crack down on Hamas. Rabin may well have been doubtful of his ultimate commitment to a genuine two-state solution but expected to put it to the test at the right moment. Yet it is indeed likely that in the absence of a final status agreement Rabin would have nonetheless been able to settle on a less ambitious goal and to avoid a head-on collision on the scale of the Second Intifada that broke out after the Camp David summit of July 2000. The plausibility of this counterfactual scenario is compounded by several historical facts and developments that did occur: Netanyahu's victory in 1996 was narrow and eminently avoidable; the peace process continued in 1996, as Netanyahu evacuated the city of Hebron in compliance with the Oslo II agreement and agreed (but did not implement) in 1998 to hand over another 13 percent of the West Bank; Ehud Barak in 2000 and Ehud Olmert in 2008 made far-reaching offers to the Palestinians going well beyond what Rabin was offering in October 1995; and Ariel Sharon, of all people, took Israel out of Gaza unilaterally in 2005 and was ready for a smaller scale unilateral withdrawal in the West Bank before falling ill.

And yet it can be said that Amir did indeed inflict a severe blow on the peace process of the 1990s. Rabin uniquely combined a determination to proceed in the peace process with expertise in Israel's national security agenda, the trust and support of a large part of the Israeli public, an excellent relationship with President Clinton, and Arafat's respect. His removal from the scene—and eventual replacement by Netanyahu, who promised to respect the Oslo Accords but in fact emasculated the Oslo process—interrupted the historical process that began in 1992 and destroyed its momentum. A full-fledged effort to resolve the Israeli–Palestinian and Israeli–Syrian conflicts was resumed by Barak in 2000, but the four-year hiatus had a devastating effect on an inherently fragile process. Israel and the Palestinians are still locked in conflict.

The assassination also had a deep impact on Israeli society and politics. Since 1977 Israel's politics have shifted to the right. Except in 1992–96 and 1999–2001 the Labor Party failed to win and hold power. Sharon and Olmert, who held power from 2001 to 2008, shifted from the right to the center and sought, in dif-

238

ferent ways, to resolve or at least consolidate Israel's relationship with the Palestinians. But during most of the nearly forty-
plus years since 1977 power has been held by the Likud, relying
on its "natural allies" (in the Israeli political idiom): the settlers and the Orthodox and ultra-Orthodox parties. Rabin's and
Barak's electoral victories in 1992 and 1999 demonstrated the
fact that Labor could win only when led by a centrist, authoritative leader with distinct security credentials who could reassure the anxious Israeli electorate that he was able to proceed
toward peace without undermining security. At the time of the
assassination's twentieth anniversary it was clear that the center
left of Israel was hard put to challenge Netanyahu and his right-
wing allies.

Rabin's assassination looms as an important landmark in
Israel's journey toward the right and away from a genuine quest
for a two-state solution. Among the developments that reinforced and accelerated the country's voyage on its current path
are that the Israeli state failed to punish the larger circle that
incited and called for the killing of Rabin; that Israeli society
did not go through the requisite soul-searching after the assassination; that religious Zionism failed to do so as well; that a red
line was crossed when a prime minister was assassinated; that
the assassin and his camp were in fact rewarded for the crime.

It is sometimes argued that the settlers' leadership was
shocked and moderated by the assassination and that, under its
impact in 2005, it restrained its constituency when Sharon evacuated and destroyed the settlements in Gaza in order to avoid
bloodshed and a potential civil war. Perhaps so. Some argue
that the restraint exercised by the settlers' leadership in 2005
led to further radicalization of their constituency in the coming
years. In any event, the settlement project in the West Bank
continues to expand, and the traditional leadership has been
outflanked from the right by messianic, violent groups. These
may not all be direct results of Rabin's assassination, but they

are definitely by-products of the opening of the floodgates on November 4, 1995, and during the preceding months.

In the wake of the assassination there were those on both the Left and the Right who hoped this violent act would become a unifying event. They argued that the fear of divisiveness and rupture should prod the two camps to rally around a determination to root out political violence and around Rabin's legacy of leadership and statesmanship. But this failed to happen. Instead, some on the left felt that scores needed to be settled, maintained that Rabin's true legacy was his peace policy, and insisted he be remembered and commemorated for his quest to resolve the Palestinian issue. To the Right this was an unacceptable legacy, and Rabin's memory and commemoration became contentious issues in a deeply divided Israel.

When Israeli presidents and prime ministers pass away they are commemorated by the State of Israel through the Council for the Commemoration of Presidents and Prime Ministers, an agency in the Prime Minister's Office chaired by the current prime minister. They are, naturally, commemorated differently and on different scales. For three former prime ministers, special laws were enacted by the Knesset. The first was Israel's founding father, David Ben Gurion. In 1996 a law was passed in the Knesset to commemorate Rabin and to support the establishment of the Rabin Center and its maintenance through the state budget. It was also determined that a state memorial ceremony would be held at his grave on the day of the assassination as well as a special memorial session in the Knesset. These decisions were widely supported, a reflection of the sense that the assassination of a prime minister had to be acknowledged and remembered at a level distinct from other deaths. Independently of the government's decision, numerous public facilities were named after Rabin.

Since Rabin's commemoration was undertaken by the state and since the state has been dominated during most of the past twenty years by the right, the underlying tension surrounding the remembrance of Rabin has surfaced on several occasions. Thus it has been difficult for Rabin's family and supporters, the keepers of the flame, to accept Netanyahu as a speaker at the ceremony held annually at the grave site. At the ceremony held in 2014 Rabin's sister, Rachel, an impressive woman in her own right, directed a barbed comment at Netanyahu when she spoke after him on behalf of the family. "We remember who was on that balcony," she said, referring to the violent rally held in October 1995. And yet Netanyahu and other right-wing leaders have found a way, as they must, of going to memorial events and of recognizing the need to support the Rabin Center.

Dealing with Rabin's memory in the Israeli educational system has been another source of tension. It erupted forcefully in 2016, when the text of a new civics textbook was leaked to the media. The project had begun five years earlier and had unfolded in a Ministry of Education headed by three successive ministers: a right-wing one, a centrist one, and a radical right-wing one. Naftali Bennet is the leader of the new incarnation of the settlers' party, the Jewish Home, and the textbook was completed on his watch. In it, Rabin's assassination is dealt with in two ways. In one section it is put in the context of the history of political violence in Israel and prestate Israel, together with the *Altalena* affair and the assassination of Emil Grinzweig, a peace activist. As we have seen, responsibility for the meaning of the *Altalena* affair has shifted over the years from Ben Gurion to Rabin, and the juxtaposition of his assassination with that episode raised a storm of protest. In a different section, the authors quote two opinions regarding the incitement that preceded the assassination, one of them from a former attorney general who argued there was no legal proof tying the assassination to the incitement. This particular quotation and the moral equivalence created by citing the two opposing perspectives on the incitement drew another round of loud protest. As a result, the publication of the textbook was temporarily suspended, but the whole affair reflected the influence the Right has acquired over the bureaucracy of the Ministry of Education as well as the radical right wing's lingering discomfort with the assassination and with the role in the incitement that its detractors attribute to it.

And yet it is clear that over the span of twenty years and more, the right wing's veneration and sensitivity with regard to Rabin's assassination have diminished. This is certainly true of the Likud as a party, and specifically of Netanyahu. In the first months after the assassination Netanyahu felt vulnerable to the accusation that he had taken part directly and indirectly in the incitement. He was particularly worried that such a development would affect his prospects in the May 1996 elections. His victory in these elections and his subsequent ability to return to and hold power have reduced this sensitivity. Neither is he entirely indifferent to comparisons with Rabin's leadership and statesmanship that cast a negative light on his own stewardship of Israel, but in the scheme of things this is not a major concern. On the other hand, the settlers and religious Zionism in general have been more sensitive to the charges of being responsible for the assassination. They have responded by arguing that it is wrong to blame a whole segment of Israel's population for the criminal acts of a tiny minority, by upholding a conspiracy theory using the role of the agent provocateur, Avishai Raviv, as a proof of sorts, and by exploiting the *Altalena* affair in order to present Rabin as someone who was himself responsible for the killing of fellow Jews. In this context, Amir himself, during his interrogation, said, "Rabin was responsible for the cannon fire and the sinking of the ship *Altalena* that in 1948 carried weapons for the Irgun forces in the Land of Israel."[2] Religious Zionism's failure to go through a real soulsearching after the assassination has haunted this segment of Israel's Jewish population. The settlers' mainstream leadership was shaken in 2015 by having to deal with violent revolutionary elements on its right. It was embarrassed to find that radical, violent elements affiliated with the Kahane movement have not only committed crimes against Palestinians in the West Bank but also established an underground organization seeking to replace the State of Israel with what they call the Kingdom of Israel.

The disagreements among Rabin's devotees about the proper way to commemorate him are less dramatic, but they do exist. They have been manifested in the arguments over the mission of the Rabin Center, the main memorial, and over what the character of the annual rally held in Rabin Square on the day of the assassination should be. The organizers of this privately sponsored event have largely given it a political orientation, seeking to turn it into a rallying event for a new peace policy. Others have contended that its political content should be toned down and that Rabin should be commemorated as a great national leader with a broad appeal to the Israeli public at large.

Indeed, it is wrong to remember and commemorate Rabin as a dovish leader. Rabin was a centrist leader preoccupied with Israel's security, and he came to the conclusion that the country should seek to moderate and eventually settle its conflict with its Arab neighbors. To him, the quest for peace was intimately connected with the quest for security. He was willing to make painful concessions, but he scrutinized such concessions through a security lens. His willingness to make them was vilified by his right-wing critics and ultimately resulted in his assassination. The Left, on the other hand, tended to cast him as much softer than he really was. He was a statesman who wanted to settle Israel's conflicts with its neighbors through a peace settlement grounded in solid security arrangements. During memorial events held in Boston soon after the assassination, even Rabin's friend and admirer Henry Kissinger began to feel unsettled as speaker after speaker paid tribute to a dovish Rabin, praising his absolute devotion to peacemaking with the Palestinians. "Yitzhak was not a flower child," he muttered quietly.

At some point I considered as a subtitle for this book a line written by the poet Shaul Tchernichovsky: "The image of his native landscape." Rabin was in many respects the quintessential sabra, the native-born Israeli: childhood and adolescence in the mainstream of the Labor movement, the Kadoorie school, the Palmach, the 1948 generation, a rough exterior concealing a inner sensitivity.

The 1948 war was the formative experience of Rabin's life, and he devoted the next nineteen years of his life to building the powerful IDF he led to the spectacular victory of June 1967. The small, vulnerable State of Israel that emerged from the 1948 war was transformed into the powerful post-1967 Israel. But victory had a price. For the past forty-plus years Israel has benefited from some of the war's achievements but has also had to contend with its other by-products, first and foremost the new incarnation of the Palestinian issue. And the country itself changed. The "native landscape" that shaped the young Rabin was vanishing. His second term can also be seen as a valiant effort by a soldier-turned-statesman to use most of the territory he captured in 1967 to consolidate, save, and preserve that original landscape. His assassination became a crucial step on the road to its transformation.

Prologue

1. Michael Karpin and Ina Friedman, *Murder in the Name of God: The Plot to Kill Yitzhak Rabin* (Tel Aviv, 1999), 40 [in Hebrew].
2. Arthur M. Schlesinger Jr., *A Thousand Days: John F. Kennedy in the White House* (Boston, 1965), 1029.
3. Ibid., 1027.

Chapter 1. The Making of a Soldier, 1922–1948

1. Henry Kissinger, *White House Years* (Boston: Little, Brown, 1979), 1:355.
2. Yitzhak Rabin, *My Father's Home* (Hakibbutz Hameuchad, 1970), 8 [in Hebrew].
3. Letter written on November 11, 1919. Private collection.
4. Rosa's departure from Russia and arrival in Palestine are described in detail in a book about her by Eliezer Smoli, a well-known educator and writer in prestate Israel. Smoli was Rabin's

teacher in elementary school and decided to write a book about Rosa after her premature death. See Eliezer Smoli, *Rosa Cohen* (Tel Aviv, 1940) [in Hebrew].

5. No date, private collection.

6. Letter, private archive.

7. Yitzhak Rabin, *The Rabin Memoirs* (Boston: Little, Brown, 1979), 10. *The Rabin Memoirs* is the translation of Rabin's memoirs in Hebrew titled *Service Diary* ("Pinkas Sherut"). The translation is not complete, and there are differences between the Hebrew and the English versions.

8. Mickey Haft testimony, Palmach Museum.

9. Nathan Shacham, *Shalom Chaverim: Pages from a Private Collection* (Tel Aviv: Dvir, 2004), 135–36 [in Hebrew].

10. These testimonies are in the archives of the Palmach Museum.

11. Yoram Kanyuk, *1948* (Tel Aviv, 2010), 131 [in Hebrew].

12. *The Rabin Memoirs*, 29.

13. Ibid., 45.

14. Col. David ("Mickey") Marcus is remembered in Israeli history for two reasons: first, a former colonel in the U.S. Army, he was the most senior volunteer from abroad who came to help the IDF in the 1948 war and was given a very senior position by Ben Gurion; and, second, because of his tragic accidental death. His life story was commemorated both in Herman Wouk's novel *The Hope* and in the movie *Cast a Giant Shadow*, in which Kirk Douglas played Marcus.

15. Yemima Rosenthal, ed., *Yitzhak Rabin, Prime Minister of Israel, 1974–1977 and 1992–1995: Selected Documents* (Jerusalem, 2005), 1:23 [in Hebrew].

16. David Shippler, *New York Times*, October 23, 1979.

17. Ari Shavit, *My Promised Land: The Triumph and Tragedy of Israel* (New York, 2013). And, more specifically, Ari Shavit, "Lydda, 1948: A City, a Massacre, and the Middle East Today." *New Yorker*, October 21, 2013.

18. Anita Shapira, *Yigal Alon, Native Son: A Biography* (Tel Aviv: Hakibbutz Hameuchad, 2004), 371–77 [in Hebrew].

19. Ibid., 382.

20. *The Rabin Memoirs*, 35–36.

21. Letter to Yigal Alon, February 10, 1949.

Chapter 2. From Independence to the Six-Day War, 1949–1967

1. Yitzhak Rabin, *The Rabin Memoirs*, expanded edition (Berkeley: University of California Press, 1996), 45.

2. Letter (undated), private collection.

3. Rosenthal, *Yitzhak Rabin, Prime Minister*, 58.

4. Ibid., 52.

5. Efraim Inbar, *Rabin and Israel's National Security* (Baltimore: Johns Hopkins University Press, 1999), 60–61.

6. Rosenthal, *Yitzhak Rabin, Prime Minister*, 72–120.

7. Inbar, *Rabin and Israel's National Security*, 59.

8. Elad Peled, Lecture at the Rabin Center, October 24, 2012.

9. Shabtai Tevet, *Moshe Dayan: A Biography* (Tel Aviv: Schocken Books, 1971), pp. 404–405 [in Hebrew].

10. Rosenthal, *Yitzhak Rabin, Prime Minister*, 265.

11. Ibid., 318–21.

12. Ibid., 337.

13. Ibid., 417.

14. Asaf Siniver, *Abba Eban: A Biography* (New York and London: Overlook Duckworth, 2015), pp. 213–45.

15. *The Rabin Memoirs*, 75–76.

16. Ibid.

17. Ibid., 80–82.

Chapter 3. Ambassador to Washington, 1968–1973

1. *The Rabin Memoirs*, 139.

2. Foreign Relations of the United States, 1964–1968, document 322. https://history.state.gov/historicaldocuments/frus1964-68v20/d322.

3. Kissinger, *White House Years*, 348.

4. *The Rabin Memoirs*, 164.

5. Yitzhak Rabin, *Service Diary*, 248 [in Hebrew].

6. Moshe Bitan, *Political Diary, 1967–1970* (Tel Aviv, 2014) [in Hebrew].

7. *The Rabin Memoirs*, 182.

8. Foreign Relations of the United States, vol. 24, document 301.

9. *The Rabin Memoirs*, 189.

10. Ibid., 203.

11. NARA document, declassified on April 16, 2009.

12. Eran's testimony, Rabin Center Archive, 186.

13. Letter from Rabin to his father and sister. Undated, probably early 1970. Private collection.

14. Undated. Private collection.

15. *The Rabin Memoirs*, expanded edition, 142.

Chapter 4. First Tenure, 1974–1977

1. *Yediot Acharonot*, April 23, 1974.

2. *The Rabin Memoirs*, 239.

3. Jonathan Shapiro, *An Elite Without Successors: Generations of Political Leaders in Israel* (Tel Aviv: Poalim, 1984) [in Hebrew].

4. http://mfa.gov.il/MFA/ForeignPolicy/MFADocuments /Yearbook2/Pages/22%20Joint%20statement%20US-Jordan%20 and%20Israel-s%20reaction.aspx.

5. Ibid.

6. *Haaretz*, December 3, 1974.

7. These quotes were included in the documentary film *Rabin in His Own Words*, released in November 2015 as part of the commemoration of the twentieth anniversary of Rabin's assassination.

8. William B. Quandt, *Peace Process: American Diplomacy and the Arab-Israeli Conflict Since 1967* (Berkeley: University of California Press, 2005), 242.

9. William B. Quandt, *Decade of Decisions: American Policy Toward the Arab-Israeli Conflict, 1967–1976* (Berkeley: University of California Press), 276.

10. Quandt, *Peace Process*, 244.

11. *The Rabin Memoirs*, 277.

12. *Haaretz*, May 12, 1976.

13. From the documentary *Rabin in His Own Words*.

14. Ibid.

15. *Haaretz*, May 16, 1976.

16. Pattir's diary, cited in Amos Shifris, *Rabin's First Government, 1974–1977* (Tzur Yigal, 2013), 70 [in Hebrew].

17. *The Rabin Memoirs*, 284.

18. Ibid., 293–94.

19. https://history.state.gov/historicaldocuments/frus1977 -80v08/d20.

Chapter 5. Fall and Rise, 1977–1992

1. Yitzhak Rabin, *The War in Lebanon* (Tel Aviv: Am Oved, 1983), 10 [in Hebrew].

2. Yitzhak Navon, *All the Way: An Autobiography* (Jerusalem: Keter, 2015), 384 [in Hebrew].

3. Amnon Strashnov, *Justice Under Fire* (Tel Aviv: Yediot Acharonot, 2004) [in Hebrew].

4. Association for Diplomatic Studies and Training, NARA, Oral History Interview, Interview with Ambassador William Brown.

5. Available at the archive at Yad Tabenkin.

6. Gad Yaacobi, *Grace of Time* (Tel Aviv, 1991), 356 [in Hebrew].

7. Ibid.

Chapter 6. Rabin's Peace Policy, 1992–1995

1. Cited in Itamar Rabinovich, *The Brink of Peace: The Israeli–Syrian Negotiations* (Princeton: Princeton University Press, 1998), 91–92.

2. Uri Savir, *The Process: 1,100 Days That Changed the Middle East* (Yediot Achronot, 1998) [in Hebrew].

3. *Haaretz*, June 10, 1998.

4. Published in *Maariv*, September 12, 2003.

5. Ephraim Sneh, *Navigating Perilous Waters* (Tel Aviv, 2002), 22–23 [in Hebrew].

6. Rabinovich, *The Brink of Peace*, 104–8.

7. Martin Indyk, *Innocent Abroad: An Intimate Account of Amer-*

ican Peace Diplomacy in the Middle East (New York: Simon and Schuster, 2009), 91. And see also Dennis Ross, *The Missing Peace* (New York: Farrar, Straus and Giroux, 2004).

8. Rabinovich, *The Brink of Peace*, 117.

Chapter 7. Politics, Policy, Incitement, and Assassination, 1992–1995

1. Cited in Karpin and Friedman, *Murder in the Name of God*, 9–10.

2. Quoted in ibid., 10. This book alongside Yoram Peri, *Brothers at War* (Tel Aviv, 2005), Carmi Gilon, *Shin-Bet Between the Schisms* (Tel Aviv, 2000), and several oral interviews are the main sources for this passage.

3. Peri, *Brothers at War*, 38.

4. Karpin and Friedman, *Murder in the Name of God*, 96–102.

5. Ibid., 121.

6. Cited in Peri, *Brothers at War*, 39.

7. These quotes are taken from Karpin and Friedman, *Murder in the Name of God*, 123–32, and Peri, *Brothers at War*, 39–47.

8. Karpin and Friedman, *Murder in the Name of God*, 156.

9. Gilon, *Shin-Bet Between the Schisms*, 240–41.

10. Karpin and Friedman, *Murder in the Name of God*, 253.

11. Ibid., 135.

Epilogue

1. *Haaretz*, October 26, 2015.

2. Quoted by Amnon Barzilai in *Haaretz*, June 14, 2013.

ACKNOWLEDGMENTS

I AM grateful to Yale University Press for commissioning me to write Yitzhak Rabin's biography. I had worked closely under Yitzhak Rabin and thought I knew him well. Yet, while researching and writing this book I learned much more about his life, career and character, and about the full significance of Israel's loss on November 4, 1995.

I would like to specifically thank Yale University Press's director, Mr. John Donatich; Mr. Leon Black, who initiated the Jewish Lives series; the series' three general editors, Prof. Anita Shapira, Ms. Ileene Smith, and Prof. Steven Zipperstein, my editor Ms. Erica Hanson, and Ms. Marika Lysandrou, Ms. Margaret Otzel, Ms. Heather Nathan, and Ms. Elizabeth Pelton.

My research was facilitated by three members of the Rabin family: Yitzhak Rabin's sister, Ms. Rachel Rabin-Yaacov, and his children, Dalia and Yuval. The staff of the Rabin Center,

Ms. Dorit Ben-Ami and Ms. Nurit Cohen-Levinovsky, were most gracious and helpful.

Special thanks are due to my three research assistants: Arik Rudnitzky, Revital Yerushalmi and Maddy Taras. Dr. Tamar Yegnes and Ms. Hanne Tidnam were very helpful as they have been with earlier books.

The transcripts of dozens of interviews kept at the Rabin Center were an invaluable source for my research. I also had the benefit of personal interviews and conversations with a large number of individuals to whom I am most grateful: Mr. Uri Avneri, Gen. Yaacov Amidror, Mr. Uzi Baram, Mr. Nachum Barnea, Dr. Michael Bar-Zohar, Dr. Yossi Beilin, Prof. Haim Ben-Shahar, Gen. Amos Chorev, Mr. Eitan Haber, Dr. Yair Hirschfeld, Mr. Amos Eran, Dr. Oded Eran, Gen. Shlomo Gazit, Prof. Moti Golani, Mr. Haim Guri, Dr. Martin Indyk, Mr. Chezi Kalo, Dr. Igal Kipnis, Ms. Niva Lanir, Mr. Dani Litani, Mr. Dan Margalit, Mr. Dan Meridor, Mr. Shlomo Nakdimon, Mr. Amir Oren, Mr. Amos Oz, Gen. Elad Peled, Mr. Yaacov Peri, Prof. Yoram Peri, Mr. Zvi Rafiah, Ambassador Dennis Ross, the late Mr. Yossi Sarid, Mr. Uri Savir, Justice Meir Shamgar, Mr. Shimon Sheves, Ms. Ora Teveth, the late Mr. Dov Tzamir, Dr. Hagai Tzoreff, and Mr. Dov Weissglas.

In addition to archival and other primary sources, I had used the extensive secondary literature written about Yitzhak Rabin's life and death. In this context, several authors deserve my gratitude for their contribution: Dan Efron, Yossi Goldstein, Michael Karpin and Ina Friedman, Yoram Peri and Robert Slater.

Itamar Rabinovich
Tel Aviv, August 2016

INDEX

ambassador to Washington (1968–73),
67–96; agenda of American–
Israel relationship, 70; American
Jewish community, relationship
with, 68–70; cabinet position,
Rabin's desire to move into,
92–94; ceasefire violated by
Egypt and Soviets, 84–85; Eban
disagrees with positions of,
80–82, 92; end of mission, 95–96;
interim Mideast settlement proposal, 87–89; Johnson administration's focus on territories
and peace plan, 70–74; Meir's
relationship with Rabin during,
80–81, 89–90, 92; military deals
for U.S. weapons, 74; Nixon's
Middle East policy, 77; nuclear
development as issue, 74–76;
peace negotiations with Egypt,
proposals for, 90–91; Rabin's
effectiveness as, 68, 86–87, 96;
Rogers Initiative (1970), 83–85,
87; Rogers Plan (1969), 78–79,
83–84. See also Kissinger, Henry;
Nixon, Richard
Amer, Abd al-Hakim, 48, 54
American Israel Public Affairs
Committee (AIPAC), 69
Amin, Idi, 128–29
Amir, Hagai, 231
Amir, Yigal, 2–3, 228–31, 237–38
Amit, Meir, 64, 134
Amital, Yehuda, 234
"Arab Cold War," 48, 54
Arab political parties in Israel, 169
Arab Revolt of 1936–39, 10
Arab summit conferences: Khartoum
(1968), 71; Rabat (1974), 113
Arafat, Yasser: Asad and, 202;
complicated negotiations with,
177–78; fails to live up to his
commitments, 237; Fath and, 48;
Husseini vs., 183; Israeli public
response to, 217; Netanyahu's
views on, 237; Oslo process and,
190; relocates from Lebanon to

Tunisia, 148–49; returns to take
charge of Palestinian Authority,
191–92, 208; signing of Oslo
Accords at White House
(September 13, 1993), 200–201;
signing of Paris Protocol
agreement (April 29, 1994),
201. See also PLO
Arens, Moshe, 149, 153, 158–60, 162–65
Argov, Shlomo, 82–83, 148
Armistice Agreement with Syria
(1949), 40–41
arms deals. See military weapons, U.S.
sales to Israel
Asad, Hafez al-: Arafat and, 202;
attitude toward neighboring
countries, 120; Hezbollah and,
185, 192–94, 234–35; in Jordan
situation (September 1970), 86;
Kissinger and, 120; Lebanon
intervention and, 121–22; meets
with Clinton (January 1994),
203–4; meets with Clinton (October 1994), 207; peace process
(1974) and, 110; peace process
(1975) and, 119–20; peace process (1983) failure and, 153; peace
process (1984) and, 154; peace
process (1993–94) and, 176, 182,
185, 196–98, 202–4, 208–12; peace
process (1996) and, 234. See also
Syria
assassination of Rabin: aftermath of,
1–4, 232–35; Amir as killer, 2–3,
228–30; analogy to other assassinations, 1–3; chain of inflammatory events leading up to, 227–31,
241–42; commemoration events
for, 240–43; conspiracy theories
on, 229, 242; extremist rabbis
sanctioning killing of Jew under
certain circumstances, 225–27;
failure of Rabin to employ
security measures, 230; failure of
state to punish those inciting,
239; funeral, 233; GSS failure to
adequately protect Rabin, 231,

(1967) and, 60–61, 64; on West
Bank compromise, 123; in World
War II, 12
de Gaulle, Charles, 2, 59
demilitarized zone on Syrian border,
40–41, 43
Democratic Movement for Change
(DMC), 134, 139
Deri, Aryeh, 170, 193, 216
Dinitz, Simcha, 82, 116
Djerejian, Edward, 184–85
Dobrynin, Anatoly, 78
Dori, Yaacov, 34, 36–37
Druze, 52
dual containment strategy, 179–80

east European Jews, 3, 135, 150
Eban, Abba: Dayan and, 106, 126; deals
with Rusk on territories, 70; leads
opposition to Rabin, 92, 94, 106;
Meir and, 81, 126; negotiates
U.S. military weapons sales, 74;
opposes escalation with Egypt,
80–82; opposes Rabin appointment as U.S. ambassador, 68, 80;
Rabin avoids working with, 81,
104; seeks diplomatic solution to
May 1967 crisis, 59; snubs Rabin
on visit to Washington, 80
economy, 105, 159, 219
Egypt: disengagement agreement
(1974) and, 117; effect of
Nasserism's decline in, 48; Jordan
and, 54; October War (1973) and,
98; peace deal with Israel (1979),
212; peace negotiations (1949),
30–31; remilitarization of Sinai by
(1960), 43; retaliatory attacks on,
urged by Rabin as U.S. ambassador, 80, 83; Sinai II agreement
(1975), background and conclusion of, 102, 109–19; Suez Canal
hostilities (1969), 71; Syrian
reaction to Sinai II signing of,
120; in territory negotiations with
Johnson administration, 72–73;
United Arab Republic (UAR)
and, 43, 48–49; War of Independence and, 29–30; Yemen
involvement of, 47, 48. *See also*
Mubarak, Husni; Nasser, Gamal
Abdel; Sadat, Anwar
Eilat, 31, 58
Eini, Giora, 145
Einy, Giora, 200
Ein Yabrud (Ofra settlement), 123–24
Eisenhower, Dwight, 70
Elazar, David, 46
elections. *See specific political parties*
Entebbe (1976), 128–32
Eran, Amos, 92
Eshkol, Levi: appoints Rabin as chief
of staff, 45; appoints Rabin as
U.S. ambassador, 68; Begin and,
134; Ben Gurion's opinion of, 56;
Dayan's opinion of, 61; death of,
80; defense portfolio held by,
108; Johnson and, 69; on nuclear
development, 75; Rabin's security
policy and, 53; reprimands Rabin,
55–56; Six-Day War (1967) and,
59–60, 63–64; Syria and, 52
Etgar Circle, 100
Ethiopia, 42
Etzel. *See* Irgun
Etzyoni Brigade (of Palmach), 19
Evron, Ephraim ("Eppy"), 69
L'Express smear of Rabin, 143–44

Faction B, 13
Fatah: attempts to roil Palestinians,
156; establishment of, 48–49; first
terrorist act of, 51; hostage taking
at Tel Aviv Savoy Hotel (March
1975), 128; Syria and, 51–52
Feiglin, Moshe, 225
Feinberg, Abe, 69
First Gulf War, 167, 174–75, 206
First Intifada (1987–91), 155–58, 162
First Lebanon War (1982), 148, 151,
153–55
Fisher, Max, 70
Fogel advertising firm, 143
Ford, Gerald, 109, 112, 115–16, 118, 125

Peled, Matti, 46, 123
Peres, Shimon: as acting prime minister (1976), 133; compared to Rabin, 104, 166; Entebbe (1976) and, 131–32; *Entebbe Diary*, 131; European orientation of, 42–43; as foreign minister in Rabin second administration (1992), 170–71; forges working relationship with Rabin (after 1981), 144–45; "good fence" policy of, 121; Hussein's displeasure with, 206; Labor party leadership and prime minister nomination, challenges to Rabin, 63, 101–2, 105, 107, 142–43, 214, 218; as Labor Party nominee for prime minister (1976), 133; Lavi Project and, 160; London Agreement (1987) and, 161–62; meets with Crown Prince Hassan (October 1993), 205; meets with King Hussein (November 1993), 205; in Meir's 1974 cabinet, 99, 103; as minister of defense in Rabin first administration, 103, 107, 127, 161; multilateral working groups, role in, 177; in national unity government (1984–85), 151, 160; on nuclear development, 74; Oslo process and possible challenge to Rabin in next election, 186–92, 196, 198; Palestinian autonomy plan (1989) and, 163–66; as prime minister candidate (1974), 101–2; as prime minister candidate (1977), 108–9; public dissatisfaction with animosity between Peres and Rabin, 135; Rabin assassination, on platform with Rabin at, 229–30; Rabin's depiction of, in memoirs, 142–44; Rabin's disagreements and compromises with, 42–43, 45, 102–3, 108–9, 125–27, 131–32, 135, 151–52, 218; Rabin supports as Labor leader, 150–51, 168; settle-

ments issue and, 123–24, 142; Shamir fires (1990), 166; signing of Oslo Accords at White House (September 13, 1993), 199–201; succeeds to prime minister upon Rabin's death, 233–35; Tsur as chief of staff, support for, 44, 107
Peri, Yoram, 97–98
PLO (Palestine Liberation Organization): Black September (September 7, 1970) and, 85; First Intifada and, 156; First Lebanon War and, 148; formation of, 50–51; Iraq and First Gulf War and, 175; Jordan's reaction to Oslo Accords with, 202, 204–5; Kissinger and, 120; Lebanese crisis (1976) and, 146–47; local West Bank leaders to solve Palestinian issues instead of, 165; Oslo process and, 178, 183–84, 186–92, 195; in peace process negotiations, 138; Rabat Arab summit conference (1974) and, 113; Rabin as prime minister (first term) and, 123, 137; recognition as "sole legitimate representative" of Palestinians, 113; relocates from Lebanon to Tunisia, 148–49; returns from Tunisia, 192, 201, 208; Sinai II agreement (1975) and, 110–11, 118–19; in South Lebanon, 121, 146; Syria and, 122; U.S. relations with, 118, 162. *See also*, Arafat, Yasser
politics (1992–95), 215–31; denouncements of Rabin by political opponents and right wing, 223–24; domestic policies, 219–20; drift to right after Rabin assassination, 232, 238; economic development, 219; fragility of Rabin's majority, 217; hawkish groups' and right wing's response to Oslo Accords, 215–16, 221; infrastructure development, 219–20; Peres-Rabin relationship

JEWISH LIVES is a major series of interpretive biography designed to illuminate the imprint of Jewish figures upon literature, religion, philosophy, politics, cultural and economic life, and the arts and sciences. Subjects are paired with authors to elicit lively, deeply informed books that explore the range and depth of Jewish experience from antiquity through the present.

Jewish Lives is a partnership of Yale University Press and the Leon D. Black Foundation.

Ileene Smith is editorial director. Anita Shapira and Steven J. Zipperstein are series editors.

PUBLISHED TITLES INCLUDE:

Rabbi Akiva: Sage of the Talmud, by Barry W. Holtz
Ben-Gurion: Father of Modern Israel, by Anita Shapira
Bernard Berenson: A Life in the Picture Trade, by Rachel Cohen
Sarah: The Life of Sarah Bernhardt, by Robert Gottlieb
Leonard Bernstein: An American Musician, by Allen Shawn
Hayim Nahman Bialik: Poet of Hebrew, by Avner Holtzman
Léon Blum: Prime Minister, Socialist, Zionist, by Pierre Birnbaum
Louis D. Brandeis: American Prophet, by Jeffrey Rosen
David: The Divided Heart, by David Wolpe
Moshe Dayan: Israel's Controversial Hero, by Mordechai Bar-On
Disraeli: The Novel Politician, by David Cesarani
Einstein: His Space and Times, by Steven Gimbel
Becoming Freud: The Making of a Psychoanalyst, by Adam Phillips
Emma Goldman: Revolution as a Way of Life, by Vivian Gornick
Hank Greenberg: The Hero Who Didn't Want to Be One,
    by Mark Kurlansky
Peggy Guggenheim: The Shock of the Modern, by Francine Prose
Lillian Hellman: An Imperious Life, by Dorothy Gallagher
Jabotinsky: A Life, by Hillel Halkin
Jacob: Unexpected Patriarch, by Yair Zakovitch
Franz Kafka: The Poet of Shame and Guilt, by Saul Friedländer
Rav Kook: Mystic in a Time of Revolution, by Yehudah Mirsky
Primo Levi: The Matter of a Life, by Berel Lang
Groucho Marx: The Comedy of Existence, by Lee Siegel
Moses Mendelssohn: Sage of Modernity, by Shmuel Feiner
Moses: A Human Life, by Avivah Zornberg
Proust: The Search, by Benjamin Taylor
Yitzhak Rabin: Soldier, Leader, Statesman, by Itamar Rabinovich
Walter Rathenau: Weimar's Fallen Statesman, by Shulamit Volkov
Mark Rothko: Toward the Light in the Chapel, by Annie Cohen-Solal

Solomon: The Lure of Wisdom, by Steven Weitzman
Steven Spielberg: A Life in Films, by Molly Haskell
Barbra Streisand: Redefining Beauty, Femininity, and Power,
    by Neal Gabler
Leon Trotsky: A Revolutionary's Life, by Joshua Rubenstein